COOL WET KISS

COOL WET KISS

American Values
degraded, debauched, and debased
by the Obama Cool Rules

C. G. London

COOL WET KISS

American Values
degraded, debauched, and debased
by the Obama Cool Rules

Relax, bro, it's just a parody.

Published in the United States by
think buy INDIE
P.O. Box 5617
Scottsdale, AZ 85261
Books@thinkbuyINDIE.com

Library of Congress Control Number: 2014486429
ISBN-13: 978-0-692-26964-0
ISBN-10: 0692269649

PRINTED IN THE UNITED STATES OF AMERICA

For Mary and Ted, unsung American parents

&

R.L., an unapologetic American

CONTENTS

Cool is as cool does.

FOREPLAY

It was C. S. Lewis who, in his unforgettable "Screwtape Letters," wrote: "The greatest evil is not done now in those sordid 'dens of crime' that Dickens loved to paint. It is not even done in concentration camps and labor camps. In those we see its final result. But it is conceived and ordered (moved, seconded, carried and minuted) in clear, carpeted, warmed, and well-lighted offices, by quiet men with white collars and cut fingernails and smooth-shaven cheeks who do not need to raise their voice."

Well, because these "quiet men" do not "raise their voices," because they sometimes speak in soothing tones of brotherhood and peace, because, like other dictators before them, they're always making "their final territorial demand," some would have us accept them at their word and accommodate ourselves to their aggressive impulses. But if history teaches anything, it teaches that simple-minded appeasement or wishful thinking about our adversaries is folly. It means the betrayal of our past, the squandering of our freedom.

Excerpt from President Ronald Reagan's "Evil Empire" Speech, March 8, 1983

QUINTESSENTIAL COOL

Cool is profoundly American. Cool has been an American way of life at least since George Washington. Jazz didn't birth cool nor does hip-hop street-beat poetry own it. Cool was on the continent long before California claimed to have invented it. The counterculture didn't hallucinate cool. Nor did the metallectuals headbang it. There is no old cool nor new cool. There's no smooth cool, no authentic cool. Liberals aren't inherently cool just as conservatives aren't innately uncool. The gangstas attempt to use it as a weapon but cool does not disfigure, mutilate, nor intimidate. Cool is not dead. Cool never dies. The Brits might teach cool by way of Aristotle's Nicomachean Ethics, yet they are too brilliantly ironic and self-deprecating to break free and truly get cool.

Furthermore, there are no arbiters of cool. Whether it's the big "C," the small "c," or the 4th "C," it's time for an honest portrayal of the cool ethos rather than a co-opting of cool to airbrush history to suit one's need to publish something, nay, anything.

Cool is the embodiment of all it means to be an American. A new and revolutionary way of living occurred when the American flag was planted. The blessing of self-government took root. A new paradigm of living freely became possible. Living in the New World was a paradigm shift. Uniquely forged through the birth of the Republic with all the grit and tenacity it took to bring the United States into the 21st century, cool is the expression of that American spirit of independence that gives rise to American values. Cool is only cultivated in a society that is immersed in these American values.

No other country in the history of the world has enjoyed the freedoms that are unique to America—freedoms and privileges explicitly stated and protected in the Constitution of the United States. The Bill of Rights, summarized in the First Amendment, reinforces these Creator-endowed unalienable rights: "Congress shall make no law respecting an establishment of religion, or prohibiting the free exercise thereof; or abridging the freedom of speech, or of the press; or the right of the people peaceably to assemble, and to petition the Government for a redress of grievances." These God-given natural rights exist by virtue of our humanity not because a benevolent government deigned to grant them to us.

The United States of America is the only country where the cool way of thinking could have emerged. Once the Declaration of Independence threw off the shackles of tyranny and denounced the King of Great Britain, the colonists' boldness and assertiveness lay the groundwork for the formation of the cool American approach to solving problems and building their lives. They identified with the reality of life and knew that justice, domestic tranquility, and liberty for all were the only path to form a more perfect Union.

The Declaration of Independence is truly the genesis of cool, that American passion for independence. Think of all the generations of Americans that drew on the Declaration for inspiration and guidance to help them understand their principles and beliefs as a people. A crucial component was and continues to be limited government deriving just powers only from the consent of the governed through a representative democracy that respects fellow citizens and their right to life, liberty, and the pursuit of happiness. This freedom demands responsibility from the citizens which in turn creates a value system of self-reliance, courage, and integrity where all Americans can live together and prosper. Citizens speak with other citizens as equals, actually practicing democracy without imposing their rule on one another. This is how America became the land of the free, the home of the brave, and the nation of the cool.

For too long, certain groups have trivialized the word "cool" by using it as a throwaway when they can't think of something else to say—like using the words "nice" or "interesting." Many musicians, actors, artists, and athletes use cool to market themselves even though almost all musicians, actors, artists, and athletes consider themselves cool. They are unable to identify their unique selves or, perhaps, their creative juices have dried up. They compete with each other using a catch-phrase image trying to best the other's middling façade. Just as well they cannibalize and dilute their "images" of cool for this style of differentiation is defunct and just plain intellectually lazy.

Advertising execs armed with their grass-roots intel chase cool, chase trends for the next big fad. They convince their clients of a guaranteed commercial success if they can only get the latest *American Idol* winner to endorse it. The competition most assuredly has their own marketing gurus touting another mega-million dollar fad if they can launch it, of course, at the Super Bowl. A plug on reality TV would suffice. Then, in a commercial-minute, it's on to the next craze perpetuating an exhausting, feverish circle. They soon learn that cool cannot be corralled in photos, on paper, on YouTube, nor in cinema. Once they think they have cool captured, Zen-like, it's gone.

Even academics try to hold cool hostage by turning it into research projects for their grad students and post docs to publish under the grand master's name lest they perish. What government grants pay for thesis-driven, severely-noted, obediently-indexed, ad nauseam-acknowledged, secondary- and tertiary-sourced textbooks of finding, keeping, birthing, demising, comparing, measuring, or losing American cool? Besides, cool is forward-looking not backward-reviewed as most writers pedantically assert.

The intrinsic meaning of cool defies any of these contradictory uses. We need to restore cool to its rightful place in the world. Cool is simply and elegantly the quintessential American philosophy of life, our cherished system of values by which we live.

Why, then, is President Barack Obama referred to over and over as cool? As leader of all the people of the United States, does he share the same values that most Americans share? Does he live by those American values that we revere? He most certainly reflects the exceptionalism of America where anyone from anywhere can aspire and become anything they choose. Yet, let's remember what cool is. Cool is a style of living, a certain way of looking at the world, with a set of values that are distinct American values. Cool is not an artifice, an image contrived to gain favor. Nor is it an illusion used to manipulate and obfuscate. Cool is not about spectacle but rather clarity. Cool is not self-absorption. Cool keeps moving forward never dwelling on the negative. It's an elevated way of viewing the world and your place in the world. Cool is never disingenuous. Cool is real.

Consider this logic: The "Obama" name is synonymous with big government. Big government is a collection of institutions. Institutionalizing groups of individuals make them easier to regulate and control. Cool cannot be institutionalized; cool cannot be regulated; cool cannot be controlled. Big government exists to regulate, therefore, cannot be cool. Bottom line, Barack "Big Daddy Government" Obama is not cool.

Many people admire Obama. Many people voted for him. Many people voted for him because they thought he was cool. Whether you agree with his politics or not, we can all agree on this point: *Obama used cool to get elected president.*

It's truly stunning how Barack Obama, who blatantly disregards American values while feigning to use "our values as a compass," can throw a mesmerizing mantle of cool over himself, instantly wrapped in those same American values that he disdains, and presto!, become President of the United States. Audacious. Disturbingly audacious.

OBAMA COOL RULES

Rule 1935
Badass Power

Obama:
Mirror on the wall, who has power over all?
Mirror:
You, my President, have power over all.
Obama:
Mirror, who on Earth has power over all?
Mirror:
You, my Emperor, have power over all.
Obama:
What about the Solar System?
Mirror:
You, my Royal Ruler.
Obama:
The Milky Way?
Mirror:
You, my Supreme Leader.
Obama:
The Universe?
Mirror:
You, my Lord.
Obama:
Mirror, you remind me of my mother.

Strategically placed throughout the White House, Air Force One, Marine One, the treadmill, the basketball court, and his golf bag are self-assuring, narcissistic, looking glasses that bolster the oversized ego that is our 44th president. Barack Obama is on a quest to honor himself with the distinction of being the most powerful, most solipsistic man that ever lived or will live forevermore. He is the center of the universe, the Higgs boson, the "God particle" that caused the Big Bang.

Somewhere between Punahou Academy and Chicago, on his journey of self-exploration, looking deep within to discover his authentic self, this abandoned, lonely, uprooted, little boy named Barack Obama chose the I-want-power path. He would have us believe that his best game is basketball and most oft-played, golf. Not so. His best game is power—unabashed BADASS POWER. Not only can he play at this level, he lives it, breathes it, devours it. Existentially, power is his morning wake-up call, his burger with Dijon mustard, his secret cigarette break, and his go-to aphrodisiac.

Lust for power is not a new concept. Many people want power. But not everyone that wants power needs to have the most powerful position in the world, the President of the United States. Given Obama's seemingly traditional upbringing and career path, where, oh where, did his "power" gene activate?

We know he served Baskin-Robbins ice cream cones as a teenager in Hawaii. What a coincidence! Frank Marshall Davis, a progressive black poet, was one of Barack's favorite customers. He would share his Chicago activist stories and dirty limericks over jars of whiskey. Frank had significant credentials and was well educated. In *Dreams from My*

Father, Barack fondly recounted Frank's sage remarks as Barack was setting off for college. Almost as a father, Frank cautioned Barack that he was going to college to get trained "to manipulate words so they don't mean anything anymore ... [to] be a well-trained, well-paid nigger." That was quite an inspirational sendoff. Frank had a gift for expressing himself, shall we say, frankly.

A few years later, Obama was in New York jogging, er, running around Central Park after his political science class and he just happened on the Black Power lecturer Stokely Carmichael, also known as Kwame Ture, the former Honorary Prime Minister of the Black Panther Party. Was that destiny or what?

The next day, Obama relaxed in a Columbia classroom, dreaming of becoming a famous writer. This fantasy could easily have become reality since he was discussing modern fiction with the prolific literary theorist, Professor Edward Said. For extra credit, Obama adopted Said's mockery of American culture, especially the Declaration of Independence and the U.S. Constitution. Both master and student reaped the benefits of education and privileged lifestyles in the United States, yet believed America was a despicable nation built on exploitation, oppression, and genocide—views wildly promulgated at their alma maters of Columbia, Harvard, and Princeton. Said was considered the Palestinians most ardent political advocate. Kismet! As if Allah himself brought them together.

Obama, now in Chicago, decided maybe he should attend one of those fancy Ivy League law schools for future "access" purposes. The law school applications were laborious not to mention all those reference letters. Fortune favored the conventional Obama again. Khalid Abdullah Tariq al-Mansour, a Muslim lawyer and a black nationalist, wrote a letter of recommendation to Harvard Law School for Obama. This type of luck happens for everyone, right? Al-Mansour reviled America, Israel, and all white people. Besides advising such Saudi billionaires as Prince Alwaleed bin Talal, the world's richest Arab, al-Mansour was known for helping these fat cats "invest" their vast wealth in hand-picked minions that advance their agendas all over the globe.

So while regular college students pursuing the American dream play it NFL Rulebook straight, salute the social order, work hard, take the right courses with the right professors, strive for high GPAs, write the best essays, build outstanding resumés, take on exhaustive extracurricular projects, and solicit merit-based recommendation letters, Obama aligned himself with power coaches. These mentors, eventually benefactors, whispered in Obama's ears throughout his formative, failing-upward years. Their words of wisdom were as gold. They showed him a faster and more efficient way to get power. It's an old technique taught by Karl Marx: It's easier to take power than to labor day-to-day at building it. Saul Alinsky, a kindred progressive spirit, put his own spin to what's-yours-is-mine: The Haves hold power; the Have-Nots want to take it away. The Alinsky "truism" may be a little too glib and pedestrian, but the Marx method offered all sorts of lifestyle options for the you-want-me-to-work-for-a-living!, aloha-spirited Obama.

Obama wants power. Obama wants power to control you. His philosophy about power is more Machiavelli and less Eckhart Tolle; more Robert Moses, less Oprah. "Executive power," "command and control," and "rule by emergency" suit him like a Cabretta-leather golf glove. Obama wields power based on his, and his alone, own judgment. Even though he was schooled at one of the most famous lawyer factories in the world, he has almost no regard for precedents. He may not have learned the art of dance or how to balance a checkbook, but he certainly learned that the rules tend to favor the people who make the rules. He found his stride. He found his cool. And when you know your cool, you write your own rules.

John Llewellyn Lewis is the inspiration for Obama Cool Rule 1935, an homage to the creation of the National Labor Relations Act of 1935, otherwise known as the Wagner Act.

John L. Lewis was the president of the United Mine Workers of America for forty years until 1960, and the founding president of the Congress of Industrial Organizations (CIO). He also worked for the American Federation of Labor (AFL) for six years as a national organizer. During the 1930s, John L. Lewis was the godfather of the labor movement.

Lewis rallied when he witnessed mine workers union membership decline from 500,000 in 1922 to 75,000 in 1933. He was a fierce lobbying force and found a receptive spirit in Franklin D. Roosevelt who was elected president in 1932. The National Labor Relations Act of 1935 became one of FDR's Second New Deal signature legislation. This Act gave employees in industry the right to self-organize and bargain collectively with their employers, thus challenging American businesses. The National Labor Relations Board was also conceived to serve as a quasi-judicial body to oversee the law.

With FDR now on his side, Lewis sprang into action. The ink was still wet on this new Democratic buy-more-votes legislation when Lewis organized 92% of all the country's coal miners using the slogan: "The President wants you to join the union!" Lewis took some liberty with this message since FDR did not explicitly order him to conduct the campaign. We're beginning to see where Obama may have learned some of his fancy footwork on the court of collecting votes.

A gifted orator, the David to the Goliath-corporate-titans, national-union-membership organizer, and tireless lobbyist for federal legislation, Lewis was on a roll. He could even use fisticuffs when needed like at the 1935 AFL convention. He provoked the United Brotherhood of Carpenters' President William Hutcheson with a few slurs, then proceeded to leap over a row of chairs while knocking Hutcheson to the ground and punching him in the face. Wasn't there a similar incident between Illinois Senators Obama and "Hollywood" Hendon in Springfield back in 1998 or thereabout? Didn't Obama provoke a kick-your-ass altercation with some pushing and shoving, even foulmouthed expletives? Not only did the thin-skin Obama have to be physically restrained, but they also had to pry him off of one of the most charismatic figures in Illinois politics. He obviously learned the fine points of building coalitions from Lewis.

Lewis's mission wasn't a game. It was real. The people were real. Lewis knew his union members because he was one of them. Like his dad, John was a coal miner. He championed the coal workers. He thought bigger and played tougher to protect them. He knew to make a difference he had to get power and leverage his way into a top spot. Alinsky was small ball; Lewis played in the big leagues. Lewis wanted power and was going to get it at any cost. Enter Barack Obama.

Obama's first foray into community organizing was in 1985 in Chicago, two years after having graduated from Columbia College. He was twenty-four, impressionable, and eager to learn. With a liberal arts degree in hand, what else does a middle-class college graduate do if he's not going to law school and really doesn't like numbers? Of course, become a supercilious writer; or better still, a snooty novelist. This was his ultimate goal but he needed some gritty, plantation-politics type of material, the kind of stuff that civil-rights legends are made of, such as Martin Luther King Jr. duking it out with Mayor Richard J. Daley. Jerry Kellman, a seasoned organizer looking for the not-too-smart-but-smart-enough candidate, offered Obama a perfect entrance into the South Side of Chicago. Imagine the edgy, civil-rights grist for the future E. L. Doctorow!

Kellman hired Obama as a wet-behind-the-ears community-organizer apprentice. You would expect that a newbie community organizer would use Saul Alinsky's *Rules for Radicals* as the official organizer's guidebook; however, Kellman thought Alinsky's biography of John L. Lewis was profoundly more incendiary in teaching wannabes how to secure power. In time, Obama would eclipse even John Lewis's appetite for domination and bankrupt the very industry that Lewis struggled so long and hard to build. Fighting global warming by busting up the coal industry catapulted Obama into supremacy Lewis never imagined.

"It's a POWER thing! X" was the trademarked, pervasive slogan for the 1992 Chicago voter registration drive coordinated by a branch of Project Vote. The "X" was a tribute to Malcolm X and his call to take power "by any means necessary." Project Vote founder, Sandy Newman, hired Barack Obama to "community organize" mass amounts of ostensibly nonpartisan, minority voters whose members have different ethnic, racial, national, religious, sexual, political, linguistic, or other yet-to-be-identified characteristic. There was something though about the Malcolm X call-to-action vibe that appealed to an African American voting-block.

By 1992, Chicago black-voter registration and turnout were the lowest on record. Black voters became despondent without their beloved leader, Mayor Harold Washington, who died of a heart attack at City Hall in 1987. Registration was so low that even a modicum of effort would increase the numbers. Mayor Washington proved that when the African American community was motivated, he could wave the wand and sign up 120,000 new voters.

Obama, channeling his idol Mayor Washington, muscled his own Chicago-style power grab. Money was not an issue for the campaign so Obama and his team, mainly volunteers, could get creative. Media saturation drove the strategy. Registering people at food-stamp locations and welfare offices proved exceptionally fortuitous. ACORN-like bounties encouraged registrars to find signatures. Unsuspecting church ladies at Sunday services looked like they were collecting for the poor. Minority-owned businesses set up registrar stations and even paid for advertising. Labor unions jumped into the fray.

In the end, 150,000 new African American voters had been registered for the national elections. This energized group pledged allegiance nearly lockstep to the Democratic

Party and helped elect the first black president, Bill Clinton; Carol "anti-Clarence Thomas" Moseley Braun to the U.S. Senate; and Bobby Rush, the founder of the Chicago Black Panthers, to the U.S. House of Representatives.

Obama's power play worked. Project Vote set him apart from the Jesse Jacksons and the Bobby Rushes and gave him notoriety within the Democratic Party. Obama discovered he had a knack for creating a believable villain-versus-victim plot that would bring voters to the polls. This was even better than being a writer.

As a community organizer, Obama persuaded volunteers to do his bidding, to do God's work. Hallelujah! All that manpower for free—a rather benign form of slavery. And those doing the tough grunt work felt good about themselves, saving Chicago and all. This freed the con artist to do the things he loved. While running Project Vote, he and his then-fiancé Michelle managed a trip to Kenya and even their own wedding in Chicago. Obama has a penchant for disappearing during the heavy lifting. He much prefers to "lead from behind" or lead *in absentia*—both styles are oxymoronic and cowardly, yet safe. Best to play just outside the key rather than under the basket—too many sharp elbows and he might get hurt. It's even safer to play remotely on a smartphone.

Obama became the Grand Poobah of voter-registration and voter-turnout though on a relatively small scale. Which brings us to the other talent that Obama developed while working on Project Vote: hobnobbing with the prominent, liberal Chicagoans with big checkbooks. Oh, and did I mention kibitzing with the infamous, unrepentant terrorist disguised as a University of Illinois-Chicago professor, William "Bill" Ayers?

Whenever, wherever, and however they "officially" met, Barack Obama and Bill Ayers were complexly entangled by the creation and the eventual failure of the Chicago Annenberg Challenge.

In December 1993, alongside President Bill Clinton in the White House Rose Garden, Ambassador William H. Annenberg, a Nixon appointment and a supporter of Ronald Reagan, announced his noble gift of $500 million to America's public schools. The funds were meant to *challenge* public schools to promote improvement in the students' academic performance and in the schools themselves. Lest we gloss over the irony here: Annenberg was a self-made billionaire, staunchly Republican, who spent the latter half of his life giving away his wealth to such causes that, unbeknownst to Annenberg, allowed anarchists and communists (small "c") to further their agendas. This is known as *voluntarily* redistributing your own wealth, thank you very much. Thus began the feeding frenzy for free money amongst the Windy City's progressive activists.

Ayers appeared a kid in a candy store when he heard the news. That very day he began plotting a strategy to get some of the cash for himself and his radical pals. Bill Ayers became the prime mover and chief architect of the CAC heist. This was his big break to restructure the entire school system. Chicago received a check for $49.2 million on January 20, 1995 as one of five grants awarded to big city school systems. Local Chicago business and philanthropic communities matched the award and grew the jackpot to $100 million.

Ayers could now launch his plan to fundamentally change the Chicago public schools. Far out!

Obama, without any school development experience, was ushered in as the founding president and chairman of the CAC—the chief administrator. Rumor has it that Bill Ayers recommended the appointment. But that's impossible! They didn't know each other personally. Bill Ayers was just a guy who lived in Obama's neighborhood. Ayers didn't even play basketball with the hoopster. One might consider this effort at "distancing" slightly disingenuous, or it might be flagrantly hiding the truth. Only Bill, Barack, and all their CAC friends know what really happened.

Sitting on boards of the Joyce Foundation and the Woods Fund of Chicago served only as stepping stones for Obama's great leap forward—chairing the CAC. If Obama had any executive experience on his lawyerly resumé, the CAC was it. Using the term "executive experience" when referring to Barack Obama is a gross injustice. A stereotypical liberal, Obama stacked his credentials with flimsy high-and-mighty-sounding titles absent substantive accomplishments to back them up. Think quantity, not quality. Any serious, business person that ever worked hard to get an executive title cringes at the thought of an inexperienced, glad-hander sitting at the head of the table. Lobotomized, group-thinking, corporate bureaucrats wouldn't know the difference.

Obama's version of executively experiencing the CAC meant shelling out the cash—end of story. There was no accountability for grantee performance other than future funds would be cut off. The price of admission to the CAC was an oath to now and evermore pay allegiance to Obama. No support, no grant money—a simple straightforward progressive formula. The greenbacks spread around primarily by the CAC fortified Obama's political relationships with key players in Chicago. After all, he was just trying to make the schools better.

The CAC, though a miscarriage in helping the children in the Chicago public school system, set the trajectory for Obama's ascent to more and more power. He cleverly used the CAC funds to build his extensive network. Obama leveraged his connections to help secure the Illinois Senate seat in 1996. In an overreach attempt, he failed miserably to oust Bobby Rush from a Congressional seat in 2000. Undeterred, Obama continued the ruse of networking and campaigning on behalf of the little Susies and the Johnnys until the music stopped in spring 2001 and the CAC ended.

In the extensive reviews conducted by the Consortium on Chicago School Research, the researchers chose their words gingerly: "In summary, the failure of the Challenge to achieve an overall effect on school improvement could be due to a number of shortcomings in the design and implementation of the Challenge itself. These include the breadth of its goals and the vagueness of its strategies for school development . . . general weakness in the levers for change . . . weaknesses in the capabilities and resources of the External Partners [the grantee sycophants]. . . . Little evidence of an overall Annenberg effect on school development or student outcomes across the schools it supported. . . . The Challenge's only real accountability mechanism was the threat of discontinuing its financial support to schools and Partners. . . . 'Not only do we want to lure you into these relationships with the money.' . . . The Challenge's stated goals were intentionally rhetorical, not made to set benchmarks for determining its success or failure but to draw attention to and mobilize support for a particular vision of educational reform. . . . The Challenge promoted a reform agenda that often collided with specific system policies, which created tensions and dilemmas for principals and teachers at the school and classroom levels. . . . [The founders wanted] to change the structure of schools as we know them."

The Challenge lasted five years. Were the schools so irreparably dysfunctional that they defied improvement? Did Obama deign to acknowledge the problems? Obama accepted a powerful founding chairman and president position responsible for 210 school locations fully staffed with administrators, principals, and teachers educating 50,000 students. The project failed, chaos reigned throughout the school system, and the main man walked away unscathed only to continue an illustrious political career destined for the White House. On the back of his matchbook Obama made a personal note to use that spellbinding "fundamental transformation" line as often as possible. It absolutely hypnotizes liberals! And man, oh man, what a perfect deception to obliterate American values!

During the 2008 presidential campaign, Obama resolved not to showcase the CAC. In fact, he went radio silent while the mainstream media followed on cue. The number of skeletons in the closet was too overwhelming. In the end, the CAC was a burlesque of big city school reform, full of save-the-children rhetoric while in the end using the kids as human shields to advance his political ambitions. Nothing personal—it was just a power thing.

Fast forward to 2013. The nation's third-largest school district closed fifty-three elementary schools and one high school to forestall the Chicago Public Schools' looming $1 billion budget shortfall. That's $1 billion just for one fiscal year! To save themselves physically, mentally, and emotionally, Chicago students were leaving in droves to charter schools and the suburbs. Mayor Rahm Emanuel, the former Obama White House Chief of Staff, admitted the decision to close the schools should have been done at least a decade ago. That would have been about the time the CAC failed to complete their dramatic improvement of the CPS. Needless to say, the president's staunch political ally did not concede the wrecking-ball effects of the poorly-managed, community-organized, structural makeover of children's education designed by the Obama/Ayers duo. Off on another planet, Obama was in his second term as president of the United States, golfing, surfing, entertaining, and traveling the globe—thoroughly enjoying his enchanted life while his very own daughters were tucked away in a safe, private, Washington, DC school.

The CAC farce was the pre-2008-election, flashing-red, danger sign of what the country could expect living under Obama's reign. When ObamaCare went online October 1, 2013, Obama had the entire world, beyond his small obsequious orbit, shaking their heads in disbelief. Ordering health insurance online like ordering a book on Amazon.com? This was the winter of our disenchantment with all things Obama. While trying to defend the myriad malfunctions, sloppy software architecture, and unpreparedness of his signature three-years-in-the-making Affordable Care Act, he compared the glitchy launch to an easily-remedied issue the tried-and-true, protected-by-the-spirit-of-Steve-Jobs Apple experienced with their new mobile operating system. He capped off the tortured analogy with another one of his casual "American values" lines: "That's not how we do things in America. We don't actively root for failure. We get to work, we make things happen, we make them better, we keep going." Does anyone really think that Obama gives a flying fig about using 317 million Americans as guinea pigs for an untested, grotesque, waiver-ridden, jerry-rigged, Son-of-Medicaid without any contingency plans? Of course not. He's constantly amending the law to suit his political game plan—keep the big-government Democrats entrenched and in power including progressives, liberals, democratic socialists, social democrats, Third Wayers, neoliberals, market socialists, collectivists, and other flavor-of-the-month Utopianists.

Control-alt-delete: Mandated by law to begin January 1, 2014, ObamaCare has been unilaterally rewritten by Obama himself 23 times with 41 delays . . . and counting. Rube Goldberg would be embarrassed. With his abundant tergiversating talent, Obama used "benevolent suspensions" as his justification for contorting ObamaCare. Only those in the legal-know would understand it to mean forced "contributions" to his highness; those on the outside looking in thought he was making the changes as an act of kindness and goodwill. June 2014, the Congressional Budget Office (CBO) cried uncle, threw in the towel, and waved the white flag exhausted admitting they could no longer assess the fiscal impact of the insufferable, unachievable, and hopelessly ridiculous ObamaCare. Surprise, surprise, surprise: At the end of this Bataan Death March, a government-dictated single-payer healthcare system awaits to resuscitate working taxpayers from the blood-sucking 50% plus marginal tax rate inflicted by the Obama vampires.

Vladimir Lenin has entered the building. Come on, you can say it, you can handle the truth. "Single-payer" is liberal code for soft selling Communism, big "C."

Obama seems to follow a power-grab pattern as evidenced by the CAC and many more savior-like, social initiatives presented in the following pages. He brashly refers to his technique as "Barack's 7 Badass Steps to Power Up":

Step 1 – Find a naive group of lefty activists.

Step 2 – Take control of the checkbook.

Step 3 – Throw money at favored, special interest groups.

Step 4 – Line up the voting blocks for current and future elections.

Step 5 – Dodge any expectations for measurable outcomes.

Step 6 – Appear circumspect while making a quick getaway.

Step 7 – Make sure "the family" isn't collaterally damaged.

Now it all makes sense. This is Obama's game plan for feigning governance. It worked in Chicago so it's really just a matter of scale. He can whip out the Power-Up playbook and, step by step, make like he knows what he's doing. It works for any issue, any piece of legislation, and any catastrophe in any venue, on any day, in any country. Power up TOTUS for the self-congratulatory speech and it's a three-pointer.

Obama has a crystal clear understanding that money begets votes and votes beget power. Nothing stands in the way of Obama getting his cash while making sure his adversaries do not. Witness his forceful admonition of the Supreme Court Justices during the January 27, 2010 State of the Union address. He literally scolded them for what he deemed was opening the floodgates for special interest groups during candidate elections. Only six days prior, the judges asserted in *Citizens United v. Federal Election Commission* that the First Amendment protects free speech for corporations and for unions funding independent political broadcasting in candidate elections. Obama threw a hissy fit because groups other than the Democrats can now get more creative with how they spend their campaign contributions with the Supremes' blessing.

Never one to let legal precedents get in the way, Obama demanded the Democrats push through the Disclose Act as a counter measure to the highest court's ruling. This piece of punitive legislation would force corporations, unions, and other groups to disclose their donors behind their political advertising. The Act was voted down in the Senate.

Obama, in a slick one-upmanship contrivance, went into full attack mode brandishing his most lethal weapon. He floated a draft Executive Order that would mandate companies seeking federal contracts to detail all political contributions for the last two years including donations made by senior executives. This move put political favoritism back in the procurement process, blunted free speech, discriminated against small businesses, and negated the Hatch Act. The taxpayer-funded comrades of Obama were conspicuously omitted from the "pay-to-play" Executive Order. In the end, the draft morphed into a neutered Disclose Act petition sitting on a Democrat senator's website begging for citizen signatures.

Big labor unions, political advocacy groups, and federal grant-seekers support Obama because he's a friend with a great many benefits. They all feed into and off of the vicious money-vote-power cycle of giving and taking taxpayers' money. Obama knows that even he can't transcend the superstar power of the Benjamins, especially the redesigned version with phrases from the Declaration of Independence on the front—just overlook the three-year delay, printing errors, and $4 million ink-splotch problem patriotically forgiven. Maybe our eyes are playing tricks but the U.S. paper currency is beginning to look a lot like euro banknotes. What's next, roping the U.S. into the euro zone to bailout the "exceptional" Greeks?

Buying votes is considered illegal within the public purview. Obama appreciates that; he's a scholarly attorney. But he's an activist organizer first and his mix-it-up instincts always trump his legal learnings. So he crafts a false storyline that social justice, wealth redistribution, and diversity are state-gifted rights. And he, power-to-the-people Obama, is ideologically wedded to these entitlements. He contrives the illusion that he is ordained to deliver these birthrights back to their rightful owners—his favored voting-block of the week. A vote for Obama is a vote for righteous ownership of their righteous entitlements. Is it buying votes? Of course it is, in an oblique sort of way. Social justice has and always will be Obama's siren song to get votes—illusively alluring and effective.

Obama, the social-justice drumbeater, orchestrates the victimhood cacophony, that heightens the populace anxiety, that escalates to class warfare, that crescendoes to wealth redistribution, and climaxes with new entitlements. It's the left-leaning zealots' way of building fresh, new voting constituencies and rejuvenating the old standbys. Entitlements spawn their own voters—the definitive calculation for Obama's power grabs.

Obama shrewdly knows that if he controls America's banks, energy producers, healthcare providers, educators, and infrastructure builders, he can regulate made-to-order entitlements that serve as magnets for unions of all stripes and environmentalists of every obsession. Think of the endless, social-equality options! Obama has an infinite patchwork of self-entitled voters that he can mix & match, plug & play, and summons to the voting booths by waving progressive freebies.

Social-justice gamesmanship has been recycled since Teddy Roosevelt became president, decades before he actually began waving the Progressive Party flag. It's all been done before. One would think that progressives would actually be "progressive" and evolve beyond their tired, unimaginative theories. Progressives are the antithesis of progress, tolerance, and broad-mindedness. Progressives are actually "regressives" reverting to a lesser, more restrictive, Chicken Little lifestyle that has never worked anywhere in the history of the world. Humans explore, they grow, they progress and prefer doing so without big government interfering.

Whenever liberals need a new cliché, they dust off their thesaurus and reinvent their antiquated slogan in the current decade's lingo—the more whimsical, the better. Who could forget these focus-group-tested mots justes: counterculture, sit-in, civil rights, gay pride, flower power, bra burner, hippies, green revolution, ecological awareness, affirmative action, selective buying, racial steering, corporate whore, global zeitgeist, global warming, climate change, climate disruption, climate change is Risky Business. The country's been there, done that. Searching for bumper-sticker-ready sound bites, Obama hoped-and-changed far and wide for a new angle, one that would distinguish his "historic" presidency.

Barack Obama and his Harvard devotees put on their transcendent thinking caps and agreed Obama must forge a unique legacy born of moral afflatus. What could it be? They really didn't have much to work with. Obama never built anything; never managed a company; never even heard of a balance sheet; never wrote a brief; never honestly penned a book; never designed an iconic product, not even a mediocre one; never created non-volunteer jobs; never enlisted in the armed forces; never assembled a resumé, nor curriculum vitae; never worked in the private sector; never joined the Peace Corp; never governed a state, a city, nor a town council; never played professional sports, nor intermural; never ran a charity 10K race, nor 5K; never became a Boy Scout; never belonged to a union; never joined an environmental group; never much of anything. But, he was in hot pursuit of unadulterated power. They could work with that.

The ivory-tower, armchair academics settled on "transformative" as the central theme for the lawless Obama years in the White House. Constitutional law professor and close Obama advisor Laurence Tribe was giddy over his chance to stuff the Supreme Court with resolute lefties. Economics Professor David Cutler was skipping the light fandango to unleash ObamaCare on the American peons.

Cutler devised a sexed-up 2008 Obama campaign slogan: By hook or by crook, Barack will cut your annual insurance premiums by -$2,500! The arithmetic-illiterate liberals didn't get the double negative and mindlessly pulled the Obama lever. Brainy MIT Professor Jonathan Gruber tried to weigh in but got tongue-twisted with his typo, speak-o, mistake-o. Poor boy. MIT you say? The Grand Crit himself Roberto Unger saw a wonderful opportunity to showcase his Critical Legal Studies protégé transforming through intellectual bedlam with a touch of romanticism for effect. Obama would be the transformative president fundamentally transforming America, thus delivering transformational vindication of America as seen through the eyes of the collectivistic dogmatists. With all this alchemy swirling around the Harvard Law School, no wonder the U.S. Constitution is treated like *chaos philosophorum* that must be reconstructed into a malleable, reinterpretable rule of law according to the sacred Emerald Tablet of the progressives. Cut to the chase: Where once stood the U.S. Constitution designed to preserve, protect, and promote American freedoms, the living-constitutionalists believe the government exists to command, control, and coerce every aspect of Americans' lives. Nothing is off limits.

Obama wants to be "transformational" at any cost. Consequently, his revolutionary power circuits are overloaded and he can't figure out what actually needs to be transformed—other than everything that's good about America. His lack of critical thinking skills, his mental agility weakness, and his propensity to distort reality probably resulted from marijuana and other drug indulgences during his formative years. A few of his IQ points must have gone up . . . yeah, man, up in smoke! Made small by his impaired thinking and lethargy to try new things, Obama opts for scale—bigger this, bigger that—instead of a unique, imaginative, visionary mission that uplifts and inspires. "We Do Big Things" emails carry the day and keep the grandiose illusion alive. He also relies on progressives who still live in the 1930s, 1960s, and 1970s to craft his forever-moving, forever-transforming agenda. He's fighting old wars against American exceptionalism because that's all he knows and cares to know. It's class warfare redux.

When the leader of what-used-to-be the free world elliptically talks of "fundamental transformation" of the United States, he's talking about fundamentally changing the U.S., the American people—how we view ourselves in the word, our nature, our motivations, our history. More precisely his plan is to transmogrify our lives—our ability to think, to invent, to choose, to build, to explore. Noam Chomsky, the lefties' much-loved anarchist, refers to it as libertarian socialism. Obama probably uses that term, too, but only with what's-the-password friends.

Behold Obama's grand social experiment: Make libertarian socialism the de facto and the literal law of the land; all United States citizens will have a spiritual transformation in the Marxist tradition, whether they like it or not; existing, newly established, and envisioned liberal institutions will "encourage" the Marxist transformation; the now-enlightened citizenry will yield more transformative institutions that will yield more spiritually-transformed citizens that yield more transformative institutions and on and on. A self-perpetuating, progressive machine that reproduces itself. The resulting automatons, or rather liberated human beings, are placidly ushered into utopian socialism or the left's version of Nirvana.

While in Warsaw May 2011 at the Presidential Palace, standing side by side with Poland's President Bronislaw Komorowski, Obama advised the Polish democracy to *institutionalize* and to not just protest: "What's required I think is, number one, understanding that you have to institutionalize this transformation . . . and the habits of countries have to change." He went on to say: "So part of the lesson is that you have to institutionalize change. And that is a hard process, and it's a long process." Sound familiar. The apologetic leader of the free world spreading the essence of *fundamental transformation* to the freedom fighters of Solidarity. What's the word for "farcical" in Polish?

Perhaps if Lech Walesa, the hero of Solidarity, would have attended the fete wearing his Pope John Paul II signet ring, he may have stopped Obama's specious narrative that democracy is protected by progressive institutions. Democracies are protected by durable constitutions, the rule of law, property rights, free elections, education, and inclusiveness. Walesa won The Nobel Peace Prize in 1983 for finding democratic solutions to Poland's problems. The template is American-style liberty envisioned by the Founding Fathers—mixt cultures, mixt religions, mixt free-trade. Having Walesa, the George Washington of Poland, on stage next to Obama would be like shining the light of freedom on the tyranny of superficial oratory—a glaring contrast that Obama could not have withstood.

So was it a slip of the lip or vindictiveness that caused Obama to refer to a Nazi death camp as "a Polish death camp" at the Presidential Medal of Freedom ceremony May 2012 at the White House insulting every Pole in the world? Probably sheer spitefulness that Warsaw has managed their sovereign debt with threat-to-democracy, tea-party disciplines much better than Obama's central-planning administrators. Walesa was sufficiently dissed as were all Polish American voters.

As a tribute to their country's strength and resilience in spite of their membership in the soulless EU, the Poles honored the memory of their "evil empire" crusader, Ronald Reagan, with a bronze statue in the center of Warsaw on Embassy Row.

The power vortex Obama generates belies the disintegration of the U.S. economy along with the perversion of American values. He goes to the gym, gives a speech, shakes a few hands, plays multiple rounds of golf, hosts a gala event for the most popular artists and athletes at the People's House—sauntering about like nothing is wrong. And that's just it. In the Obama radical activist playbook, everything is going as planned.

Anarchy and destruction, code-named fundamental transformation, are Obama's objectives. And we thought it was just Obama being cognitively dissonant. Instead, we Americans need to come to grips with our cognitive disequilibrium for trusting someone who has benefitted so grandly from our education system, structure of laws, free-enterprise society, and good will. Obama proclaims to be building the one indispensable nation. Rendering the nation superfluous and impotent is more like it. His deceptions are real and we are living in this absurdly inverted universe.

Imperious Obama uses the tools in his command-and-control box cunningly without remorse as if it were the new normal for the American rule of law. If you doubt that American governance has changed under the freelancing politician, step inside his parlor said the spider to the fly:

- pay-to-play
- a panoply of executive fiats
- "I've got a pen and I've got a phone"
- trade laws for fellow travelers
- strangling regulation
- discretionary enforcement
- "notwithstanding" loopholes
- technical legal minutiae
- parsing the obvious into obscurity
- confiscating the mortgage market
- anointing winners and condemning losers
- speaking with forked tongue
- redistributing wealth instead of creating it
- rope-a-doping Fox News hosts
- unbridled spending
- fudging economic reports
- fiddling with the Gross Domestic Product (GDP) algorithm quarter to quarter
- serial stonewalling
- class warfare
- clemency carpet-bombing
- shallow rhetoric
- line-item veto on steroids
- public-equity investing
- emperor-like decrees
- Harry Reid's 51ers

- extralegal proclivities
- condoning bureaucrats' political hit lists
- unilaterally suspending statutes
- politically-expedient enforcement of laws
- rewriting the U.S. Constitution
- interpretable regulations
- social engineering
- "[fill in the blank] is the civil-rights issue of our generation."
- financial engineering
- duplicitous fact-checking
- creating a world devoid of economic rationality
- taxing taxes
- Beltway creative accounting
- do-over budgets
- social-cost modeling
- cost-benefit analysis racketeering
- play-it-by-ear foreign policy, a.k.a. the Obama Doctrine
- relinquishing global respect
- zigzag diplomacy
- "calibrated" sanctioning of revanchist invaders
- finger-pointing chastisement
- pirouetting pressers
- shrewd swindling
- deriding Congress
- muzzling whistleblowers
- "sue and settle"
- blaming his speech-writers

- late-Friday-afternoon, pre-holiday-weekend data dumps
- "Madder than hell" platitudes to tranquilize wounded veterans

These are but a few of the methods used thus far. More precisely, Obama is an obstinate, I-was-nothing-and-now-I-am-everything, uniquely-purposed scallywag!

Usurping Congress's regulatory authority, Mr. Executive Power willfully surrenders his national security responsibilities—hell-bent on upending everything under the Stars and Stripes. Obama and his liberal allies will stop at nothing until they have full control over all U.S. taxpayer monies to use for their anti-exceptionalism, sanctimonious, Euro-socialist Utopia. It's a zero-sum game: They win, America loses.

THE OBAMA HEAD FAKE

Obama says one thing and does another. Sure we know his game is basketball, after all, he's LeBron, baby. Head fake right, pivot left. He's in a perpetual state of shamming his position. Yet does anyone doubt that he deliberately misleads to hide his intended move? An amorphous head fake is slippery and hard to catch in real time. Dissembling is more palatable and slightly less disrespectful to the American people than a full-frontal, bad-boy lie, straight up. As early as November 2008, the late former Secretary of State Lawrence Eagleburger saw through Obama, intuitively exposing him to be a charlatan and a phony. Comedian Dennis Miller, after four years of careful and thoughtful consideration, finally called it: “I think Barack Obama is a debonair grifter. I don’t trust a word he says.” Touché.

The main job of the American president is to protect U.S. citizens. Somehow he missed that important bit of information pursuing not only an alleged political science degree but a full law degree. He relishes power and drives directly for it, feigning that he will assume the pursuant responsibility for solving enormous economic, international, and political problems. Then the swift swivel and he’s racked up $17 trillion of debt, disparaged our closest allies, and paralyzed the political process making like he just pulled off the MVP play of the century. This is not a typical politician over-promising and under-delivering.

What’s the genesis of the wicked Obama head fake? Most believe it’s a basketball strategy. Faked out again! It’s Barack expressing his passive-aggressive feelings. “Say what you mean and mean what you say” does not register in a passive-aggressive, especially an Obama-sized, egomaniacal personality. The ethical circuits are disconnected between what a passive-aggressive says and what he does.

If Obama doesn’t get his way, he follows a strange pattern of suave nonchalance followed by a patronizing TOTUS speech. Soon after, he exhibits signs of annoyance that reveal a potentially full-blown paroxysm of disdain. That’s where Obama, with great discipline, contains it with his passive-aggressive devices. They can present in many different forms but it’s usually a mean-spirited reversal of a promise or a commitment. President Mighty Mouse dare not use physical aggression to express his rage so he reverts to relational aggression.

What does an Obama head fake look like? Michael J. Boskin, professor of economics at Stanford, published his analysis in the September 8, 2011 *Wall Street Journal* "Records Set on Obama's Watch." Where the unassuming U.S. taxpayer might consider this a list of abject failings, Barack probably considers them high-five victories. And to our chagrin, this was just the beginning—he's president for five more years! We believed when Obama was sworn into office that he would safeguard a prosperous, exceptional America. At least we were hopeful in our interpretation of that which he told us. Certainly we can trust President Obama. He's one of us. More than willing to seize the moment, Obama posed for the camera, played to the crowd, pretended he was trustworthy, pivoted far left, and started dismantling our country piece by piece.

Here are a few of the failings/victories on Obama's watch. Note the superlatives:

1. The first U.S. sovereign debt downgrade in American history.
2. The highest federal spending since World War II (25% of GDP).
3. The highest budget deficit since WW II (10% of GDP).
4. The highest federal debt since just after WW II (67% of GDP).
5. The highest long-term unemployment since 1930s (45.9%).
6. The lowest home-ownership rate since 1965 (59.7%).

7. The lowest percentage of taxpayers paying income tax in modern era (49%).
8. The highest government dependency in American history (47%).

Obama wants to guarantee his place in history as the president that added as much debt during his administration than all prior 43 presidents combined. This has been fact-checked. All 43 presidents starting with George Washington! Do you see the pattern? The head fake here is the rational assumption that any president of any organization has a fiduciary responsibility to said organization. That's inherent in having that honor. But not Obama. His responsibility is to himself. He obligingly takes the power and uses it against those that bestowed it on him.

Adding insult to injury, Obama decided to change how the United States' GDP is calculated. Waving his hammer and sickle, he ordered his bureaucratic minions to devise the Obamanomic GDP effective July 2013. Obama's economy would have its own unique formula not used anywhere else in the world. Clever liberal subterfuge—when the real numbers are bad, use those great, big, beautiful ABCs to rewrite the categories that make up GDP. Gone was the notion of measuring *real production.* No, no, no. In the Obama Nation, *spending* is the only true measure. They considered rephrasing it to Obama's Gross Domestic Spending (OGDS) but that would blow the smokescreen. To pump up the new GDP numbers, the liberal economists included research & development (R&D); pension pay-outs along with pension IOUs; artistic originals of photographs, books, movies, TV shows, greeting cards, and music. Reality shows, soap operas, newspapers, magazines, blogs, sports events, etc. have no enduring value so are *not* in the new GDP groupings. Today, the free press has no enduring value. Tomorrow, the Obama machine controls the world. Catch the tyrannical drift to absolute power? Weighing Europe's socialist proclivities, the U.S. bureau that calculates GDP may follow their lead and include prostitution, illegal drugs, and other activities in due time. Is Europhilia considered one of those "other activities"?

Beltway enema: With the 2016 changing of the White House guard not happening soon enough, the case could be made for performing a department-by-department colonoscopy on all U.S. economic data collected and reported during Obama's eight years in office. A complete forensic purge may be in order, or at least asterisking the-fix-is-in Obama and his cadre of administrators the way Major League Baseball handles serious indiscretions. Liberal job-protectors are in every nook and cranny throughout the Obama administration—DOJ, EPA, DOE, DOD, DOL, FERC, EPA, VA, etc., including the "impartial" CBO.

Sacked: How can teleworkers at the U.S. Patent and Trademark Office (USPTO) suspend a protected NFL team nickname with but a handful—yes, a mere handful—of well-paid "Native American activists" complaining about a "redskin" racial slur? The majority of American Indians have abandoned this panhandling, damn-the-white-man mentality. What gives? Who else! President Obama audibled the offensive play: "If I were the owner of the team and I knew that there was a name of my team, even if it had a storied history, that was offending a sizable group of people, I'd think about changing it." Hike! Federal government employees were his #4 contributor in 2012, jumping from #19 in 2008.

John Crudele at the *New York Post* reported since 2010 the Census Bureau has admitted that several die-hard employees had been caught red-handed manipulating unemployment reports to benefit their progressive president. Fudging the unemployment numbers in the last months before the 2012 presidential election put Obama over the top and back in the Oval Office. The "labor participation rate" was a finicky number to tally; fewer and fewer people were looking for work; more and more were giving up and dropping out. What's an ingratiating desk jockey to do? Just don't count them. Delete! Poof! Gone! The former GE CEO Jack Welch was incredulous about the bogus government numbers and tweeted: "Unbelievable jobs numbers…these Chicago guys will do anything…can't debate so change numbers."

Which the White House could do rather conveniently having taken control of the Census Bureau as soon as Obama's staff hung their West Wing nameplates. They knew the Current Populations Survey overstated the number of uninsured Americans. It must have been heaven sent: The reports justified their hyperbolic arguments for ObamaCare. Come 2014, when it was obvious that the liberals ramrodded their baseless healthcare law, well, they just tweaked the CPS questionnaire to "prove" they were right all along. Fantasyville by the numbers.

Watching Obama flex his power pecs on the international stage is one of the left's most alluring spectator sports. Almost all bodybuilders train to display their physiques, posing for the judges. Obama cuts and bulks with the world's most competitive, weighty heads of state. Come the crucial, decision-making showtime, however, Barack leads from behind the pack—a rather flaccid stratagem. Where's the scrawl-and-brawl, ground-and-pound, clinch-fighting Chicago South-Sider when you need him? That's the rub. Obama was elected using political, mixed-martial-arts techniques, certainly not because of his worldly diplomatic experience. This is not how an American holds onto the iron-willed Mr. Olympia crown for global guts. America is a nation of leaders. *Hasta la vista*, Barack!

Obama thinks, therefore, no one else exists. Typical arrogant Obama. "Leading from behind" conjures up a pack of Alaskan Huskies mushed around the Iditarod by their master, unable to find their way through the blinding snow were it not for his greatness. Or the one and only Santa Claus in his trusty sleigh heroically guiding his rudderless reindeers around the globe. The phrase must really endear the president to other heads of state. Who writes his talking points? Probably President Awesome.

Obama's realpolitiking confirms that he is a teenybopperish neophyte when handling any issue outside his narrow, progressive, domestic silo. Feeling sentimental because his mom and dad romanced in Russian class, Obama "reset" our position with Russia by completely cancelling the missile defense shield the U.S. had arranged with Poland and the Czech Republic. Not only was he trying to make nice with Western Europe who believed the shield irritated big bad Vlad, but he also felt the volte-face would make Moscow swoon over him. Poor little Putin was afraid NATO would attack him. Have no fear, Barack's here! In effect, he handed over on a silver platter our right to self-defense and got nothing, nada, zilch in return. Without as much as one single, save-Pussy-Riot-punk, human-rights concession, Obama tied the gift in a bow by rewarding the Russians with their most long-awaited access to the World Trade Organization, and signing a lopsided New Start nuclear treaty potentially more deadly than binge-drinking Russian vodka. Hey, B baby, wasn't that a little overly generous when all Vladimir Putin was askin' for was just a little respect?

During several months of negotiations, Obama didn't even bother to consult with the Poles and Czechs until after the deal was struck. Obama phoned both prime ministers the night before the prearranged September 17, 2009 news conference with the pander-to-Putin press release a click away from their email inboxes. Salt in wound: This sadomasochistic gesture marked the 70th anniversary of the U.S.S.R. invading Poland September 17, 1939 under the teeny-tiny footnote in the Hitler-Stalin Nonaggression Pact stipulating that the Soviets could invade and occupy as much of Eastern Poland as they could put in their tank-treaded shopping carts.

Fast forward five years to March 2014. Putin decided to milk his perceived vexation for as much as he could get, so he annexed Crimea with unanimous backing by the Crimean parliament. To hell with unenforceable international law, range limits on nuclear missiles, and Obama's jokester sanctions! June 2014, Obama offered up $1 billion of U.S. taxpayers' money for the European Reassurance Initiative to try to put the Putin genie back in the bottle and protect the frontline NATO states—the same ones he left twisting in the Soviets' wind.

Atomic battlefield: What happened to Russia's 3,800 tactical nuclear weapons strategically positioned to annihilate the United States' less than 500? TNWs would be discussed after the 2012 election when Comrade Obama had "more flexibility." *Psst, Dmitry, pass this take-me-I'm-yours message to Vladimir when you see him. He'll understand "flexibility," you know, his new gymnast squeeze. Tee-hee. Oh, and give him this gift, too. He'll really think I'm special when you tell him I've chopped U.S. nuclear forces to the bone waaaaaay before the 2018 New Start deadline. I'm doing it for Vlad's 62nd birthday. Thanks, bro.*

Could the comparison between world leaders be more stark? Ultra-nationalist Vladimir Putin was looking out for Russia in the 21st century; neurotic contritionist Obama indulged his peacenik donors from the '60s who wanted a cowering U.S. that's not a soupçon more powerful than Europe. And they got it! Putin was just planning ahead to destabilize Europe in order to reassemble the Soviet Empire—slice and dice Ukraine as soon as Mother Russia took the top gold-medal honors at the 2014 Sochi Olympics. Except for the radioactive Chernobyl wasteland that's uninhabitable for the next 20,000 years. He'd gladly pay someone, anyone to take the "zone of alienation" off his hands.

H-e-e-e-e-r-e's Billy! Atomically-armed-to-the-teeth Russia had already confiscated Ukraine's 1,800 nuclear weapons with the Clinton Administration's 1994 Budapest Memorandum. Canny Kiev had amassed the world's third largest stockpile of nuclear weapons. In exchange, the U.S., the United Kingdom, and the Russian Federation promised to protect and defend Ukraine's territorial and political independence. Failing to trust their aching guts about a possible betrayal, the Kiev officials gave up all of their strategic nuclear defenses. In 2008, President George W. Bush and the Brits, honoring their security commitments, proposed Ukraine and Georgia join NATO, however,

Germany and France squashed the outreach. Putin used reverse psychology on the mental midgets by feigning fear that NATO might gang up on his poor unguarded Russia. The "victim" ploy worked so Putin invaded Georgia. Mad Vlad viewed members of the North Atlantic Treaty Organization as passive pawns that could never contain the Russian Bear, in spite of their "collective defense."

Frau Merkel and Monsieur Sarkozy went wobbly about the fire-breathing Putin laying claim to all of Europe starting with Georgia, then Crimea, then Ukraine, then the Baltics, then Poland, then Germany, then France, oh my! What a predicament—Europe used their military budgets to save the planet then couldn't save themselves. Call up the Greenies! Arm the environmentalists! They'll protect carbon-free Europe with their soft-pellet hand guns, solar-paneled tanks, and wind-turbine aircraft. Industriously minding its own business, unarmed Ukraine was geographically caught in the middle, inadvertently dropped the soap, and got screwed. The cross-my-heart-and-hope-to-die Budapest Agreement was nothing but a Kiev-take-a-hike maneuver for the dominant nuclear powers.

The White House's response to the assault on Ukraine was a heavily circulated image of Obama looking sharp in his tighter jeans, casual shirt, sleeves rolled up, hand-on-hip power stance, making a 90-minute phone call from the Oval Office to Putin. 90 minutes? That's one and a half hours. A lot of horse-trading can be done in 90 minutes. So what part of the United States did Obama agree to give to Putin if he slowed down his global gerrymandering? On the other end of that photo-op, a shirtless pec-flexing Putin, walking his pet tiger with his trophy nymphette more than half his age, just snickered remembering how he made Obama crawl to him on Syria then leveraged the bogus peace process to get himself one of them snazzy Nobel Peace Prizes—just like Barack's. Earth to Thorbjørn Jagland, secretary general of the Council of Europe and chair of the Nobel Committee: Putin says to stick your "international laws" where the sun doesn't shine; he can be wooed the same way you bought Obama.

Kumbaya diplomacy: Lt. Col. Ralph Peters (Ret.) aptly crystalized the interplay between Russia and the West when he said Obama uses "group therapy" to combat Putin's "brute force." The progressive moral-relativist pansies have a hard time judging good from evil, except when scripted, digitized, and viewed on the silver screen or on Angie's List.

Hey, Vlad, how about a little quid pro quo on *containing* the Iranian nuclear expansion that you personally set in motion when you breathed life back into their defunct Bushehr nuclear reactor with Russian-made parts and rubles? Aw shucks, Mr. Putin, he misspoke. Please excuse the then-nominated U.S. Secretary of Defense Chuck Hagel. Walk it back: Obama's hand-delivered note said he meant nuclear Iran *prevention* not *containment* when he was testifying before the Senate Armed Services Committee February 2013. Of course we appreciate Secretary Hagel's distinguished Vietnam service, but what do you expect from an unremarkable, academic, national-security greenhorn from Nebraska? It's The Hagel Doody Show! Chuck, you're giving the Cornhuskers a bad name. Russia no doubt enjoys watching the U.S. twist in the wind against an Iranian ICBM. Putin's FSB (formerly the KGB) diplomacy outflanked the feckless Chicago negotiator and his puppets, flushing American values down the toilet.

Then there's Iran, our formidable foe. While BHO, the dilettante diplomat, lives in a dream state that he can calmly cajole mullahs, ayatollahs, and dictators of any persuasion, the Iranians continue to highly enrich uranium, billet by billet, with reckless abandon. Given a once-in-a-lifetime, historic, strategic choice during the 2009 Iranian "Green Revolution" whether to help the bloodied demonstrators or hang tight with the mullahs, Obama chose the path of least resistance and did diddly-squat for the brave protestors with the upshot of endorsing the oppressive Iranian regime.

Perhaps Obama thought this BFF signal would curry favor with Iran's then-President Mahmoud "wipe Israel off the face of the earth" Ahmadinejad. In the upcoming, no-more-nukes negotiations, the U.S. and its entourage requested the customary right to inspect unsanctioned, underground sites and to cease uranium production—pretty please? Iran knows if they can keep the centrifuge guessing-game going, they will have more time to keep the stockpiles growing. Strategic patience? Say what?!

And that's what they did. Iran kicked dirt in the negotiators' faces by blocking any and all future "workshop" inspections, then, sucker punched them by installing more centrifuges to make bucket loads of highly enriched uranium. They ushered the useful idiots out the door and wished them happy travels until they meet again. Iran rolled the envoy like a Persian rug, making them feel like they got a marvelous deal while Iran bought more time. Hand-knotted in their own vibrantly-colored silky diplomatic-speak, the sightseers failed to uncover: What the heck are the Iranians doing with 10,000 centrifuges? Maybe this phrase was lost in translation: global nuclear terrorism.

Like a battered lover who keeps being seduced and going back for more, Obama offered a handshake to the new "moderate" president of Iran Hassan Rouhani while visiting the United Nations in New York City. Obama wished to engage him with his finest twenty-first-century diplomacy. The opportunity to humiliate Obama on his own turf, especially at the jihad-imprinted lower Manhattan, was way too tempting for the U.S. State Department officially-designated, economically-sanctioned, state sponsor of international terrorism to resist. What else could the charming Persian politician do when faced with the opportunity to meet the "great Satan"? Rouhani refused, rebuffed, and spurned Obama's overture. Later that day, Rouhani warmly welcomed and privately dined with the Nation of Islam leader Louis Farrakhan. As a gesture of friendship, Rouhani offered to send Brother Farrakhan a few "Made in Iran" weapons disguised in cement bags for his protection from the Chicago South Side gangs. The Iranian president and his entourage also found time to personally visit the 9/11 Memorial and admire the work of their dancing-with-virgins al Qaeda departed.

Frenetically erratic best describes the rest of Obama's Middle East footprint. American-funded Pakistan harbors terrorists and disdains America. Syria bleeds and burns while militarily sheltered by Iran, Hezbollah, Hamas, and Russia; then Syria pays it forward to jihadists by sheltering them in their take-us-back-to-the-good-old-Neolithic-days terrorist training camps. Iranian Quds Force attempts assassinations of ambassadors in Georgetown restaurants. Iraq turned upside down by more than 400 senior al Qaeda death-row terrorist escapees—a come-to-papa assist by an atomic Iran. By June 2014, Iraq was bathed in blood by a reconstituted, fanatical, chopping-off-heads army, so terrifying that even al Qaeda disavowed them. President Grasping-at-Straws then reached out to his long lost buddies, Tehran's mullahs, for help to stabilize and rescue Iraq. Rapprochement mirage? The White House press secretary must have been high on something when he claimed that President Barack Obama had "substantially improved the tranquility of the global community." Pass the joint.

Obama's whipsaw foreign policy knows no limits. Obama cut and ran from Afghanistan waving a white flag like a girlie man to appease the moneyed, anti-war liberals. By feigning red-line concern yet doing nothing, Obama bolstered Syria's President Bashar "terrorist magnet" al-Assad thereby emboldening the Iranians and Russians to jockey for alpha-dog dominance in the Middle East. Nuclear zero? Global zero? The quixotic nuclear-free planet with Iran, China, and North Korea strengthening their nuclear facilities? Saudi Arabia, Turkey, and Japan now want nuclear parity to guarantee their own protection and survival. Tehran, say hello to the Saudis' little friend, the DF-3 missile with a range and payload to make your day.

Searching for his *spirit animal* in the Iranian snake, Obama single-handedly unleashed the nuclear-proliferation *animal spirits* of hostile, rogue nations worldwide.

Obama's lead negotiator with Iran was the same child-welfare social worker, U.S. Under-Secretary of State for Political Affairs Wendy Sherman, whom Clinton used to go toe-to-toe with North Korea in 1994. Dictator Kim Jong Il signed the Agreed Framework like a good little boy, and then his monster alter ego ignored the agreement and kept collecting his nuclear toys. Non-compliance was never naughtier. Iran's chief negotiator cared less about the world's children and far more about continuing enrichment and preserving Iran's nuclear program. While Wendy consulted her community-organizing notebook, Tehran agreed to nothing save full steam-turbine ahead with enriching and cranking out nukes. Mass production that Henry Ford would have envied! Mixing its messages with linguistic precision, Iran amiably agreed in a Western dialect to shut down the Arak reactor then switched to Farsi and told Obama to stuff it. Shake off the pixie dust, President Dreambeam! Concessional castration can't be reversed! Has the numbness in your groin gone away, yet? And the nuke can't be disinvented! Obama's heave-a-ton-of-bricks warning on sanction violators was spine-chillingly petrifying. Eeek! A mouse!

The tangled maneuvering begs the question: Why did Obama whip out our Uncle's checkbook May 2011 and underwrite the largest portion of the $40 billion Deauville Partnership to foment revolution in the fragile Arab Spring democracies? To beat his chest in the photo op with his Group of Eight buddies and take advantage of a tremendous opportunity to stir up chaos in the Middle East. C'mon, in his heart Obama remains a community agitator. Meanwhile back at the ranch of the most generous nation in the world, the deadliest and costliest single tornado in U.S. history ravaged Joplin, Missouri—158 killed and 1,150 injured. The tornado victims felt the Arabs' "growing" pains and had to think long and hard about the noble investment Obama had made with their tax dollars while they were homeless, toothbrush-less, and completely torn apart. Yet we all know that Midwesterners never say die, particularly those in Tornado Alley. They are generous with their neighbors, cameras or no cameras. President Obama, spare future tornado victims the "climate change as public health hazard" trope to regulate and tax CO_2 while Bay Area billionaires stage-manage an apocalypse to promote their lucrative carbon-credit exchanges. Besides, global warming registers less than 2.0 on the pollsters' Richter scales even as the president floats his new $1 billion Climate Resilience Fund. Biggest social-impact bang for your buck: The CRF proposed legislation highlights goods and services of companies that represent the holdings in most of the progressives' social-impact hedge funds. Go figure!

Sometimes an Obama head fake is just a plain old-fashioned flip-flop. The promise to close the Guantanamo Bay detention camp alone probably got him enough votes to start buying drapes for the Oval Office. Add in swapping-out military tribunals for civilian courts along with scrapping enhanced interrogation and he definitely had the keys to the kingdom. Mugged by the real world: Then came a mega dose of hard-cold reality known as presidential responsibility and, flippity-flop, he decided to just eliminate the enemy combatants by ordering "drone-caused disasters." No doubt he sensed a fault line portraying himself as Captain America slaying evil-doers with his trusty, indestructible drone-shield, primed for a macho, campaign slogan: Judge, Jury, and Executioner. The right calls this a certifiable flip-flop; the left knows they were head faked.

Club Gitmo remains open and has become a coveted, rejuvenation retreat for the New Age take-care-of-the-terrorists crowd. A nine-figure, multi-million dollar upgrade features a World Cup-style soccer field, basic cable TV, "Enrich Your Life" seminars, business courses on how to build a milk and honey farm, desert gardening classes, and, of course, the obligatory yoga disciplines. *Namaste*. Wait, there's more. An expansion of the upgrade includes a detainee & lawyer meeting complex, a hospital & senior center for the aging bomb-throwers, HD & premium cable channels, along with a 10,000 Islamic book library. And tear down those repulsive red, white, and blue rags hanging on the flag poles—the fluttering makes the incarcerated terrorists want to puke! All compliments of the American taxpayer. Is General John F. Kelly, commander of U.S. Southern Command including Gitmo, planning on retiring there?

To understand why Obama has such caustic contempt for American businesses, we need to remember that he and his lefties view all of America's wealth at their disposal and will use it to brazenly advance their progressive Utopia. Obama's life-is-good, surfer-dude, soul mates view America as the epitome of exploitative, bully capitalism devouring the world's resources causing ecological scarcity. The U.S. produces too much, too fast! We've left the rest of the world in the dust and their choking on it! The fair-chance progressives strive to minimize all things U.S. so non-U.S. countries can catch up. Their dream is that all men and women have government jobs and/or lavish government grants to pay for their do-what-you-love lifestyles rather than—dare we say this—produce things. Ignorance is liberal bliss.

Obama lives in a world of words and isn't very fond of numbers. The Harvardian needs some schooling on how the bulls and the bears "do it" in euphemistic terms even a fifth-grader can understand:

Lesson #1 – Wall Street is not Corporate America.

Lesson #2 – Wall Street is not Main Street.

Lesson #3 – Wall Street, though a symbol of U.S. economic power, is only a subset of the private sector and could not exist on its own without the larger private sector.

Lesson #4 – Wall Street is a separate industry unto itself that invents investment products using the underlying "raw materials" that are the stocks and bonds from the private sector—publicly-traded. And if the deal is juicy enough, they will also trade public-sector municipal bonds, U.S. Treasury bonds, notes, and bills.

Lesson #5 – Wall Street legally trades worldwide whatever financial products will make beaucoup profits such as quant funds, hedge funds, mutual funds, derivatives, stocks, bonds, commodities, exchange-traded funds (ETFs), U.S. Treasuries, and currencies through 31 different exchanges across the U.S., not just the New York Stock Exchange.

Lesson #6 – Wall Street traders, especially institutional traders, move the markets not the worker bees in Corporate America or on Main Street. Though Wall Street would like Main Street to think that they have great empathy for Main Street by providing resources to empower Main Street, Wall Street is a shameless, gimmicky, money-making game.

Lesson #7 – Wall Street traders don't make money unless the market moves, either up or down. That's why the market is always in motion—more money for traders. It's the bulls and the bears "dirty dancing." Tech darlings like Amazon, Facebook, and Twitter may trade on the exchanges as bottom-lineless organizations, yet traders will make money on these profit-slowpokes because their stocks are volatile, always in motion, always making money for long- and short-positions as well.

Lesson #8 – Wall Street traders of all pinstripes are addicted to government-goosed monetary stimulus, therefore, they love Obama most of the time and Mr. Quantitative Easing himself, the former Fed-head Ben Bernanke, all of the time. Hyper-money-printing excites the stock market and hyperactivates the stock traders. Main Street is left to go begging.

Lesson #9 – Corporate America and Main Street worker bees pay more taxes when government boosts the economy, thus, are stimulus-averse. Most are too busy managing their businesses and just doing their jobs that Obama can sometimes get away with his hoodwinking.

Lesson #10 – The private sector needs to be freed from government shackles to grow and create J-O-B-S.

Q.E.D.

Wall Street measures what Wall Street does—the trading volume for that day, week, month, etc. When the Dow gyrates and starts trending up, Obama is naive to equate it to "the private sector is doing just fine." In Obama's unicorn universe, he ignores the weakening greenback and flat GDP growth. Asset inflation be damned! Between January and March 2014, real GDP slipped deep into the red zone—negative 3%. Hmmmm . . . flat growth is looking better and better. Any wonder the U.S. is on the brink of financial disaster chasing the whimsies of this financial wizard? Stop-loss alert: The day after Obama won both the 2008 and 2012 elections, the stock market tanked 486 and 312 points, respectively. Obama's Midas-touch party-pooping totaled 798 points! Were Obama's college-graduate, job-seeking letters sent to Wall Street firms stamped ACCEPTED or REJECTED?

In Obama's singsong mind, nonprofit businesses are good and for-profit businesses are bad. Nonprofit schools are worthy of subsidies and for-profit schools are "predatory" liars and should be bullied, spat at, and regulated out of business. When Obama came into office, Corinthian Colleges was trading on the NASDAQ at $21/share; by July 2014 it was gasping for air at 22¢. Somebody goofed: Should have named the company after a part of the Quran, like Aakhira, rather than a book from the Bible. If only the reason for Corinthian's crucifixion were that simple. Singsonging along, the public sector is honorable and the private sector is vile. Public-equity investments steer the economy and private-equity investments wreck the economy. Grant-funded community organizers are revered while bootstrapped entrepreneurs are despised. And profits are the big, bad bogeyman—except for profits from green-energy projects.

Never mind that profits are what makes the world go round. In the private sector, both private and publicly-traded companies exist to make a profit from selling a product or service for the greatest benefit to the consumer. If there were no profit motive, there would not be an economy. Even the well-funded nonprofits at some point were endowed from profits made by someone's focus on earning profits. Just follow the money—nonprofits spend the profits someone else earned! Where did Obama acquire his millions? Profits made from the sale of his books in the private sector.

The private sector is open territory to be pillaged, plundered, scorned, vilified, disrespected, and bashed. The private sector is also the disparaged ATM that constantly spits out taxpayer dollars in the trillions to pay for the public sector that funds the nonprofits, state and local governments, universities, roads, bridges, and other civilized, shared-use amenities. As good citizens, the private sector also invests their profits to hire employees, build facilities, furnish retirement packages, sponsor healthcare benefits, and contribute tax dollars to their communities.

When convenient, Obama uses this huff-and-puff diatribe against profits to placate his liberal base. Painting the private sector as a trivial cash box downplays its role as the engine that runs the American economy. He is threatened by the immense leverage businesses have in all sectors of the economy and the American psyche. So it's easier to destroy what you fear than build a coalition.

Well, unless said coalition can be built with a private-sector business that can write jumbo checks and broadcast their support to Barack's designated causes. Money can right many make-believe injustices in Obamaland. How else can

Obama explain his close relationship with the profit-rocket born in "the cradle of capitalism" Warren Buffett? Consider this a gold-digging head fake.

As if our heads weren't spinning enough, Obama jolted the U.S. with his proposed American Jobs Act of 2011 for an additional $447 billion heaped onto the U.S. debt. To impart a sense of urgency, Obama commanded Congress to "pass this jobs bill now" eighteen times in about eight minutes. He was catering to, of course, a long list of political voting blocks, such as trial attorneys, teachers, cops, construction workers, veterans, and the long-term unemployed. Obama has a special affinity for the long-term unemployed—he social-engineered this Frankenstein and demands their five million plus votes. Repealing the Davis-Bacon Act and unlocking wages in the construction trades for public works projects wasn't even a consideration. The unions would have considered it an act of high treason with a loss of their 25% pay premium.

Sometimes we see Obama perform an accidental head fake; it has the same effect as an I'm-going-to-crush-you hustle. In the aforementioned American Jobs Act, Obama insisted that at least half of the $447 billion go to the States to spread the funds around to protect the jobs of the same ol same ol, unionized, human buffers, e.g., teachers, firefighters, policemen, etc. At first glance, it sounded generous.

Shrewdly, it boiled down to a transfer of tax dollars *from* municipal and state governments *to* the big Washington spenders *through* the hands of average investors. So while he appeared magnanimous, Obama gave cash to the municipalities, then, at the same time, changed the tax treatment for their muni bonds. Municipal bonds are purchased by moms and dads for kids' college educations, retirement, and possible health scares because of their special tax-exempt status. With a reverse two-handed dunk, Obama slammed the taxpayers' exempt cash right back to his Washington coffers. Harvey Golub, a former chairman and CEO of American Express, in his "A Jobs Bill That Boggles the Mind" summed it up as "cluelessness." Most likely it was an intentional behind-the-back pass to the burgeoning federal government—more taxes extracted along with more big-government jobs paid for with municipal bonds.

By the way, how many speeches does it take to convince Obama that the only jobs his "job" speeches create are for his Lost-Boys-in-Neverland speech writers? Fast trackin' a fine-arts scholar: Once a lowly wordsmith hunting and pecking at a keyboard, Benjamin J. Rhodes was appointed Assistant to the President and Deputy National Security Advisor for Strategic Communications and Speechwriting with a blood brother that's the president of CBS News. His unique contribution to keeping Americans safe under Obama's watch: "Don't do stupid sh**." Oh, the cleverness of thee to craft such a comprehensive and definitive U.S. foreign policy.

This trifling quote from President Obama's 2009 Inaugural Address sounds like Peter Pan: "We must pick ourselves up, dust ourselves off, and begin again the work of remaking America." At this point in the speech, the Lost Boys choreographed the Dougie into the script so that Barack & Michelle could make like Fred & Ginger in the 1936 movie *Swing Time.* One Great Depression dance duo paying homage to that other Great Depression dance team. Rumor has it that Obama can't even dance, let alone Dougie. Did you catch him on *The Ellen DeGeneres Show*—both times? In 2007, he busted a move on stage on camera and it was way too pitiful to watch. March 2014, with the Obamacare sign-up deadline looming, Obama desperately needed Ellen's demographic so he made an appearance via satellite. He was nearly in tears having to cede the selfie crown to the new queen. Don't despair. Obama still holds the world's record for photobombs—he's everywhere, he's everywhere!

Obama believes his own fabricated press that he has created "millions of jobs" since he came into office January 2009. The Bureau of Labor Statistics says it's more like 100,000 total net increase. That's a sizable in-your-face prevarication since current unemployment, all sectors considered, is upwards of 15%, not the as-promised below 8%. But Obamamaniacs are prone to exaggeration and fantasy. Just ask the 28 million part-time workers that would rather pursue their Nancy Pelosi-protected right to follow their passion to be gainfully employed full-timers.

Obama insists that governments generate jobs—a classic, progressive misconception. Any and all governments, be they city, county, state, or federal, don't exist without a tax base. The tax base is funded by the taxpayers' dollars. The taxpayers form governments and support them with their taxpayer dollars so that the governments will provide a secure infrastructure for businesses to exist, grow, and prosper. If the businesses don't exist, grow, and prosper, then there aren't any taxpayer dollars to fund the government. Liberals fail to recognize this elemental, circle-of-economic-life phenomenon. Rather, they choose to ignore it.

Every single, solitary business in America was started by an entrepreneur. Most thriving companies are taken for granted but somewhere along the line, an entrepreneur came up with the idea for the product or the service, took a chance, and made it happen. Entrepreneurs beget small businesses that beget medium business that beget large companies that beget multinational corporations. And these businesses are where jobs come from, not the government tooth-fairy. Again, another circle-of-economic-life fundamental that eludes liberals.

Obama never had a job in the private sector save the ice cream store gig to support his youthful peccadillos. Oh, right, don't forget that one-year telemarketing stint in a New York back office fresh out of college. He has next to nothing business experience. Clearly Obama doesn't know what he doesn't know.

In his incessant quest for power, Obama put a dagger in the Clintons' hearts on March 23, 2010 by signing into law The Patient Protection and Affordable Health Care Act, fondly known as ObamaCare. To secure his bid for the White House, he forced the Clinton political machine to its knees—his first major triumph. Desperate to hear them beg for mercy and surrender to the new progressive Grand Master, Obama pummeled the Clintons with this Holy Grail of socialized medicine instead of attending to the free-fall economy. It's the efficient Chicago way—take out your enemies and steal the Crown Jewels at the same time. In 1993, President Bill and his sidekick Hill failed miserably to pass a slightly, less-onerous piece of healthcare legislation called ClintonCare.

Most say ObamaCare was a mere 2,700 pages. That was during the bill's embryonic stage. According to the Americans for Limited Government Research Foundation using word-counting, they reviewed the fully-birthed statutes plus the highchair regulations, including the how-to-crawl directives, and tallied 3,600 pages and still growing. Then-Secretary Kathleen Sebelius was still tenderly feeding it enriched baby-formula over at Health and Human Services.

All 3,600 ObamaCare pages were chock-full of legalese laced with furtive taxes published in plain sight with more to come. You've heard Obama say this: "I didn't raise taxes once. I lowered taxes over the last [fill in the blank] years." June 2012, the Supreme Court ruled that ObamaCare's "individual mandate" was really a "tax" sold to the American public as a "penalty." This wasn't just a bait-and-switch; this was a supremely-sanctioned equivocation. Over ten years, $500 billion of new ObamaCare taxes will be levied on U.S. citizens. $500,000,000,000 of crushing new taxes! All those who thought they were protected from this monstrosity because they earned under $200,000 a year, filing individually, were just punked Obama-style. From the silver-tongued devil himself in a 2008 pre-presidential election ad that ran 30 minutes during prime time just about everywhere: "As President, my middle class rescue plan will cut taxes for every working family making less than $200,000 a year."

ObamaCare places more than $100 billion in new taxes on just these healthcare businesses alone: drug companies, health insurers, and medical-device manufacturers. This $100 billion new tax burden, disguised as fees on these big companies, is passed on to the consumer. Let me repeat. These are actual taxes that you are paying as the buyer of these products and services, disguised as fees on these big companies. This is Obama's "it depends upon what the meaning of the word 'is' is" dodge.

This humongous entitlement drives up the costs of healthcare for everyone while it was sold by liberals, with one voice, as a cost-cutting measure. The real cost cutting, or rather principle erosion, occurs with the Social Security Trust Fund, Medicare, and new long-term care insurance premiums. These programs will be the cash investors in the Ponzi scheme to pay for ObamaCare as House Budget Committee Chairman Paul Ryan uncovered. ObamaCare "borrows" $500 billion from the Medicare retirees and disabled to spread the healthcare wealth around, you know, everyone doing their fair share to support the Obama power grab.

It's estimated that 35 million Americans will lose coverage because ObamaCare incentivizes employers with more than 50 workers to drop healthcare coverage, pay a penalty, and move workers either to Medicaid or to the state government exchanges. By 2021, healthcare will account for nearly 20 percent of the U.S. economy up from under 14 percent in 2000. That's $1 of every $5 spent. In the first ten years, ObamaCare will cost $2.6 trillion (that's 12 zeros!) for all the additional bureaucracy, especially for more Internal Revenue Service enforcers. ObamaCare basically highjacks a giant portion of the U.S. economy.

In America, we cherish democracy and elect representatives to pass laws to make our lives better. We place our trust in them. President Obama was elected with the same duty. ObamaCare exploited our trust in government. Obama cut backroom deals wherever he could. He jammed, shoved, force-fed ObamaCare down our throats December 24, 2009 like a whole, fully-stuffed, Christmas turkey knowing that it would kill us. Shades of the gluttony death-by-spaghetti scene in the movie *Se7en* with Brad Pitt. This Capitol Hill, neo-noir, horror scene was deviously planned, coercing the Congress to vote on Christmas Eve when all of Washington wanted to go home to their families. All Senate and House Republicans voted against the bill. Even several Democrats, who risked losing their seats in upcoming elections, voted against ObamaCare. A clever "reconciliation" maneuver by the Democrats gave them the final determining edge to make ObamaCare the law of the land. Using "protect the poor" as his defensible shield, Obama carved out one-sixth of the U.S. economy to show the world he was in charge. Never underestimate Obama's psychosis for power.

Obama and the Democrat-controlled House and Senate wrapped up their euphoric spending-spree by passing ObamaCare then, woefully hung over, completely abdicated their responsibility to pass a federal budget. Having a lawful obligation to plan and restrain binge-spending cramps Obama's spendthrift style, so why bother.

The first and last time Obama signed a federal budget was March 11, 2009 with the Omnibus Appropriations Act which covered only seven months. Since 2010, the government has been freely floating on a series of Continuing Resolutions. From the time he took control of the U.S. piggy-bank, Obama's strategy has been to kitchen-sink his budget proposals sometimes in writing with actual numbers. In almost every instance, the preposterous wish-lists are voted down with zero support by both Democrats and Republicans in both houses.

His preferred dodge is the virtual budget disguised as a speech. This cloud budgeting allows the president to promise whatever spending and cuts he wishes to whatever governing body or voting block that his teleprompting targets. Besides conveniently defying any serious mathematical scoring by the number-crunchers in the CBO, he keeps the upward track of his progressive policies unchecked and unlimited, as if they were merely soft, fluffy abstractions. Unless it's for the military—that's when the sabers come out and the cost-gutting gets real.

There were promising signs that the electorate were onto Obama's head fakes and race-baiting Republicans with invectives like "they can come for the ride, but they gotta sit in back." When John Boehner assumed the Speaker position November 2010 after the Republicans took control of the House, Mr. Boehner cleverly outsmarted the fleet-footed president.

Boehner's full-court press began with Obama shooting his fair-share, more-taxes air ball followed by an extend-all-Bush-tax-cuts-for-two-years turnover. As Obama struggled to regain his balance, his proposed 2011 budget was chopped by $61 billion. Obama dribbled a few more steps and his spending mandate was hacked by $38 billion. Setting up the "clean" debt-ceiling-vote screen for his spending-without-reduction hook shot, Obama fell short, lost his rhythm, then tried to recover with balanced-approach smack talk when Boehner delivered a hard foul and blocked the shot. Obama's entire defensive game fell apart. Boehner, with a House majority on his side, out-flanked and out-negotiated Obama's blank-check-ultimatum pivots. Nothing but net!

Swearing on a stack of *Ultimate Jordan* DVDs from that day forward to never ever let Boehner outmaneuver him, Obama banded with his Senate towel boys and attacked, criticized, and demonized Boehner relentlessly until the

Speaker lost his political will and caved to a clean debt-ceiling increase February 2014. The cheerleading press somersaulted and cartwheeled for the left's victory. The monkey that jumped off Boehner's back didn't know whether to laugh or cry. In the May 2014 primary elections, Boehner cruised through with a 71.5% win, however, his trusty point guard House Majority Leader Eric Cantor was cut from the Republican team with an 11-point loss after spending $5 million on his campaign. Though adept at passing middle-of-the-road legislation, he took for granted his ability to score with his own Virginia district. Game over: The voters kept serious tabs on his lack of true-conservative stats.

Only slightly circumspect, pouty Obama proceeded to follow his liberal instincts: When in doubt form a commission to lay blame on its doorstep while appearing competent and in control. December 2010, said Presidential Commission presented the Bowles-Simpson proposal, all sixty-six pages entitled "The Moment of Truth." Needless to say, it was way more truth than Obama had planned. He tossed it aside to stay the Keynesian course of manipulating the U.S. economy with stimuli after stimuli. Deep down he knew his path to Utopia was unsustainable but, as long as he was in the White House, what a payday for the Obama loyalists and arse-kissers. Shush! It's the lost-in-theory Keynesians' dirty little secret.

Obama's real moment of truth came August 5, 2011 when Standard & Poor's had the nerve to downgrade the U.S. government's credit rating from AAA to AA+. The relentless brinksmanship that Obama forced on Washington riled S&P's sensibilities. The Republicans' only respite was Obama's tee time. Still believing S&P to be infallible, stock markets worldwide plunged while Obama took to TOTUS to save the day. The markets downward spiral was fueled by buyers' remorse of casting a ballot to put the economic-illiterate Obama in office. Still bristling from the ignominious downgrade two years later, Obama sicced mad dog Treasury Secretary Timothy Geithner and the Department of Justice on S&P with a $5 billion civil lawsuit. South Side shakedown: Always a trusty underboss, Geithner looked at S&P's enormous disservice very carefully. S&P brought a knife; President Chicago brought a gun. Deep into 2014, S&P's story was still AA+ and they were sticking to it.

The Obama vs. Boehner bout continued during the summer of 2011. Not keen on losing to the Speaker again and appearing wimpish, Obama dismissed a bipartisan Congressional plan agreed to by both the House and the Senate called the Budget Control Act. How dare they? Just the very name disrespected and challenged Obama's infinite spending authority. He kicked it to the curb. Obama had to avoid an antagonistic debt-limit fight before the next election. From his bag of legal tricks he threw down the sequester gauntlet designed to have Congress, not him, eventually run the gauntlet as a form of hardhearted punishment. A sequester would take legal possession of the U.S. taxpayer-funded government coffers temporarily until the debt the government owes is paid. Washington-speak decoded: A sequester is designed to cut spending across the board until the pain is excruciating, then all new tax revenue proposals will be approved. This is Obama's heartless idea of balancing spending cuts with new tax revenues. The threats of doom and gloom fueled the Obama media circus—millions would lose their jobs, soup kitchens would abound, children by the thousands would starve, the entire U.S. economy would come to a shivering end! Maximum pain, minimum gain, and slim to none Obama leadership. Final reckoning: Only one full-time employee lost his job because of Obama's cataclysmic sequester.

Speaker John Boehner had the last laugh. By the end of fiscal 2013, Obama's sequester boomeranged. The most blissfully-spending president since LBJ's Great Society orgy hit a wall. His spending fever began falling—not precipitously nor consciously, but on the downward slide nevertheless. Whether or not the Speaker decided he needed to appease the limited-government tea partiers, by the end of June 2014, the House voted to sue the executive branch because of Obama's aggressively tweaking laws without Congressional approval.

Washington burns while Obama tees up. In time, watch for the progressive rewrite of this historical debacle. These lackadaisical and leaderless years, with Obama pretending to be at the helm, will be reshaped by the faux truth-seekers. Obama will be recast in pure Hollywood fashion as they wished he were—strong, decisive, omnipotent, benevolent, and indubitably, larger than life. The liberals are known to take past events out of context and alter the facts in their favor under the guise of creative license.

We saved Obama's ultimate, vainglorious head fake for last—the extermination of Osama bin Laden.

It took the combined talents of all U.S. and allied intelligence agencies fifteen years of pre-Obama hunting to find bin Laden. The methodical SEAL Team Six and their brave, support network trained for ten years to implement the long-awaited mission. Without President George W. Bush hanging tough on the Patriot Act, anti-terror policies, and courageous determination to protect the United States, Obama would have encountered bin Laden's own version of Operation Neptune Spear on Pennsylvania Avenue rather than the Abbottabad homebody bin Laden shuffling around in his slippers in northeastern Pakistan.

What should have been a national triumph morphed into an excessive celebration of Obama's manliness. Obama, delirious with his newfound executioner tendencies, had a flashback to his days as Barry O'Bomber on Punahou's basketball team.

> *In spite of his overindulgence in pakalolo* (marijuana), *Barry finally made it to the varsity team his senior year. Though usually sitting on the bench because he was high-jump, touch-the-rim challenged, Barry O'Bomber received a special invitation to join the game so he would score the winning point. The referee cleared a path down the lane to the basket. The other Punahou players made like a warrior SEAL team and distracted the opposition. The coach took Barry's arm and walked him with great pageantry down to the basket. The entire staff of Punahou administrators lifted Barry up, right above the rim, touching the backboard. With obedient deference, they alley-ooped him the basketball and humbly suggested he make a decision—score now or cowardly skulk away?*

Barry, er, Barack shook off the nightmare for another, remembering how then-President "Lover Boy" Clinton was ruthlessly chastised for not taking OBL out in 1998 even though at the time he was justifiably distracted by the "I did not have sexual relations with that woman, Miss Lewinsky" scandal. Nonetheless, it was clear to Obama that his very own mocking of counter-terrorism teamwork, discipline, and the surge in Iraq was bogus. If not for waterboarding, he realized he would have missed a legacy-forging opportunity. Obama, completely mortified and embarrassed at his utter hubris, decided that it was best for his career to drop the ball in the hoop. Capitulating, Obama ordered the death of "Geronimo," a.k.a. bin Laden.

Obama ordering the far-away assassination of Osama bin Laden was neither a three-point swish nor a svelte, finger-roll layup. Obama killing Osama was a pansy gimme. He only had to show up. He only had to make one decision. He only had to give the go-ahead nod and the fifteen-year, impeccably-planned mission was complete. Swept under the carpet was the hypocritical detail that a presumably compassionate, peacenik, pro-gun control, progressive pulled the trigger. Liberals ignore this head fake and call it leadership and courage.

The photo of the White House Situation Room speaks volumes. Look closely. Obama appears the most inconsequential person in the room. Decked out in his golf gear looking like he just finished 18 holes, he had his courtside crouch going on as if it were the second quarter of the NBA championship. Obama ducked out several times to play fifteen hands of Spades with his "body man" and have a few drags to calm his nerves. While indisposed, he left strict instructions to call him back in time for the money shot. Somehow his combat-ready prowess didn't rise to the level of the illustrious portrait of George Washington crossing the

Delaware River the night of December 25, 1776 in a surprise attack against the Hessian forces. “Victory or Death” versus “Exterminate or Prevaricate.” The contrast is striking and disappointing.

A more contemporary juxtaposition is Obama’s Sit Room media-mug next to George W. Bush’s restrained, veins-bursting-at-the-temples outrage September 11, 2001. Sitting in a Florida schoolroom talking and laughing with children, W was bushwhacked along with the rest of the sane world by cold-blooded murderers. Which president epitomized composure under extreme pressure? Which president confronted an existential threat to the American way of life? Which president demonstrated that he could lead from *in front* by constructing an anti-terrorist infrastructure to protect the free world even beyond his own term in office? There’s no comparison. Bush established himself as a steady, determined leader in the face of fanatical nihilism.

Purportedly sleeping with the fishes, Bin Laden’s caliphate rushed back in with the tide. Al Qaeda was driven out of Iraq when Bush was in charge, yet fervently returned during the Obama years as a highly trained, killing machine under their new moniker ISIS (the Islamic State of Iraq and al-Sham) on Eastern Arabic odd days and their other nickname ISIL (Islamic State of Iraq and the Levant) on even days. Excellent ticker symbols when they take their biggest and meanest terrorism conglomerate public. Whatever their name, the bloodthirsty insurgents finally settled on a social-media-friendly brand for their new Islamic State: Shariaville. Abu Bakr al-Baghdadi, we know you grabbed the uranium and the eleven commercial jetliners from the Libyan airport, but what about the domain names? Forgive us, Caliph Ibrahim. We accidentally used your nom de guerre. Please don't cut our heads off.

While Obama professorially classified them as a shrinkable "manageable problem," the Islamic State (IS) made short work of reclaiming Mosul, Tikrit, Tal Afar, Fallujah, Ramadi, air bases, oil fields, and decapitating American journalists. President Retreat was found dictating soldierly maneuvers with an Xbox 360 Special Edition camouflage wireless controller. As usual, Obama holds all things military at arm's length while enjoying the ride sporting SEAL cachet. Let's hear the Commander in Chief pronounce "corpsman" again.

Let the blowback begin. Three months after bin Laden was buried at sea, thirty unescorted troops were killed in a CH-47 Chinook helicopter crash in Wardak Province, Afghanistan by a rocket-propelled grenade launcher. This proved to be the single deadliest day in the Afghan war. Seventeen of the thirty on board Extortion 17 were from SEAL Team Six. With one precise RPG, a Taliban sharpshooter sent the brave warriors to a fireball hell. The #2 man in the White House, Vice President Joe Biden, recklessly wrote Six's name on the revenge missile when he exposed their identities to the world the day after bin Laden met his Muhammad. The silent professionals sacrifice their lives while Obama and his entourage pound their chests and steal their valor. The Obama administration should stick to protecting the Mojave desert tortoises at the Twentynine Palms "nature conservancy" rather than masquerading as military strategists. Hollywood screenwriters get VIP passes to the West Wing Basement while al Qaeda runs amok.

The Obama administration's braggadocious outpouring about the details of bin Laden's demise also stole the freedom, if not the life, of Shakil Afridi. This courageous Pakistani doctor devised a brilliant DNA-collection program that directed the SEALs when and where to find bin Laden. Unbeknownst to the doctor, the head of the CIA, an Obama friend and true believer, never had Afridi's back. Once the mission was complete and Geronimo was dead, it was the "Afridi who?" shuffle. Afridi was left holding the bin Laden bag. If only then-CIA Director Leon Panetta would have "shut the f**k up!" during his starry-eyed interview on CBS's *60 Minutes*. Dr. Afridi could have plausibly denied any involvement while priority boarding with his one-way ticket to the United States.

Whether it was just one numbskull or several that mentioned "DNA samples," "a doctor," "CIA operative," and "Abbottabad" in various interviews, the information seepage delivered Afridi to the Pakistani officials. He was tortured for months and imprisoned for thirty-three years that was only recently reduced to twenty-three on a charge of treason. Was anyone in the Sit Room actually the-buck-stops-here responsible for this mission? Why wasn't Shakil Afridi and his family protected? Makes you wonder if other Special Forces and CIA operatives around the globe feel a tad bit exposed with a liberal-lawyer-politician-professor-walnut-farmer in charge of the U.S. intelligence community. Obama's head fakes and political appointments can be deadly.

Obama knows that botched, military operations can also be fatal politically. Little publicity was given to the fact that Obama insulated himself in case anything went wrong with the bin Laden mission. In a heavily, lawyered-up document, Adm. William H. McRaven, head of U.S. Special Operations Commission (SOCOM), would have been responsible, not chicken-hearted Obama. Having commanded at every level of the special ops community, McRaven stood rock-solid behind his troops and knew they would never ever ring the brass bell.

To avoid appearing overly self-centered, Obama visited CIA Langley to thank them for their part in tracking down bin Laden. Donning his Ronald Reagan mask, he used phrases like "it doesn't matter who gets the credit," "stay true to our values," and "there's nothing we cannot do." The insincere words evaporated into thin air for the CIA personnel knew they were being used for the cameras. Two of their own interrogators were being prosecuted and incarcerated by Obama's Justice Department while Agent Obama was taking credit for the operation. The two-facedness was shocking. The interrogators did what the U.S. government paid them to do. They poured water over the faces of three whack-jobs without inflicting any more pain than was necessary. This technique, known as waterboarding, led them to bin Laden. To pacify the freedom-sucking, far-left zealots, Obama nullified Reagan's spirit and threw the freedom-fighters in jail.

The CIA agents get it. They know Obama is AWOL except when he can leverage a personal advantage. To protect themselves à la Obama, many have purchased group insurance against litigation and other partisan perils. Many feel defenseless choosing to error on the side of caution and inaction rather than being stripped, flogged, and dragged into court. Obama has already shown his predilection for information leaks regardless of the sensitivity and the risk to the security of all Americans. Nothing is off-limits to the power thirsty Obama.

"Death by droning" will most likely be Obama's foreign policy legacy—his signature achievement for restoring America's standing in the world. That "responsibility to protect" sound-bite was too grownup and boring. It's more electrifying to annihilate your enemies from the air. You're in, you're out. They're dead, you're done. It's stealthy and there's almost no evidence for conviction. It's so Obama, so Chicagoesque, so warped! Tell us again why waterboarding a few butchers is evil, while droning entire villages, collateral damage included, is sacrosanct? Because it's just another Obama head fake.

Obama scuttles about community-organizing power by preaching dependence, subservience, and obeisance which he himself would never consent. The Obama Rules do not invigorate but entrap and cripple a healthy person. His power is getting you to believe in compliantly following him like the lemmings in Apple's 1985 Super Bowl commercial. He counsels you to be empowered in a world that he outlines for you. American values afforded him uniqueness, allowing him to be an individual and define who he is. Deceptively, Obama doesn't permit you to be a unique individual and chart your own lifestyle. His path to power is ultra-exclusive and forbids you even imagining that you have the capacity to think for yourself. You are crushed by conformity. George W. Bush called it "the soft bigotry of low expectations."

Besides being intellectually dishonest, Obama assaults the very values that give him a platform, give him an open-door into the lives of Americans. He throws the words "American values" around haphazardly, mocking them along the way. He oozes sham values when it suits his self-absorbed purposes, even tossing in a couple of references to the Declaration of Independence, peppering it with "self-determination" for flavor. Obama couldn't explicitly express an American value if his speechwriter highlighted, circled, double-underlined, marked in big red letters, and added a ringtone to it.

Obama did not stomp on American values by wanting to gain power. He flew in the face of American values by exerting pernicious power to take from the Haves and give to the Have-Nots. The American culture is aspirational and rooted in self-reliance, creating, and building. It's a country of doers; slackers should just move to France where 33%—yes, one-third—of their population is on welfare. The compulsion to take power, in most cases by intimidation, threats, and wickedness, is not the American way. Commanding U.S. citizens to kiss his ring isn't the American way. Transforming the office of the president into "I'm POTUS, bitch" isn't the American way either. His supporters see him as President Cool. His critics see him as President Badass.

Rule 1959
"Do You Mind If I Call You Barack?"

The seeds for Obama's eventual reinvention were sown in Hawaii September 1959 when his father, Barack Hussein Obama Sr., arrived in Honolulu from Kenya. Senior had a full scholarship to attend the University of Hawaii to study economics.

He lived in Hawaii for three years. Upon graduating, Obama Sr. moved to Cambridge, Massachusetts to pursue a graduate degree at Harvard. He lived there for another three years. When he completed his master's degree, Sr. returned to Kenya. He was in the United States a total of six years.

During his three years in Hawaii, Obama Sr. married Ann Dunham, another University of Hawaii student from Kansas. Ann and he met in a Russian class, had several amorous rendezvous, and married February 2, 1961. Obama Jr. was born August 4, 1961.

By the time one-year-old baby Barry was about to say "dada," Obama Sr. was history. The Harvard gods were calling. He packed his bags and moved across the ocean, way across the country hoping to never be seen again by his polygamied, Hawaiian-pleasure, mixed-blood papoose. Back in Africa, the Kenyan Luo tribesmen killed the fatted calf and praised his decision to exorcise his sullied lineage. Obama Sr. was a real wham-bam-thank-you-ma'am kind of guy. "Pure blood" deemed thicker than "mixed blood," Sr. gave his young brother Onyango a generous hand up to relocate from Kenya to attend a Cambridge elite boys' school. Obama Jr. would make his own Cambridge debut twenty-six years later without Sr.'s selective benevolence.

Mostly in his mother's care, Barry crossed the Pacific Ocean at least six times, racked up nearly 25,000 air miles, and had seven known addresses by the time he was ten. Ann was a dedicated, doting, single parent with itchy feet. In time, baby Barry would discover that he was competing with his mother's wanderlust disguised as transcontinental degree-seeking.

Fortunately for baby Barry, Ann's respect for the life of the unborn fetus overrode her feminist instincts. Before the quasi-celebrated birth, Ann with Barry in her womb decided to forgo the pilgrimage to the mainland to visit fellow Kansan, Dr. Jack Tiller, at his abortion clinic. Were it not for the generosity of her parents, government grants, and government food stamps, Ann would not have been able to afford little Barry. Wrapped carefree in her entitlement orthodoxy, she knew which government safety nets would catch her as she self-actualized.

Monetizing *Roe v. Wade*: Dr. George Tiller carried on his father's abortion legacy largely empowered by his politically-funded protector, then-Kansas Insurance Commissioner and later then-Governor Kathleen Sebelius of the ObamaCare fiasco fame. After *Roe v. Wade* was decided in 1973 by the Supreme Court, the late-term abortion business boomed. The kill-the-baby demand was so good that George Tiller had to expand his inherited clinic. In 1975 he held a grand opening of his own Women's Health Care Services butcher shop to make it more convenient for women to have their right to privacy while depriving the child in the womb his and her right to life. As sole owner, Tiller became a wealthy man. He cornered the hookup market coming and going—protect the right of feminists to hookup whenever wherever, but kill the silent egg that was forced to hook up with the doing-his-duty sperm. Dr. Tiller was ahead of his time.

Ann was an only child and wanted for nothing. There were no siblings vying for her parents' love and affection. She mothered her only child with the same generous spirit by pampering him with her time and attention. Mama Obama was Barry's affirmation goddess.

She chose never to go to the dark side about his wretched father. Instead she went overboard with building up the storybook image of Obama Sr., filling Barry with subtle lies that his father was incredible and should be his role model. Ann Obama skirted the incontrovertible truth that baby Barry was actually one of eight children in Obama Sr.'s tribe. Was Ann apologizing for her horrible mistake of falling for such a philanderer? Probably, yet Barry would benefit in spite of the subterfuge. His inheritance was more than an extended family spread out all over the world. Obama Sr. bequeathed Obama Jr. his lust for the ladies, which is never, ever, ever discussed, referred to, hinted at, or acknowledged in Jr.'s "story of race and inheritance."

After Obama Sr. left for Cambridge, Ann and thirteen-month-old Barry moved in with Ann's parents, Madelyn and Stanley Dunham. Their home was spacious and humble, their hearts loving and charitable. The Dunhams offered baby Barry stability along with the necessary care and feeding of a growing boy. Obama's grandfather became Barry's role model.

Stanley fussed over Barry like a son and spoiled him like a grandson—beaches, snorkeling, bodysurfing, fishing, feasts, friends, and friendship. Together, he and his boy enjoyed Hawaii with gusto. Barry's grandparents lavished him with kindness for they were exceptionally proud of their princely grandson. It was as if Ann, Madelyn, and Stanley had made a solemn pact that Barry was never to suffer from self-esteem issues. They showered him with enough praise to inoculate him for the rest of his life.

Barry lived a fortunate and privileged life. His main struggle was puzzling out why he deserved such a charmed existence. He also wrestled with those pesky Midwestern values. Naming him after his great-grandfather, Ralph Waldo Emerson Dunham, may have prodded Barry to be more self-reliant. We'll never know. He also needed some nudging on respect and honesty. For some reason, it made perfectly good sense for Barry to besmirch his Kansan great-grandfather as a philanderer and wife's suicide instigator, but had a brain fart about his own biological father sexing it up on various continents. Anointing the young child Barack Hussein Obama, "the blessed, handsome, crooked one," was prophetic though the Swahili version of "loose with the truth" would have been more suitable.

Barry rode the wave in and through the idyllic, elite Punahou School. Cowabunga! Entrance to this private prep academy came compliments of his grandfather parlaying his connections and the school's affirmative-action deficiency. This suited the laid-back Barry just fine. It became his signature success strategy throughout his life: leverage affirmative-action dictates at the top-tier institutions; add a dose of friendly backscratching; stuff your "pool file" to make like you actually competed to get there; then assume the position as if you were entitled to it. It worked at Punahou, Occidental, Columbia, Harvard Law School, and the University of Chicago Law School—all liberal-leaning institutions that have been absolved of their slave-owner guilt by promoting affirmative action.

Barry was living the easy, breezy, squishy, good life—food, clothing, shelter, car, education, drugs, alcohol, entertainment, travel, vacations, money, an inheritance, love, affection, autonomy, and privacy in a tropical paradise. All of it paid for by his steadfast grandparents. But it just wasn't coo-coo-ca-choo good enough for the heir apparent to the Luo tribe.

"Do you mind if I call you Barack?" opened up new vistas for Barry. When a female Occidental student asked him this question, he was awakened, stimulated, empowered. "Barack" was so exotic and lyrical; "Barry" so twangy and hick. Time for Obama Cool Rule 1959. Time to reinvent.

"Strange how a single conversation can change you." That's how Obama recounted his decision in *Dreams* to pursue his black Barackness. The flip side was to condemn and renounce all ties to his version of other worlds that were not black. All the white people that helped him along the way, that sacrificed and put up with his growing-up shenanigans, were tossed aside, including his mother, grandmother, and grandfather. Thus began the calcification of Barack Obama's technique for civil-rights justice—chew 'em up and spit 'em out.

Charles Ogletree, Harvard civil-rights professor and blame-the-assistant plagiarist, saw Obama as a kindred spirit steeped in the black-studies movement. During his idle abstract musings, he pictured Barack one day becoming the president of the United States since his protégé was cut from the same socialist cloth as the much admired Hugo Chavez of Venezuela. As with all the gloating Harvard Law professors after the fact, Ogletree waxed quixotic about Obama's lifelong, insurmountable, racial obstacles: "Black identity was not given to him—he sought it." And seek it he did.

Obama embarked upon an exhausting, angst-drenched journey of self-discovery filled with self-involvement, self-devotion, self-promotion, and a whole bunch of navel-gazing. His objective was to emerge as a black man that birthed himself—sans mother, sans father. This was his decisive act of self-creation. He shed the live-and-let-live Barry persona and became Barack, the composite black, made up of fictional traits and even some real characteristics. Whatever he needed to roll smoothly in and out of the black communities, is what he chose to assimilate.

Unfortunately, his bygone-era templates for 'buked-and-scorned blackness focused on activists, protesters, agitators, militants, and reparation-seekers which were outdated and out of touch with reality. The ready-to-wear causes of his life were dredged-up issues that had been resolved many years prior. He was stuck in the past and down with the radical brothers.

The "I'm Barack and I'm Proud" makeover, like the James Brown funk, didn't happen overnight. Piece by piece, Obama meticulously exchanged ivory mores for ebony ethnicity in every aspect of his life. The keystone of this transmutation was his selection of inspirational, black, father figures that guided him to establish his home base in a large, urban center with thriving black leaders. His pad was in an area with a substantial number of black brothers and black sisters. To certifiably purge his whiteness, Obama assembled a pure black family: stand-in black fathers, surrogate black mothers, a black wife, and black babies. And, most important, he staked out an essential black cause. All the building blocks were in place to realize his own fundamental, black transformation.

If Obama were genuinely serious about reclaiming his consummate blackness, his biological father's heritage, why didn't he move back to his father's country, Kenya? Obama had several fork-in-the-road moments to decide if he should make Luoland his own. Giving him considerable pause were more than a few factors that scared the hell out of him: he didn't like the sound of Swahili nor the Queen's English; soccer was the national sport not basketball or golf; their marathon runners put him to shame, especially the women; he didn't want to live in a hut; he wasn't much attracted to the native African women—until he laid eyes on and lusted after that Luo hottie, Lupita Nyong'o, who won the Oscar for best supporting actress in *12 Years a Slave*; and lifting his Luo family out of poverty was really, really hard work. Obama admits to this day that he leans toward laziness, even though he deplores it. Once a sloth, always a sloth.

Another alternative was for Obama to return to a Muslim Arab country. His entire name, Barack Hussein Obama, is of Muslim Arabic descent—not even close to a black African name let alone a black American name. By the way, didn't the Arabs trade slaves in East Africa before the British shut the despicable business down? What a Pandora's box if the connection were made between Obama and his possible slave-owning, slave-trading ancestors! Game over!

Instead, Obama chose the path of least resistance, greased and sweetened with affirmative action sponsored by esteemed, liberal, *American* institutions. He would pursue his *black* metamorphosis in the United States—the homeland he inherited from his *white* family.

Drawn to black, father figures known for reinventing themselves, Obama studied their life histories from every angle. His goal was to identify their traits that gave them prominence in the black community, compile their qualities into a wannabe list, and embrace them for his own ends. Frederick Douglass, Malcolm X, and Martin Luther King Jr. were his favored black fathers for all three had compelling black narratives.

Frederick Douglass was an unbroken, biracial slave that became an instigating abolitionist maturing into a self-taught intellectual. This documented slave rose to be nominated for vice president of the United States in 1872. Even though thoroughly impressed, Democrat Obama was forced to overlook Frederick's fatal flaw: "I recognize the Republican party as the sheet anchor of the colored man's political hopes and the ark of his safety." Nonetheless, he made Obama's top-three list because Douglass loved to preach and people of all nationalities flocked to listen to him.

From thug to self-educated scholar to black-manhood personified, Malcolm X was the black prince of self-invention. His dream of becoming a lawyer was waylaid while he found self-enlightenment in jail. He, too, drew huge crowds for his respect-demanding, "by any means necessary," invective preaching. Malcolm, too, loved the podium.

The liberal media darling, Martin Luther King Jr., began as a Baptist pastor, grew into an African American Gandhi, and blossomed into a $50 billion, restitution-seeking televangelist. Never mind he pirated his PhD dissertation and cheated on his wife numerous times, he was a reinvention genius. Obama knew he could never achieve King's sainthood status but he envisioned the heavenly possibilities if he could duplicate King's black cadence and inflection.

Douglass, Malcolm, and King all reinvented themselves, all loved to preach, and all were media magnets—even babe magnets. Obama could relate; this was exactly what he wanted out of life. His adopted-father icons did it and he could, too. All he needed was a stage and a microphone. Obama summed up his feelings in *Dreams*: "Because it [preaching] makes *me* feel important. Because *I* like the applause. It gives me a nice, cheap thrill. That's all." He knew Frederick, Malcolm, and Martin felt the same way.

Reverend Jeremiah Wright was a postscript father for convenience sake. He and his church were window-dressing for Obama's networking activities—and the best Sunday stand-up shtick in town. Black liberation theology was Wright's method of differentiating himself from the other black preachers on the competitive South Side. The

Reverend's "MIT" ("Ministers in Training") program was a marketing tool to reel them in and pluck their pockets. After all, the man had to pay for the roost and feed those prodigal chickens. Even so, Obama would never disown Wright. Obama was a true believer, a believer that Wright's down-and-dirty, eternal-damnation, racial-moral-authority, preaching technique would come in handy someday.

Constructed from his chosen fathers, Barack Hussein Obama was the resulting composite—the ersatz African American.

Having lived in the first and second most densely populated cities, New York and Los Angeles respectively, Obama put down roots in the third largest metropolis. With its uncontested, #1, top-of-the-charts, most-segregated distinction, Chicago was the chosen city; the South Side the chosen community; and Hyde Park was the perfect place for Obama's crib.

Like King before him, Obama needed to find a city where he could nonviolently exploit racial inequality and stir up anger, resentment, and maybe a riot or two. Imagine the national media frenzy! Obama wanted to pick up where King left off with his Chicago Freedom Movement, the most ambitious civil-rights campaign in the North. Obama felt he could out do King if given half the chance. Damn, he could even use King's demands on Chicago City Hall as his barnstorming template.

As the Census Bureau will attest, Chicago remains the most-ghettoized U.S. city, particularly when combined as one big megalopolis with the Milwaukee Metro. Each census cycle, Chicago and Milwaukee trade the dubious, discrimination honor while New York chomps at their heels. It's one of those plus-ça-change conundrums. NYC prides itself as ground zero for progressivism and the standard-bearer for rounding up more Democrats than Republicans—a six to one ratio.

Where, oh where, did Obama find a black, replacement mother? The black church ladies, of course. These church moms served many purposes, especially as volunteers. Handing out pamphlets, voter registration, gathering signatures, collecting donations, relationship advice, what to wear, what movie to see, were just a few of the tasks they performed for Obama. They enjoyed being his proxy moms.

Obama didn't even have to hide his church moms from his future wife's family like he had to do with his white mother. Nor did he feel any guilt or regret for leaving them behind while he went on Louis Farrakhan's Million Man March, be they cancer-ridden or not. His black moms were very low maintenance. They just wanted to give and give to their sweet, innocent, adopted, black son.

Marrying the right, black woman was of the utmost, strategic importance for his long-term career plans. Obama's mating checklist had several nonnegotiables. Her skin color had to be a special shade of black—not too dark, not too light. Her street-wise, fist-bump rhythm had to be dead-on—the brothers would size her up in a split second. Their secret sharing of the *shaka* sign would be reserved for their annual, Christmas, hang-loose vacations in Hawaii, since it was a white-family vestige.

With a lot of beach time on the horizon, Obama's lady had to fill out an itsy, bitsy bikini without detracting from his vain, ab-publicity stunts. If she wasn't a Halle Berry body double, no problem—Obama would settle for access, not of a sexual nature but sheer, political access, as in access, access, and more access. She had to personally know all the right people in town like Jesse Jackson, Mayor Daley, John Rogers Jr., Reverend Wright, etc., etc., etc.

The spousal specifications continued. Her income had to be at least six figures in case his book project went bust and Obama was forced to actually work for a living. Excessive worship of everything Obama was an absolute must-have on the prerequisite list. And she had to agree to make precious, black babies as soon as she met the aforementioned qualifications. Obama was compelled to start his own, authentic, black tribe.

Obama found his black, life partner in Chicago, as obliged. She fulfilled his every fantasy even introducing him to a ghostwriter that could fabricate one of those *Profiles in Courage*, political-introduction "autobiographies" to launch Obama's narrated notion of ascent. But, he still lacked a critical component: a black cause.

Perhaps Obama's essential black cause was and is to launch the twenty-first-century civil-rights movement. Jerry Kellman, who first hired Obama as a community organizer, knew that Obama "was looking for a civil-rights movement." Of course he was looking for a juicy, civil-rights battle. Progressives are born with politics coursing through their veins. They live and die asserting their versions of inequality and acceptable lifestyles on mere mortals. Their noble cause is perfecting lesser humans to be more like themselves. Didn't a 1930s wealthy, land-owning, fascist, sociologist justify eugenics using statistically-measured income inequality? Didn't he rationalize using the left's favorite inequality measuring stick—the Gini coefficient? Isn't eugenics still a basic tenet of progressivism? Packaged ever so palatably, the liberals soft-pedal "controlled selective breeding" through income inequality, abortion on demand, and birth-control pills as women's vitamins.

Yes, it's possible that Obama is trying to reconceive the civil-strife years of Douglass, Malcolm X, and King Jr. Yet this is a man who lacks imagination. His entire life has focused on imitating others. No need to plunge the depths of Obama's psyche, his philosophy, his thought processes. Obama's essential black cause is essentially Obama, his skin-deep self. It has and always will be about Obama's self-aggrandizement.

Back to the *Profiles in Courage* fascination of the budding, half-black, half-white John Fitzgerald Kennedy.

With the rising-star status afforded him from his new position as the president of the *Harvard Law Review*, Obama was given a $150,000 advance to write a book on a scholarly topic, like voting-rights law or even affirmative action. The publisher's expectation was for Obama to dispel current myths surrounding civil rights and discuss the brutish reality of race relations. However, telling the truth, the whole truth, and nothing but the truth was an anathema to Obama.

After he artfully had half the advance in the bank, Obama altered the project from a critical analysis of legal realities to a mythical autobiography of a thirty-year-old, namely himself. The impressionistic book format gave him the freedom to hazily sketch and vaguely generalize his life that began in the white world, yet longed for the opportunities that were ripe for the picking in the black world. If only he could harness that "estrangement from whites" theme, he'd be in tall cotton.

When first published in 1995, *Dreams from My Father* was used as a vehicle to trash Obama's white, conservative-leaning ancestry and ingratiate himself with the black, liberal community. *Dreams* also played well to the guilt-ridden, trust-fund, liberal, white big-spenders who especially love irresponsible blacks for their white-rescue possibilities. The liberals and blacks feasted on the unsentimental folktale about the victimization of Barack. They would literally weep when he expressed his pain: "I wish I had a father who was around and involved." Boohoo. If only it were true.

With his debut on the national stage in 2004, he decided he especially needed the white, female, liberal vote as much as those black, church ladies. In an instant, Obama added a new introduction offering up three sentimental paragraphs praising his deceased, single, Kansan mother and suggesting the possibility that he might have focused too much on the absent, Kenyan father. This indulged the New-Agers, making them feel special and better than the rest of humanity. Of course, this admission of guilt was bogus because the book was still marketed and read as poor, confused, baby Barry desperate to find his unfairly persecuted and unjustly brutalized black father—who never really wanted him.

Comparing *Dreams* to the autobiographies of G. H. Williams and J. McBride in the fawning blurb was patently bootlicking. All three were first published in 1995; all three classified as biographies; and all three referred to in the *Dreams*' book-cover appetizer as *memoirs*. From there it was open territory about what was true, fantasy, or simply made up. And it really didn't matter—every which way was editor-endorsed. Apparently back then, publishing houses were trying to fashion a new genre: black male inner-odyssey. This was the perfect example of the liberal press driving their racial-oppression leitmotif and ignoring free-market forces. Obama's *Dreams* only sold 10,000 copies after an extensive book tour. So much for left-leaning publishers pushing their agendas at the expense of loyal readers looking for honest literature.

For all those progressive, liberal arts majors who fancy themselves literary connoisseurs and feel they know Obama through his books, take note: *Dreams* is not an autobiography; it's not even a memoir. Obama describes it as "an honest account of a particular province of my life" and "a meditation on the absent parent." Translation: It's a methodically, distorted portrayal of history with a thimbleful of hard facts—better known as a tall tale. Obama and Bill Ayers probably laugh themselves silly over the madness for *Dreams*. It was written to lampoon the New-Agers and appeal to Oprah's audience. Grow up!

Dreams targeted the modern *Catcher in the Rye* crowd. The black mindset was in vogue so why not seize the moment. The Obama personage was developed into the contemporary version of the existential hero, Holden Caulfield. Adolescent readers were fixated on the anguish, isolation, turmoil, and anti-establishment rebellion, set in a more current context with racial tension, semi-complex characters, and no emphasis on sex. Obama's overseers advised against any implicit or explicit references to s-e-x. It would tarnish the scrubbed, ascetic, Spartan image they had crafted for the son of a global, self-contained, progeny production line. Obama was molded into the perfect American male hero—at least for liberals.

Catcher in the Rye, like *Dreams,* was written for adults but read mostly by adolescents. J. D. Salinger, and now his estate, has sold 65 million copies and counting. Not a bad post-White House annuity if Obama can keep the legend spinning. Maybe *Time*'s literati will continue paying homage and post it to their list of 100 best English-language novels of the 21st century.

Yet isn't this whole, Obama script a twenty-first-century rewrite of the 1979 movie, *Being There,* based on a novella by Jerzy Kosinski? Chance the gardener is replaced by Obama the community organizer. The white stooge role is replaced by the black stooge.

Peter Sellers's character, Chance, is on the fast track to becoming the president of the United States controlled by forces way beyond his sphere of influence. Well into his forties, Chance has lived his entire life watching TV in the confines of his benefactor's estate, never venturing beyond its gates. When his benefactor (most likely his father) dies, Chance is thrust into the world completely on his own without family, education, money—nothing except what he learned from watching TV for forty-some years.

Obama, too, was weaned on TV, movies, and other modern distractions. Abandoned by both parents, Obama was forced to find his way in the world by venturing beyond the protective shores of Hawaii. Where Chance created his reality through TV personalities, Obama created his world by drawing on the civil-rights generation of black leaders that he found in history books, TV, and movies. Chance mimicked TV characters and Obama mimicked radical, racial dogmatists from the '60s. Louise, the benefactor's housekeeper, captured the film's absurdity:

> "**LOUISE**: *It's for sure a white [black] man's world in America. Look here: I raised that boy since he was the size of a piss-ant. And I'll say right now, he never learned to read and write. No, sir. Had no brains at all. Was stuffed with rice pudding between th' ears. Shortchanged by the Lord, and dumb as a jackass. Look at him now! Yes, sir, all you've gotta be is white [black] in America, to get whatever you want. Gobbledy-gook!*"

Louise saw it for exactly what it was—a farce to place the destiny of America in the hands of a puttering gardener. Which begs the question: How absurd is it to have a community organizer, "dumb as a jackass" on all things economic, in charge of the world's strongest and largest economy? More precisely, Obama wanted to raise taxes during a recession. Even strict Keynesians don't raise taxes while the country is struggling. Someone tell the pop-cultured president his economic illiteracy is showing.

When garnering support or collecting votes, Obama temporarily pockets his blackness and conveniently assumes the white pose. Lacking in creativity and substance like Hollywood executives remaking tried-and-true favorites, President Mutability generally opts to wear the mantle of a popular, deceased American president. The Lincoln that didn't suspend the writ of habeas corpus and the U.S. Constitution, or the FDR that didn't intern Japanese-Americans are his usual lily-white reincarnations. Obama strutting around in a General Eisenhower uniform spouting foreign policy and playing war games looked far-fetched. For picture perfect occasions with his wife and daughters, he conjures up the faithful family man, the liberals' beau ideal—JFK. When he really wants to stretch the imagination, he play-acts Ronald Reagan for the day.

A wee bit Irish: Sizing up the thirty-four million, Irish American votes, Obama took a cue from Reagan and visited Ireland. Having virtually disowned his white European heritage, Obama and his entourage set off for Moneygall, Ireland, birthplace of his great-great-great-grandfather on his mother's side. They drank Irish stout and pulled a pint with goodwill all around, though Obama and his wife appeared tortured with the bighearted festivities. It was obviously beyond Obama's capabilities to express Ronald Reagan's genuineness, kindness, cheerfulness, and beautiful-person aura. Nonetheless, Obama's mission of insincere glad-handing on the Emerald Isle was accomplished—gobsmackingly so.

His Hollywood handlers ought to give their acting protégé less demanding sketches. Obama as Reagan?! Barack Obama is to Ronald Reagan's luminous leadership, as Roger Moore is to Sean Connery's canniness, as Randolph Scott is to John Wayne's screen dominance, and Paul McCartney is to Mick Jagger's, well, everything. No comparison. No contest. Don't even try. Better a horseback-riding, cowboy-hatted, B actor leading the land of the free and home of the brave than a head-faking, b-ball dribbling, conniving, beseeching, BS artist wrecking and reducing it.

Red Rover, Red Rover, send Ronnie and his "bedrock values" over! So intent on pulling off the perfect crime against moral-compassed humanity, Obama hung Reagan pictures all around the Oval Office, had a few on his nightstand, packed his bookshelves with inspirational Reagan biographies, and ordered all of Dutch's movies with regular showings in the First Family's private theatre. All invitation-only guests received elegant Reagan Ranch t-shirts flaunting "Faith, family, work, neighborhood, peace, and freedom" with President Reagan's signature. All smoke and mirrors.

Steeped in honor and committed to "strengthening our community of shared values," Reagan signed Executive Order 12291 to focus the federal bureaucracy on reinforcing American values. He sought to diminish the size and scope of government which he strongly believed impeded the American way of life. "Regulatory action shall not be undertaken unless the potential benefits to society from the regulation outweigh the potential costs to society" became his acid test to maximize the net benefits [of regulations] to society. This gave birth to *cost-benefit analysis* purposely designed to contain the expansion of federal regulations. Then Americans' rendezvous with destiny ran face first into Obama's values-twisting head fake.

The Reagan ruse was all for show. Within days of taking office, Obama resurrected Bill Clinton's EO that had put the kibosh on most of Reagan's EO. Obama then proceeded to unceremoniously, and with great pleasure, revoke George W. Bush's EOs that were designed to reinforce Reagan's by requiring agencies to identify a "specific market failure" to justify a regulation. Obama would have none of this conservative hooey. Instead, Obama contrived an *informal constitution of the American regulatory state*. Social engineering codified. Woohoo!

Obama's EO 13565 would "take into account benefits and costs, both quantitative and qualitative. . . . each agency may consider (and discuss qualitatively) values that are difficult or impossible to quantify, including equity, human dignity, fairness, and distributive impacts." No directive at all to cost-benefit improvements to advance America's *human capital*—more progressive to drive institutions down to the lowest common denominator. While the majority of Americans were working hard to meet their taxpayer obligations, Obama institutionalized social justice and income redistribution buried deep within his EO and even deeper in the Federal Register. Instead of resolving social ills, he would inflame them and use them to his advantage. But then again lawyers and community organizers don't solve anything. They enhance their cred and wealth by stirring conflict that will last in perpetuity.

Every federal agency could cost-benefit-analysis its own social-justice crusade using whatever long-sword or great-axe spreadsheet would guarantee them save-the-planet conquests. Where once stood crystal clear Reagan-solid values now stood contentious social issues leveraged into "rights," dismissing responsibility, and promoting anything-goes-as-long-as-it's-left lifestyles. The values-based message that only Obama can deliver the way that Obama delivers: more votes for big government. All the entitlements the liberals could ever dream of were neatly packaged and insinuated into Obama's "mini-constitution" for the regulatory state—his official edict to nudge, prod, bump, shove, and jolt his subjects into submission. Long live the living-constitutionalists! Hip, hip, hooray! Hip, hip, hooray!

The final curtain came down: And that's the tale of how American values were bastardized and fundamentally transformed into progressive government institutions—all the better to enslave uninformed voters, my dear. The ghost of President Reagan offered some advice to the misguided whippersnapper: "Anyone who seeks success or greatness should first forget about both and seek only the truth. The rest will follow." Not about to invest one iota in the Gipper's syrupy truth-business, Obama destroyed all of his Reagan banners, books, and dorky lifeguard tips. If Barack says it's true, it will be so . . . or else.

Single-minded about his globetrotting competition with then-Secretary of State Hillary Clinton, Obama stopped off in London after his social call to Ireland. Scotland Yard had too-clever-by-half Obama sized up and code-named him *chalaque,* a Punjabi word meaning "smart aleck." The British police, along with the entire United Kingdom, had unfriendly memories of the surprise, wooden crate marked "BRITISH TRASH" showing up at the British Embassy in Washington back in January 2009. Evidently, one of the first things Obama did when he physically moved into the White House was to expeditiously replace the bust of Winston Churchill in the Oval Office with the bust of Martin Luther King Jr. Obama figured he got a retaliation-twofer by returning Winnie: first, revenge for his Kenyan grandfather and father who lived under British rule, thereby assuaging the Obama family's anti-colonialism rage; and second, vengeance for his benefactors in Palestine who were also under the Pax Britannica since the end of WWI. Mahmoud Abbas, the president of the Palestinian Authority, bundled a president-to-future-president influential gift and, in return, all Obama had to do was insult the Queen and her loyal subjects. Well, at least until June 2014 when the PA formed a government with Hamas, a State Department-designated foreign terrorist organization, and the PA's annual $400 million transfusion of U.S. taxpayer money needed Obama's presidential protection. Languishing in his ennui, Obama wrestled with possibly returning the Statue of Liberty back to the French and replacing it with an urbane statue of Karl Marx, Chairman Mao, Ho Chi Minh, or Joseph Désiré Mobutu. Decisions, decisions.

Johnny to the rescue! October 2013, Obama's Republican punching bag, Speaker John Boehner, hosted the dedication of a new bust of Winston Churchill to be permanently nailed down, immovable, affixed for eternity, and on display in the Capitol Building. Aye, Aye, Speaker!

With his travels to Ireland and Britain, Obama was reliving his inner-Frederick Douglass years from the 1840s. Someone remind Obama that he's the president of the United States and need not perform a theatrical representation of Frederic Douglass's pilgrimage. It is transparently patronizing and a waste of taxpayers' money. The Brits raised the funds to purchase Douglass's freedom from his American owner 170 years ago. The slave-breaker that bound him is long gone, in the grave. Get over it! The rest of the world has evolved beyond the retro-serfdom mentality.

Barack Hussein Obama Jr. eventually became president of the United States in spite of his blatant disregard for American values. In the end, he concocted someone that was unrecognizable. He became at least twenty-five different archetypes but deliberately excluded the most important one—a true American. This might explain why he remains bewildered about who he really is.

Rule 1964
Bespoke Street Cred

"Equal Employment Opportunity is THE LAW" growls a laminated, watchdog poster found in every breakroom in the U.S. with 15 or more latent offenders. Just in case anyone forgets, the Equal Employment Opportunity Commission reminds "Private Employers, State and Local Governments, Educational Institutions, Employment Agencies and Labor Organizations" not to discriminate on the following bases: RACE, COLOR, RELIGION, SEX, NATIONAL ORIGIN, EX-CONVICTS, and PREGNANT WOMEN. Done! Equal opportunity, enforced by the EEOC, is the official law of the land. Or is it?

The stated purpose the Civil Rights Act of 1964 was to create a color-blind society where equal individual rights would prevail under the protection of the federal government. The separate-but-equal, government-policed Jim Crow laws were overruled and discrimination towards blacks was banned. Even MLK Jr., the patron saint of equal rights, galvanized his universal dream with all of God's children "will not be judged by the color of their skin, but by the content of their character." Equal individual rights meant equal opportunity for *all* U.S. citizens.

Though used as a legislative catch phrase to guarantee the passage of the Civil Rights Act, "equal individual rights" is the cornerstone of American values clearly spelled out in the Declaration of Independence. No one would oppose memorializing, once again, a founding principle of the United States. But something happened on the way to not just writing the legislation but actually practicing it in the real world beyond Washington. Where once stood equal individual rights for all, racial group entitlements sprung forth to advance but one race, one color, one minority group. Can you say "black people"?

One hundred years after the Emancipation Proclamation was signed by President Abraham Lincoln, President John F. Kennedy delivered his "Civil Rights Address" June 11, 1963. JFK emphatically stated: "This Nation was founded by men of many nations and backgrounds. It was founded on the principle that all men are created equal. . . . In short, every American ought to have the right to be treated as he would wish to be treated. . . . This is one country. It has become one country because all of us and all the people who came here had an equal chance to develop their talents. . . . [T]he Constitution will be color blind." These words were historic and set the stage for the nation's touchstone civil-rights legislation based on *merit*.

Two days before President Kennedy's assassination, his signature civil-rights initiative, fortified by the House Judiciary Committee, was formally reported to the full House. Within five days of JFK's death, the newly sworn-in President

Lyndon Baines Johnson picked up the equal-rights baton to honor JFK's memory. Almost three months later, the final version passed the House on February 10, 1964. LBJ wasn't considered the politicians' pol for nothing.

With much consternation, the Senate began debates March 30 with Senator Edward "Ted" Kennedy dedicating his first speech to his departed brother's equality-of-treatment crusade. Senator Hubert Humphrey even offered to literally eat the bill to prove that Title VII of the 1964 Civil Rights Act did not require quotas or percentages. LBJ exercised a fair amount of arm-twisting, cajoling, and backroom wrangling to help break the 54-day Senate filibuster. The president and the senators all knew the big carrot was the huge amount of votes in the offing. July 2, the bill passed both houses of Congress and was signed into law by President Johnson.

Expansively interpreting seven, unvarnished words from the U.S. Constitution known as the Interstate Commerce Clause, the proponents of the Act trotted out their equal-rights Trojan horse. Fully barded from nose to tail with "To regulate Commerce . . . among the several States," the victory trophy was ceremoniously wheeled straight into the core of American culture, commerce, and common sense while trampling States' rights and individual liberty along the way. As if it were masquerading malware sitting invisibly in an infected computer, the Trojan bill unleashed its social-engineering hackers in the form of the EEOC.

Created to enforce Title VII of the 1964 Civil Rights Act, the EEOC used this bureaucratic, simple-minded, and crippling logic: An employer was accused of self-evident racism if he did not have the same percentage of blacks on the payroll as existed in the general population. This crude formula was enough to judge the employer guilty as charged unless the employer could prove otherwise. The burden of proving innocence resided with the supposed-racist employer. The employer was then forced to manage the business based on quota and percentages, rather than performance and loyalty. This pernicious quota system was born as protective armor shielding the EEOC, diametrically opposed to JFK's original aspiration of an America built on talent and merit.

Less than a year later, LBJ spoke with both guilt and condescension at a Howard University Commencement Address. He blamed white hatred and prejudice for the plight of the American Negro: "But freedom is not enough. . . . Thus it is not enough just to open the gates of opportunity. . . . We seek not just legal equity but human ability, not just equality as a right and a theory but equality as a fact and equality as a result. . . . To this end equal opportunity is essential, but not enough, not enough." This sweeping, costly, and gratuitous quid pro quo was gifted within minutes of President Johnson, a former high-school public-speaking teacher, swapping it for an honorary degree of doctor of laws, i.e., JD or PhD. File this under a lesson in collecting scholarly status without the investment of time, money, and brainpower—just surrender the country and all of its citizens.

The don of give-and-take upped the ante. A few months later, LBJ'S Executive Order 11246 gave unparalleled enforcement authority to the Secretary of Labor, a U.S. Cabinet-level position, to guarantee that all federal contractors and subcontractors comply with its non-discrimination and affirmative-action provisions. Like the Black Plague that descended on the masses during the Middle Ages and killed nearly half the people in Western Europe, no average U.S.

worker was safe from the debilitating effects and killing-the-spirit experiences of LBJ's equality-of-result scourge.

With more teeth than the EEOC, the Office of Federal Contract Compliance Programs (OFCCP) was designed to police EO 11246. To put this in perspective, it controls the workplace experience of nearly 22% of the total civilian employees, about 26 million people, and the disposition of $200 billion plus in prime contracts paid for with taxpayers' dollars. Their mission from God: Prosecute with impunity; punish them all; spare no one.

With sleight of hand, the fraud squad enforces compliance not with numerical goals but rather with utilization analyses of under-utilization, over-utilization, backward-utilization, sideways-utilization, upside-down-utilization, and inside-out-utilization of qualified individuals. Cryptogram for numerical quotas on steroids. On the one hand a contractor cannot be penalized for not meeting goals, while on the other hand failure to comply with the goals may result in contract cancellation, termination, or suspension. The contractor may be debarred . . . but there's no penalty for not meeting goals! But there aren't any goals! Who's on first?

Finessing more magic tricks, the Department of Labor annually bestows several best practices awards. The most blatant, double-talk prize is the Exemplary Voluntary Efforts (EVE) award given to contractors with outstanding affirmative-action programs. The operative word here of course is "voluntary," meaning without legal obligation. Even though an employer can rationalize following federal guidelines to protect a contract and preserve jobs, the average-Joe worker is often times oblivious to the behind-the-scenes stacking-the-deck that the government mandates. The company's Human Resources department really isn't there to protect the "human resources" but to adhere to the rules of the game dictated by the government overseers. For most employee issues, the HR department serves as the company's firewall to protect the sacrosanct government contracts. And you thought the HR wellness questionnaires tracking your BMI and blood glucose levels were a token of their love for you? Nah, ObamaCare makes them do it.

With eyes wide shut, the politicians that repackaged "equal individual rights" with "racial group entitlements" debased the U.S. Constitution, debauched individual liberty, and degraded a fair and just society by confusing, intimidating, and blinding it with color. Racial group equality, racial group entitlements, selective reverse discrimination, and equalizing outcomes became the law of the land. The "Advance to Go" card was replaced with the reparative "Play the Race Card," better known in polite society as jumping the queue, cutting in line, go to the head of the class, and racial preference. All government sanctioned. Americans felt the tectonic plates of social-exchange rules shifting under their feet but weren't quite sure why. Ever wonder why the race baiters have the *cojones* to push people around as forcefully as Jesse Jackson's Rainbow PUSH Coalition does? They use the EEOC enforced by the OFCCP as their weapon of choice.

Barack Obama thought he had ferreted out the secrets to being black. Reverend Jeremiah Wright and the Trinity Church helped him with that fire-and-brimstone, preachified delivery. For a little variety, he could even color it with fake stammering or phony stuttering to lower his highfalutin tone. Obama's favorite pitch, though, was the crack-the-whip imperative when he really wanted to command attention. Unfortunately, his words stung like cat-o'-nine-tails and had the reverse effect. When they heard Obama shout at them, the defenseless listeners knew instantly they were completely shut out, no heartfelt discussion, no intellectual exchange, no negotiation. They interpreted his words as "do what I say or go straight to hell!"

Walking side-by-side with Louis Farrakhan at the 1995 Million Man March was extremely valuable. The very nature of the happening reeked of racism and sexism—all black, all male. No matter. Obama learned how to jiggy with the Islamists, a rare talent. But he still came off as snooty and pretentious living in Hyde Park, teaching at the University of Chicago, Harvard law degree, so on and so forth. A regular, gentrified, Punahou-preppy, Hawaiian homeboy. His book of *Dreams* was to have mystically dispelled any notion of his whiteness but that fabrication only went so far. Damn, he even cultivated his basketball jones mastering head fakes and pivots, swishes and swooshes. The vertical leap still eluded him—obviously a congenital, whitish predisposition.

To gain the respect of his black brothers and sisters, he needed street cred and he needed it bad. Most of the blacks viewed him as an Uncle Tom and not black enough. It was apparent to the black community that this sissified black/white man had no idea what it meant to grow up in the hood with gangbangers carrying AK-47s. Not only did he not command their respect, he didn't deserve their R-E-S-P-E-C-T. The old fist bump wasn't cutting it. He craved to get to the heart and soul of what it meant to be his brothers' and sisters' keeper. Authentic blackness became his neurotic quest. Cracking the black psyche was the buried treasure.

Obama hit pay dirt when he plunged straight into the belly of the black-victimization beast. The exclusive trademark of black civil-rights activists was leveraging black oppression over white bigotry. Guilting whites to repent for black irresponsibility was extraordinarily intoxicating, particularly for Obama. Liberal whites were easy to shame in exchange for redemption and forgiveness. He couldn't go wrong as long as liberal blacks never ever swear-on-their-ancestors'-graves admit to taking responsibility for their own lives.

Granted, Obama knew he couldn't reach all blacks. Many were dependable, conscientious citizens and took pride in their accomplishments. They knew Obama's black bravado was a swindle and kept their distance. These blacks considered themselves Americans. Obama saw them as his arch enemies.

No, Obama was after the true believers, the whitey-is-sticking-it-to-me blacks. He struck a grand bargain with these freeloaders: Obama would protect their convenient powerlessness, never expect them to be responsible, and abolish any paths to empowerment. His dedicated homies, in turn, would have his back no matter what.

His next step was to find some good old-fashioned racism that he could artfully package into gross amounts of new-fangled racial entitlements. Obama's motto: Never let baited, contrived, or centuries-old racism go without restitution. With the U.S. government's checkbook in hand, Obama would pay for the black voters' mortgages, education, healthcare, food, cars, O-phones, dishwashers, washing machines, clothes dryers, microwave ovens, air conditioners, internet access, Detroit's drinking water, and other take-care-of-me living expenses ad infinitum. Such benevolence would prove he was the guardian of the black race. His place in history was certain—right next to LBJ.

The Obama Cool Rule 1964 became his ultimate street credential, tailor made to testify to his adroit blackness. Dressed down street-style, he Motown-shuffled into the hoods and hearts of black Americans; spit-and-polish dressed up, he wielded Cool Rule '64 in Washington like a Chicago gangsta.

There were several elements that LBJ used to pass the Civil Rights Act that Obama wished he could patent as his own legislative engineering marvel. The elasticity of the Interstate Commerce Clause was classic—such dexterous, shrewd abuse of seven, innocent, lawful words. Who would have the guts to take an outdated, throw-away, constitutional concept, like "States' rights," and obscure it with a postmodern, subject-to-interpretation twist? Sheer genius! The EEOC warmed the crowd up with omnipresence before the show-stopping OFCCP dropped the heavy hammer of federal omnipotence. Smack talking the opponents into submission in the backroom with liberal white guilt was a black-activist MO, yet LBJ got a pass on the piracy since he used it to the blacks' advantage. And the coup de grâce was legislating from the grave. Everyone knew, and LBJ made sure everyone knew, that JFK put forward the initial legislation even though its true intent was somewhat lost in translation by the time the bill was finally signed.

Obama jotted down "How to pass unpopular legislation" and put the crib sheet in his pocket to use for a later date, circa December 2009. When signing ObamaCare into law March 2010, Obama added a BHO exclusive to one-up LBJ: a blue "Tedstrong" bracelet. After 47 years, the deceased Senator Ted Kennedy's universal healthcare was signed, sealed, and delivered though under the chichi Obama moniker. Note to Obama's self: A "LillyLedbetterstrong" 2009-version bracelet would be a nice touch; include them in the gift packages to the Title VII trial attorneys.

With the lawmaking angle stashed away in the future-use file, the fun part of his bespoke street cred began. Man, he couldn't believe how easy it was to shuck and jive in the black communities. Obama could tell them almost anything as long as the statement included "racism," "entitlement," and "it's not your fault." He had them eating out of his hands! And, if they elected him president, they would all feed from the trough of government goodies that they so rightfully deserved.

This unsophisticated, Jesse Jackson-approach worked for most of the Chicago South Side with lower income blacks. Obama delighted in the one-way nature of the transaction. He didn't have to invest anything of himself yet basked in their adulation. A quick flick of dare-to-be-near-me dirt off his shoulders and he was their urban messiah. Not much was expected of him as long as he showed his groupies a mere scintilla of interest—a haughty trait he continued to nurture through the years. Obama's real hangout, where he actually formed friendships and give-and-take was de rigueur, was the more affluent section of the South Side, namely Hyde Park. Here he had to up his game.

Obama collected a prized, hermetically-sealed entourage made up of present and former Hyde Parkers, like Valerie Jarrett, Arne Duncan, Austan Goolsbee, Cass Sunstein, Elena Kagan, Desiree Rogers, and David Axelrod. The ex-Weather Undergrounders, Bernadette Dorn and Bill Ayers, took refuge but four blocks from Obama's multimillion dollar home. They lived so close that Ayers walked Obama's scribbled, cathartic journals down the street, up the stairs, and right into his just-a-guy-in-the-neighborhood writing den. The other Hyde Parker that resided within four blocks of Obama was the controversial leader of the Nation of Islam (NOI), the Honorable Minister Louis Farrakhan.

In the 1996 general elections, Farrakhan took credit for inspiring an additional 1.7 million black men to vote after his Million Man voter-registration event on the National Mall. Obama rallied shoulder to shoulder with the black-male-only, no-whites-allowed group just one month into his first ever political campaign. Feeling obliged to Farrakhan for hustling the brothers to jump start his political career, Obama knew he had to clandestinely return the favor. Even if Obama believed Farrakhan's diatribes, any association with the anti-Jew, anti-white minister was considered political suicide. However he repaid him, it had to be on the q.t.

Normally Obama can slip brown-nosers some skin and send them on their way with token appreciation. Farrakhan, however, helped him get to Springfield and eventually to the White House. Besides the NOI wielded a powerful paramilitary, the Fruit of Islam, that protected the heart, soul, and backside of the minister. The Fruits were not to be trifled with. Disrespecting someone could cost you your life: Witness thuggish Chicago-operating procedure at City Hall, Logan Square, Woodlawn, Washington Park, or Hyde Park. Brother Barack, knowing the consequences, had something extraordinary in mind for Brother Louis.

All Windy City politicians have sworn to uphold the Blagojevich Oath. As Commander in Chief of all U.S. military assets, Obama figured he had these things and they were [expletive] golden. He wasn't about to give them up for [expletive] nothing or just anyone. Obama proceeded to earmark the Navy for Kenya because the SEALs had it too cushy on Coronado Island; the Air Force for China to goad the Japanese; the Army for Egypt's Muslim Brotherhood and Hamas; all nuclear capabilities for Iran to insure WW3; the Coast Guard for his Somali pirate peeps; both houses of the pesky Congress for Russia as promised pre-2012 election; all traditional media for Al Jazeera; and Hollywood for the Emir of Qatar. But the Honorable Minister Louis Farrakhan, on behalf of his NOI Black Muslims, deserved something extra, extra special.

How many times had Minister Farrakhan schooled Obama that Islam is Mathematics and Mathematics is Islam? The minister, formerly known as Louis "Calypso Cat" Walcott, even signs his Saviours' Day cards with a festive *Mathematically Yours*. The Nation of Islam teaches that "Blacks, the Original People, dominated the planet for trillions of years, achieving astonishing feats of science, until the calamitous rise of the white race. Whites were the result of a genetic experiment gone horribly wrong, the work of Yacub, 'a black scientist in rebellion against Allah.' These monstrous creations were permitted to oppress other races for six thousand years until God became incarnate in the man, Wallace Fard, an event signaling the beginning of the end of white supremacy. Imminent Armageddon would be initiated by the Mother Plane, a colossal UFO that would annihilate America and the white powers." (Philip Jenkins, *Mystics and Messiahs: Cults and New Religions in American History*, [New York: Oxford University Press, 2000], 109-110). This is NOI orthodoxy, not Hollywood fiction!

"[Fard] taught that the Muslim religion was intended to help free black people from oppression by white, the blue-eyed devils, and their deceitful religion of Christianity. 'The black men in North America are not Negroes but members of the lost tribe of Shebazz, stolen by traders from the Holy City of Mecca 379 years ago. The prophet came to America to find and to bring back to life his long lost brethren, from whom the Caucasians have taken away their language, their nation and their religion.' . . . so Fard offered the prospect of a regathering in Mecca." (ibid, 108).

Obama humored Farrakhan about the minister's views on Islam spun from Arabian mythology with Star-Trekster religious make-believe. No self-respecting traditional Muslim would accept that anyone or anything could reincarnate Allah, certainly not Wallace Fard from Detroit. Having been a prayer-rug student of Islam himself, Obama knew this whole Islamic magic-carpet ride started in Arabia back in the 7th century with the Quran-thumping prophet Muhammad. Along with many learned progressive scholars, Obama believed his Arab Muslim brothers were probably the very slave traders that ignominiously cast his black brothers out of Mecca to North America.

Yet both sides of the who-enslaved-whom debate had one thing in common: The mainstream Muslims in Mecca at Temple #1 and the Chicago NOI at the Gadhafi-funded Temple #2 believed that Muslim scientists and inventors discovered *all* truths that sustain the modern world starting with mathematics, architecture, medicine, astronomy, navigation, optics, hydraulics, and beyond. Both the South Side Chicago Muslims along with the Arab Muslims believed they had been disenfranchised from their rightful place in the annals of scientific discoveries. Obama, firmly seated in the Oval Office with the help from his Islamist backers, seized the chance to work both sides of the globe by inviting all believers of Muhammad into the official "Oppressed Muslims" tent.

With one deft head fake, Obama made amends on behalf of the American citizens to Minister Farrakhan and the Arab world. Farrakhan, fearing the same fate as Muammar Gadhafi, was ecstatic that Obama delivered him in the Allah tradition. Brother Obama tasked the newly-appointed administrator of NASA, Charles Bolden, to perform some heavy-duty community outreach. In a July 2010 interview with Al Jazeera, Bolden outlined President Obama's mission for NASA to foremost "find a way to reach out to the Muslim world and engage much more with dominantly Muslim nations to help them feel good about their historic contribution to science . . . and math and engineering." So, the United States is liable for Muslim victimhood not only around the globe but also in low Earth orbit and deep space!

Mission accomplished. Reparations were made to a song-and-dance cult leader and the hugely-rich, oil-producing, Islamist countries. NASA is now a mere shadow of its original self with most of the space programs canceled or handed over to the Russians. The U.S. pays Russia $70.7 million per seat for a one-way ticket to the International Space Station. Heavens to Murgatroyd! It's the only ISS taxi service available and the Soviets control it. The oldest surviving shuttle, Discovery, still rarin' to go for the next twenty-five years was forced into early retirement. Even the Chinese soft landed their first lunar lander-rover combo in December 2013 with a home-grown, professional taikonaut waiting in the wings. The insecure Muslims feel better about themselves while America surrendered unparalleled achievements along with handicapping NASA for many, many years. And morale at NASA? Shattered. The country was neutered to third-rate status in space exploration and became the galaxy's victim magnet. Obama threw the Mercury, Gemini, and Apollo astronauts a bone by giving them legal permission to sell their own personal memorabilia from their missions. Thank you, master! WOOF!

The Arab-world, fossil-fuel producers knew that money talks, especially with the pliable Obama. They wanted more than the paltry Global Entry expedited-airport-clearance and they could buy it at any cost.

The Arab Muslims lobbied Obama heavily after they helped get him into the White House. Mohamed Abdul Latif Jameel, the sixteenth wealthiest Arab in the world with a net worth around $5.1 billion give or take, sought Obama's endorsement for his international community initiative. Obama kissing Jameel's ring while bowing before him wasn't necessary. The president of the country founded on Judeo-Christian values didn't even have to prove that he heard the *azaan* five times a day, turned to Mecca, Saudi Arabia and recited the *shahadah* from memory. The most important Islamic declaration of faith goes something like this: "Allah is Supreme! Allah is Supreme! Allah is Supreme! Allah is Supreme! I testify that there is no god but God, and I testify that Muhammad is the messenger of God." Obama whispered that he thought the prayer was prettier than rapper Pharrell's "Happy" song—blasphemy worthy of a sharia flogging. Instead, Jameel needed the Obama administration network to open a few doors and create buzz for his interactive exhibition—*1001 Inventions*.

After a skeptical *New York Times* review while at the New York Hall of Science, the show received gushing praise in Los Angeles with a personal video introduction by Obama's then-Secretary of State Hillary Clinton. By the time it reached DC in August 2012, the exhibit had won the museum equivalent of the Academy Award for Best Touring Exhibition of the Year.

The exhibit was aptly called *1001 Inventions*, a modern version of the fantasies conjured up in the *One Thousand and One Nights*, a.k.a. the *Arabian Nights*. The tales spun in the *Nights* are generally considered by the Arab literati as rubbish and trivial. The wizardly rewrite of history depicted in *Inventions* was akin to reimaging Medieval Aladdin into Aladdin Las Vegas. Masterful Muslim-only feats from the 7th to the 17th century were showcased à la Planet Hollywood. What was once known as the Western Dark Ages was—shazam!—transformed into the Golden Age of Islam.

The embellished self-promotion was eclipsed only by the lack of a scholarly foundation based on facts not implications and errors. The show exaggerated its assertions by attributing 1,000 years of scientific discovery to only Muslims, as if the rest of blaspheming humanity were intellectually challenged. Time out! Sharia faithful condemn the Western world, the very engine of economic prosperity and modernity, yet believe that their own repressed society was actually responsible for changing the course of history without nurturing the creative talents of all of its citizens regardless of religion, gender, nationality, or sexual orientation. Really? The producers knew to package this illusory exhibit with gobs of glitz and glitter. All the better to fleece the American hedonistic infidels!

Time for a little truth in advertising here: When the Prophet Muhammad declared the Word of God in the Quran to be the only truth known to man, Islamic scientific discovery ceased to exist, vanished, and went dark. Scientific thought was viewed as a corrupting force never to be pursued again. The Christian West filled the void. Ever wonder why Pakistan, Afghanistan, Somalia, and Sudan, to name a few, appear to be living in the dark ages? Because they are! What comes to mind when you hear the phrase "Middle East"? Oil, warring countries, terrorism, and suicide bombers.

Islamic extremists don't care about advancing, let alone preserving culture and heritage. They get their jollies from truck-bombing priceless works of ancient civilization, including their own. Moneyed Muslims want their Quran cake and eat it, too. Watch what happens to Indonesia's tourism trade as the country with the largest Muslim population gets cozy with Islamic purists packing machetes and attacking popular Western-influenced attractions. Pack your bags: Arguably the #1 Natural Wonder of the World, the Grand Canyon in Arizona is a non-denominational, machete-free zone for travelers looking for world-class amazement. And it's neighbor, "Don't fence me in!" Nevada, is a playground for any and all, protected by gun-toting States' militias if Senate Majority Leader Harry Reid's federal enforcers get too big for their britches.

Obama defied gravity to cash in on the multibillionaire Arab's inflated vanity and the U.S. multiculturalists' penchant for enlightenment. Sticking it to Sarkozy and France's newly created Islamic Art department in the Louvre, was a side benefit. The wealthiest Arab in the world, Alwaleed Bin Talal, contributed $23 million to the French museum to display the Muslim backstory to *all* civilizations' advancements that had been *inadvertently* attributed to other cultures for centuries. Only time will tell if the mini-Louvre in Abu Dhabi, possibly the richest city in the world, will grow to accommodate the Paris-based antiquities made homeless by lack of French government funding. The entire museum may end up in the bejeweled desert by the time the Froggies wake up from their socialist stupor. And we all know what happens to antiquities when the free-the-world-from-idolatry Wahhabi demolition teams get a hold of them to make more room for the burgeoning religious tourism business. Unless al Qaeda in Paris (AQP) gets to the Louvre and the Eiffel Tower first.

Prince Alwaleed also owns sizable shares in U.S. companies, namely Citigroup Inc., Apple Inc., Time Warner, and News Corp. Soon employee welcome-packages will include prayer-rug mouse pads and wall posters with catchy Quran quotes. Obama would have preferred dealing with the #1 Arab on this Islam rewrite of world history, yet opted to keep two degrees of separation from his early benefactor that helped him get into Harvard Law School.

Recently, Prince Alwaleed expressed his anxiety over Saudi Arabia's defenselessness against abundant U.S. shale reserves. As the prince fussed and fretted in his flowing, ankle-length thobe and turban, the U.S. was officially crowned the world's largest producer of oil and gas. Wahhabi World Records: Saudi Arabia happens to be the world's largest producer of crude oil, the world's biggest bankroller for radical Islamists, and the only country in the world where *only*

Muslim prayer is permitted. The whole country is considered one enormous sacred mosque and all Saudis are Muslim from birth. Christians are "unbelievers" and "evil-livers." Better dead than sharing the earth with enlightened Islamists.

Two roads diverged at the White House and Obama took them both. Not only did he take credit for the private-land fossil-fuel extravaganza stateside, Obama also reassured the Arab prince he would dismantle the fracking industry posthaste. Somebody's got to save the al Qaeda slush fund. Ever so discreetly, Obama's courier delivered to the Saudis the president's very own personal list of the most rabid U.S. environmentalists with links to their nonprofit donation web sites. Moral dilemma: How will the sanctimonious secularites of the Sierra Club and the Environmental Defense Fund deal with praying to Muhammad five times a day after they've sold their quasi-scientific souls? Once again, Obama took credit for America getting closer to energy independence in his UC Irvine Commencement Address June 2014, performed for his California climate-change cronies: "America produces more renewable energy than ever, more natural gas than anyone. And for the first time in nearly two decades, we produce more oil here at home than we buy from other countries. And these advances have created jobs and grown our economy, and helped cut our carbon pollution to levels not seen in about 20 years. (Applause.)" Who believes these whole-cloth stories? Liberals do because it's a story and it came out of Obama's mouth. A simple formula for progressive simpletons.

Covering his multi-pronged promises, Obama piggybacked the green agenda on top of the shale gas success by offering state and local governments inducements to develop wind and solar alongside fracking by creating

Sustainable Shale Gas Growth Zones. Gas gusher: The fracking revenue blowout underwrites the financially-unsustainable renewables. Ever keen on cross-subsidizing without breaking a sweat, the fracking convert learned a new technique—horizontal drilling into taxpayers' savings accounts to fund yet another energy experiment.

Obama realized the quickest path to legitimate street cred was to make it socially acceptable for victimized AA (affirmative action) recipients to come out of the closet. He had to breathe life back into the moribund civil-rights issues even though the RIP head stone was firmly planted in concrete with institutional rebar protecting it from every angle. Blacks of all ethnicities, including American, Caribbean, and African, and their equally underrepresented minority brothers, Hispanics, were now encouraged not to hide in the shadows but to be proud of their concealed competitive advantage bestowed on them by multicultural-thirsty administrators from liberal institutions. Affirmative action became a badge of honor and a birthright for a few chosen minorities. Lower-class whites, Mormons, ROTC cadets, military types, 4-H club members, National Future Farmers of America, Pentecostals, social and political conservatives, born-again Christians, rural and small-town people, ranchers, working class white ethnics, older students, wheelchair users, and others don't count toward disadvantaged minority quotas. Russell K. Nieli, Princeton University professor, shed light on this topic with his July 2010 paper "How Diversity Punishes Asians, Poor Whites and Lots of Others." Skin color is the definitive diversity factor.

One of the first affirmative-action-preferenced blacks to hear Obama's clarion call was a professor from their beloved Harvard. One need only read Henry Louis Gates Jr.'s major signifyin(g) scholarly work to understand that Ivy League schools bend their admissions and grading rules to accommodate certain ethno-racial groups. And students look up to this educator? He must have some very rough days in class trying to keep up with his students. Thank you Harvard admissions team for putting this disadvantaged black on a flight to fame and fortune not available to the negative-actioned minorities. And Samuel L. Jackson, when you complain about Obama dropping off "g's" from the end of his words, know that it's his dog whistle to his bros at Harvard and the hood signifyin(g) he really, really, really is black. This undermines his lectures about the "authentic way" of behaving blackly to followers of his My Brother's Keeper project. Who says the president has to be congruent?

July 16, 2009, Gates was arrested, handcuffed, and obliged with a CV-ready booking photo for disorderly conduct during a misunderstanding of a potential burglary into his own home. Obama raced to the White House bully pulpit to reprimand the Cambridge popo for messing with his Harvard homeboy while doing their job. The president quick to lash out that Sgt. James Crowley "acted stupidly" added "that there is a long history in this country of African Americans and Latinos being stopped by law enforcement disproportionately. That's just a fact." Facts aside, Obama didn't even have the full story before wielding his racial-profiling sword.

An independent panel ruled that the incident had nothing to do with race. Since the truth was irrelevant, Obama lit the whole incident ablaze and made it *all* about race. This was just a glimpse of Obama's slash-and-burn tactics to free blacks and Hispanics from their white oppressors, never mind that President Lincoln already claimed that victory. To recap: The truth was irrelevant.

Believing that one good turn deserves another, Gates came out of the shadows again to help the president anoint Eva Longoria, *Desperate Housewives* actress, as Obama's face for Latino votes and fund raising. After having sampled her DNA for a documentary series, Gates discovered that Longoria wasn't the Mexican/Native American ancestral blend that afforded her free passes throughout her career. The inconvenient truth that Gates uncovered was that she was 70% European, 27% Asian/Indigenous, and 3% African. Both Obama and Longoria were more than "a little shaken" by the news, yet were overjoyed that at least she wasn't 100% Anglo-WASP.

The twin impostors, Barack and Eva, forged ahead with their unique American stories, delivering them in an emotional manner as if talking to family. The uninformed Latinos whipped out there crying towels and fell for it. Do you think Longoria modified her resumé after the big DNA reveal? Obama put his hands over his ears and screamed "La, la, la, la, la, I can't hear the facts." It made absolutely no difference to him that she wasn't an authentic Latina. Again, the truth was irrelevant. *Precaución al comprador*. Buyer beware. With Obama ignoring the caveat-emptor gaffe, Longoria had a presidential pass to tout her Latino Victory Project as a "non-partisan" non-profit though forged with DNC dollars. *Muchas gracias*.

Obama forgave Dr. Gates for the mixed chromosomal message. A political scientist himself, Obama knew better than to use quantifiable, verifiable data to support his latest pseudo-science subterfuge. Best to have no evidence, ergo, no negative effects, like the same-sex marriage arguments before the Supreme Court. Witness Obama having shot himself in the foot trying to draw a causal relationship between guns and violence. Relying on a small sample of general scientists' answers to a two-question online survey collected by a master's student, Obama tweeted that "97% of climate scientists agree: #climate change is real, man-made and dangerous." Then there was Obama's Justice Department using the Herfindahl Index, sans empirical certainty, to halt legitimate corporate mergers. As with all the social and behavioral sciences, particularly political science, conclusions are usually ambiguous because the data is too weak. Guns don't kill people; people kill people. Market share need not be squared unless you're an antitrust lawyer manipulating real data to create a distorted marketplace. Facts in the physical science world are stubborn things. However, in the Obama world of relative make-believe, facts are mere words that are meant to bend and flex to suit his immediate ambition. Obama's facts can be whatever he wants them to be. And Gates Jr. got it!

His made-for-PBS soul mate understood completely how to exploit street cred. Look no further than The Hiphop Archive that Gates established as the director of the W.E.B. Du Bois Institute for African and African American Research at Harvard.

As stated on its website: "The Hiphop Archive's mission is to facilitate and encourage the pursuit of knowledge, art, culture and responsible leadership through Hiphop." Its rubric is the counterpublic or underground.

Translation: Political dissidents, guerilla warfare, internet hacktivism, demonstrations, and social movements to challenge, agitate, and assert themselves without compromise. Within the lofty, academic rhetoric that would elude most hip-hop lyricist's wildest mental-complexion, Gates conveniently created a space for hip-hop artists as "oppressed" people. Yeah, that's the ticket! Poor, tormented thug *rappers* spewing hatred, misogyny, violence, and murder rebranded as hip-hop *artists* spewing hatred, misogyny, violence, and murder are now legitimately canonized as victims of society and its educational system. This fit ever so neatly into Obama's narrative as the Robin Hood of the Oppressed.

Try to solve this liberal, suspend-reality brainteaser. The Forbes Five wealthiest hip-hop entrepreneurs include Puff Daddy, Jay-Z, 50 Cent, Dr. Dre, and Birdman. These aspiring-billionaire multi-millionaires are heralded as oppressed by Harvard's Hiphop Archive. Suffering from post-oppression stress disorder and in need of constant attention, these tragic figures must be chauffeured in $8 million Mercedes Maybach Exeleros, visit the Hamptons in their personal jets, acquire private islands, form oil and gas exploration companies, create hoodlum clothing lines, act in Hollywood movies, hawk ghosted autobiographical books, negotiate baseball contracts while hauling stacks of cash to banks and brokerage houses. The abuse is unbearable. For additional therapy, these lost souls practice yoga, eat vegan, meditate with maharishis, compare notes with power coaches, collaborate with Parisian culturists, mentor disruptors in the Garage, and memorize Gary Zukav's *Seat of the Soul*. Oh, so much tax-deductible, market research to get close to their customers' POV, yet the pain just won't go away. What's the solution?

The answer, of course, is to institutionalize hip hop. Let collectivization shine. Lock down the inmates. Control the code. Structure the street beats. Stifle creativity. Make it uniform, dull, and unimaginative. Straightjacket it. Make it obey. Organize the oppressed hierarchy. Bring it into the system. Manage the raw human aggression. Replace the artists with buildings and desks and computers. Make it mainstream. Take it to the suburbs. Surrender it to the Ruling Class. Enshrine hip hop at all the Ivy League schools. Proclaim moral authority. Offer degrees at every level to certified, licensed, professional hip-hopsters. Make it into a non-profit. Well, not thaaaaat institutionalized.

Instead, build Fortune 500 multimillion dollar marketing campaigns around hip-hop swagger. Honor the code: no bling, no thing. Spread the wealth. Everyone can ride the hip-hop gravy train. Never mind the sleazy icons of gansta rap have vulgar backgrounds connected with using and selling illegal drugs, dropping out of school, violent gang shoot-outs, drive-by murders on the Las Vegas strip, pimping sex slaves, fathering multiple children with multiple mates then abandoning them, along with Jerry Maguire-imitations of shoplifting the pootie. Besides, enticing the white MTV audiences was always the intent of hip hop. But bro, we be eavesdropping on the black-thug ethos.

The manufactured menaces that morphed into family entertainers just followed Obama's secret sauce for fame and fortune: write a new life story, erase the seedy indiscretions, reformulate to be endearing, and invent a more saleable brand. What an exit strategy! Obama's way is far more lucrative than death or prison. Degenerates and reprobates can whitewash, well uh, blackwash their bios, too! Spin is spin, no matter what color. Anti-social behavior can be overlooked and casually forgotten if the media cabal gets a first-class seat on the g-train.

A hallmark of institutionalization is the coveted, venerated, and puffed up Doctor of Philosophy degree, or PhD. An Ivy League university awarded a student, Marc Lamont Hill, a PhD in Education which is considered the lowest-level doctorate in the intelligentsia caste system and generally pursued by those with the least amount of zeal for teaching. His thesis was "(Re)negotiating knowledge, power, and identities in Hip-Hop Lit." Dr. Hill is now an associate professor at another progressive Ivy League school, soon to be a distinguished professor of African American Studies at an all-male historically black college to augment his frequent s**t-eating grin, TV guest appearances as a combative expert on hip-hop culture and just-for-the-hell-of-it militancy. You might call him a tweet-addled metaphor for race hustling. Makes you wonder how many SAT points were added to his "holistic" scores to check-off his affirmative-action entry box. Teachers, listen up! The guilty-white system you buy into with your liberal votes, emboldens the likes of Hill to end-run the step-and-lane gulag while you slog away semester to semester picking up credits here and there like slaves bowing to your progressive masters. Hello!

An accredited university in Iowa awarded a PhD in Communications to another student, Aaron Dickinson Sachs, with a dissertation entitled "The hip-hopsploitation film cycle: representing, articulating, and appropriating hip-hop culture." Dr. Sachs is now an assistant professor of media, technologies, and culture at a college in California. Substitute "rock 'n' roll" in either of the above mentioned dissertations and see what liberal-minded university would take it seriously. Yogi Berra would just call it as he saw it: 1970s blaxploitation déjà vu all over again. Best not to expect too much originality from the professors' lounges.

If the academics would deign to step out of their cushy salons, they might learn what the real world is saying about President Obama. Felonious Munk captured the sentiment oh so delicately with his "Stop It B! OBAMA PAY YOUR &*%$#% BILLS" on YouTube August 10, 2011: "How the f**k do you owe China, B? ... the biggest Communist country on the f**kin' planet ... President Obama, personal to you. All the black people was proud. We got a black president. You actin' like one right now, B. Pay your f**kin' bills on time." There's a whole lot more of Felonious on YouTube.

Rock 'n' roll was considered taboo for corrupting generations of juveniles. Elvis, the King of Rock 'n' Roll and accidental iconoclast, was counterculture having grown up in African American neighborhoods idolizing black gospel singers. His swiveling hips and pulsating legs were judged too-hot-to-handle pornographic. His "Jailhouse Rock" music video is brilliant, kinetic poetry. Yo, rock 'n' roll ain't keepin' it real! Take a good hard look—it is reality! Today rock 'n' roll has become classy, tailored, even refined compared to the down-and-dirty, expletive-laden rapping. Puff Daddy's hip-hop clothing line is playing catch-up to well-financed clothiers like Bespoken, where Savile Row meets rock 'n' roll. Or another dynamic duo, Thom Sweeny custom-clothing for Steve McQueen types. Good luck, Sean, using hip-hop thuggery to compete with rock 'n' roll-loving Arab money and Brit bespoke tailoring.

So what's the fuss over the hip-hop religion, spawned in sexual and scatological nursery rhymes? Is hip hop merely an expression of the human condition? Jesus, Mary, and Joseph save us! Hip hop should emulate its multinational, multicultural, inclusive predecessor. Does inspiring the savage Islamist Jihad-Z to get down with the rapper beat while beheading American journalist and practicing Catholic James Foley count as multiculturalism? Rock 'n' roll welcomes all cultures—black and white, straight and gay. Rock 'n' roll isn't about hate and debauchery. Rock 'n' roll doesn't glorify killing innocents, abusing women, and sanctioning criminal activities. While pushing many social boundaries, rock 'n' roll performers don't degrade their ardent listeners or cut their heads off.

Motown expressly created a platform for the world to experience the distinctive, treasured, and coveted essence of its black entertainers—soulfulness. Ask Smokey Robinson. The Motown sound had nothing to do with Detroit; it had everything to do with the humanity of the warm-hearted, sensitive black singers. Like the Motor City's financial collapse, rap and hip hop bankrupted the very culture the Motown artists dignified with their music. If they ever had any soul, foul-mouthed rappers expose how lost these souls really are. Would Chuck Berry tweet the following after the 2011 Japanese earthquake and tsunami the way 50 Cent did with "Look this is very serious people I had to evacuate all my hoes from LA, Hawaii and Japan. I had to do it. Lol."? Would Chubby Checker's debut twist album have Dr. Dre-inspired song titles about "F**k wit Chubby Day," "The Day the Niggaz Took Over," "A Nigga Witta Gun," or "Bitches Ain't Sh*t"? Would Donna Summer, Tina Turner, or Whitney

Houston make like Nicki Minaj and demand "Somebody please tell him who the eff I is" while bragging that "We're high than a motherf**ker (3x)" and toss in a phrase about "entrepreneur n*ggas . . . Then the panties comin' off" just for emphasis? A Nicki-pink-shade different from a few decades ago when the Beatles sang a gently provocative "Why Don't We Do It In the Road?"

Postscript: Obama keeps Minaj's songs on his iPod in spite of Nicki's off-the-reservation street-beating: "I'm a Republican voting for Mitt Romney/You lazy bitches is f**king up the economy." Both Barack and Michelle enjoy hip hop and condone rapper lyrics by inviting the likes of Common and Pharrell to the White House. Jazz replaced Negro folk music, as hip hop replaced jazz to become the new cultural signifier, conjuring up connotations of discrimination, second-class citizen, n*gger, the whole black-versus-white scene. In Obama's retro, reconstituted, raging-racist world, what's not to enjoy!

One can only conclude that the Obamas' daughters also listen to hip hop, including the repugnant and obscene lyrics. Highly unlikely. Different rules though for his sensationalized, sound-bited, adopted son. Delinquent, hoodied, and high, Trayvon Martin marched to his own hip-hop drummer. Ay, *güero*, if he can coldcock a white Hispanic pretending to be a community organizer, he can listen to whatever he wants! Like father, like son. Tell us, almighty bigotry squad, do invectives like "creepy ass cracka" or "peckerwood" justify hatred, censure, and retribution? Again, different standards for the genetically oppressed and disrespected.

Why institutionalize hip hop? Is hip hop even worthy of institutionalization? Profit alert: Bigger hip-hop markets equal bigger dollars. The mash-up of bling aspirations with drug-addled lyrics and white-guilt forgiven was bigger than the inner-city, crack-cocaine, smash-mouth contagion. No thinly veiled racial attack here. Black or wigger, no matter, it's all green. The hip-hop culture became the darling of American brands packaged and promoted to appeal to Americans' pocketbooks. On the way to the MTV Awards, the rappers stoked the fires of hate and became racism profiteers. These trash-talkers demean and dumb down the culture and Madison Avenue calls it the newest "embodiment of cool." Has Corporate America realized yet that hip-hopcrisy undermines and betrays American values? Not at all.

One man's rap is another man's rubbish: Silicon Valley venture capitalists with billions of dollars to invest encourage America's youth to feel the rappers' stories, make the hip-hop lifestyle their own. Forget about what their acerbic words mean. Become the rapper. Suffer the lyrics. Savor the tension. Mainline the rhythm. The computer-coded nerds praise the rappers as great philosophers not the least bit interested in making money. Arrggh! What would Socrates say to these humanities-stunted geeks and rhyming gangsters that don't give a rat's rump about what things mean, about the pursuit of knowledge, you know, the essence of philosophy? Plato's "universals and particulars" were the precursors of software engineering "instances and classes"? Computer logic has rewritten epistemology and ontology? This gives new meaning to artificial intelligence masquerading as gee-whiz clever. Their self-absorbed inanity defies explanation regardless of how many billions of dollars and fans back them.

Debasement was exactly what Obama had in mind and hip-hopped rapper music was the vehicle to deliver it. Gates delighted in the con. Obama relished the scam. If feigned persecution was the bait, so be it. Bottom line: Entice new buyers. Thus began Obama's Pied-Piper oppression procession to the White House for cathartic poetry readings, lyrical pity parties, chummy chillin', smoking weed with Snoop Dogg in the john, and OD'ing on crass witlessness. Ditch the Dalai Lama! Take him out the backdoor trash door. Don't want the high rollers faced with any moral dilemmas while they're getting it on in the People's House.

Occasionally to recharge and get back to his roots, Obama returns to his old stomping grounds—Chicago, the murder capital of the U.S. His loyalty to his adopted hometown is seen in the steady stream of shout-outs and kisses he sends to the Bulls and the Bears at the expense of dissing every other national league team. Though not Olympic host-city material, the "Let Friendship Shine" Chicago campaign may have overstated their ability to welcome international guests safely—well, for that matter, any guests or even residents. Weighing Chicago's soaring crime rate and Illinois' tanking credit rating, the International Olympic Committee just didn't feel the warm and fuzzies. Nor did the IOC muckety-mucks want to infect the peaceful, friendly, and fair-minded spirit of the global games with the local Chicago culture famous for if-you-can't-beat-'em-then-you-drop-'em goon rules. Even though Obama brought his very own six-pointed star power to the party, it still wasn't good enough. Leave it to the Chicago Blackhawks' Stanley Cup wins in 2009 and 2013 to restore honor to the besmirched city.

Scarcely phased by the IOC's poor judgment, Obama keeps strong ties with his financially insolvent and politically corrupt Chicago. Movin' and groovin' in the most segregated city in the U.S., Barack soothes his South Side soul and reaffirms his elusive blackness. To keep the welcome vibe going, the Obama campaign/donation office is perpetually in motion and only a 5-minute hop, skip, and jump to City Hall. For Big Data enemy-targeting and cold-cash trolling, Google's new penthouse offices at the Merchandise Mart are only a 10-minute toddle from O's never-ending Campaign Central. Connecting 150 yottabyte dots for the c4 Organizing for Action, formerly known as the c3 Obama for America, requires special Googler expertise. And ultra-convenient for the "vacuous cipher" Valerie Jarrett who doesn't even have to swap her 4-inch heels for walking shoes. Her partner-in-crime David Axelrod despises the walk though desperately needs the exercise. Rumor has it that Obama & Friends are rechristening the Democratic Party, The Obama Party. Clintonistas take heed!

The only company that could afford to move to downtown Chicago, Google redirected 3,000 newly acquired Motorola employees from the solvent, affluent, northern suburbs to Chicago and Cook County. Democrats Mayor Rahm "Dead Fish" Emanuel along with Governor Pat Quinn made them a $110 million offer they couldn't refuse. With a Gallup poll reporting that 50% of Illinois residents were desperate to *move out* of Illinois, the progressive putzes had to do something. Not jumping for joy at this effort to redistribute wealth and help feed the imploding unfunded Chicago pension coffers were the Googleized Motorola employees that had an additional fifty-mile commute. The thousands of Motorola nonessentials chopped pre- and post-Motorola purchase were too traumatized and jobless to weigh in. After all, this was only mundane, terrestrial fly-over country. Why would the Google gurus want to waste their government discounted fuel to shuttle their corporate jets to and from no man's land? They might even agree to pay California taxpayers the $5.3 million for the science-research-that-looked-a-lot-like-beach-parties, business-expense dodge if pushed a little by the Pentagon. A few months later and overflowing with tons of working capital, Google bought Moffett Federal Airfield and washed away the boys-will-be-boys bad press. The obsolete WWII Moffett Field NUQ was assigned a stellar, interplanetary, location identifier—GOOGLE.

The Googleplex Californians that struck the deal with Motorola never had to hazard white-out blizzard conditions on I-94. Their sun-drenched Venice Beach campus was more to their liking. Nor did they want their employees to drive in those conditions either. The method to their madness was to have those suburban commuters feel the pain and relocate to the downtown, concrete jungle. The West Coast liberals support the EPA smart-growth subterfuge to drain the suburbs and pack everyone into congested urban enclaves to reduce carbon emissions. Chicago would be held up as the exemplary sustainable community—better than New York and Los Angeles. Even Toronto! The HUD-DOT-EPA interagency would proudly send Chicago all sorts of federal grants and award monies if they just shuffled Illinois taxpayers around.

The 2012-13 winter was enough for the Santa Claristas. By January 2014 they called it quits with Motorola, Chicago, and those damn potholes! When Lenovo's chairman offered Google's executive chairman Eric Schmidt his homemade kung pao chicken and $2.91 billion for Motorola, Eric broke out his sandals and sunscreen and caught the first flight out of the Prairie State back to California. The tech gods delivered him back to Governor Jerry Brown and the land of "the smart people." Google would find a way to rationalize the negative ROI on Google's original $12.5 billion investment. They really only wanted Motorola's treasure trove of patents and a reason to set up their metadata analytics operation in the strategic center of North America. Topographic map check: Rugby, North Dakota is the official Geographical Center of North America. Google knows this, however, there's fewer than 3,000 people living there and the local truck stop is the best restaurant in town. Think of the delicate sensibilities of the Silicon Valley gourmands!

Google's ambassador-at-large for government outreach, hand holding, and thought leadership, Schmidt solely angel-funded and mentored the Obama campaign data-crunchers' new company, Civis Analytics. Spun off to exploit commercial opportunities from their offices in Chicago and Washington, DC, Civis Analytics monetizes the teams' lofty lefty goal of solving the world's biggest problems with Big Data. If these homegrown and H1-B troglodytes ever emerge from their algorithm haze and screenly-lit cave, break the news softly—for fear of shattering their liberal Utopian worldview—they now closely resemble a capitalistic, money-making, profit-driven collection of startup brainboxes. The real rude awakening will come as they limit their marketing efforts to "Democrats Only" while the Democratic Party transforms itself into tyrannical, invasive eyes-in-the-cloud cruising around in black helicopters. In the free-market world, emphasis on *free*, customers vote with their dollars.

And when they're hunkered down in the backroom and nobody's looking, the cave dwellers might even sneak a peek at conservative Gmail emails. Who needs a secret court order when Obama's National Security Agency "unwittingly" sponsors a hackathon dragnet of telephony records galore and calls it PRISM. Clever. PRISM. American citizens' "private information" reflected, refracted, dispersed, reverted, inverted, shifted, bent, displaced, and deviated into harmless rainbow colors to distract the world from the subterfuge. Go get 'em, boys! Collect it all!

Also, Google's new Big Brother search algorithm innocuously called "Hummingbird" omnipotently assumes "customer intent" when conducting an online search. Everyone's privacy, softly sold as "the people's data," is now a negotiable currency for sweet mega-million cloud-computing contracts. Yet Schmidt is shocked and enraged that the "cookie monster" NSA is spying on the company's data centers. Google and its C-suite executives are protected by impenetrable firewalls having purchased their immunity as the #3 contributor in the 2012 presidential campaign, up from #4 in 2008. Google's $1.6 million gift exchange with Obama almost bought them net neutrality—deep-discounted, consumers-pay, internet pipes—until the DC federal appeals court put the brakes on the Federal Communications Commission's anti-competition tomfooleries. Google's Friedmanian cri de coeur: There's no such thing as a free internet! Never mind the court's decision, Eric, my good friend, my best buddy—paleeeeease fix HealthCare.gov!!!

Fessing up to their left-tilting financial gifting, Google realized they needed conservative friends in high places, too. Their Big Tent of Washington lobbyists currently houses an even number of Republicans and Democrats. Obama campaign posters have been replaced with pictures of the Founding Fathers—and replicas of the U.S. Constitution with the "unreasonable searches and seizures" Fourth Amendment expunged. Yet Google wasn't so fortunate in Europe. June 2014, the EU high court ruled that when requested, Google would have to remove an individual's information that the search engine displayed when the individual's name was inserted. At last, a European society-protecting idea that makes sense—the "right to be forgotten."

Here's the $6 billion pattern-recognition question: Who benefits most from Obama's proposed imperially-mandated tax on every American's cell phone to cover the cost of free Wi-Fi, with unlimited coffee refills, to every student in every classroom in every city in every state? Google believed they even trumped Steve Jobs' Apple-computer-in-every-classroom coup back in the day. Starbucks will no doubt run the tax-payer-funded coffee concessions.

Pitchman Obama: Stunned that one of his proposals went down in flames, Obama made it up to the avowed liberal Starbucks' CEO Howard Schultz and their much-loved pitch-lady when he occasioned an "impromptu" walk to the local DC Starbucks coffee oasis for a cup of Oprah chai tea June 2014. This bit of native-advertising theatre went headline virile while Iraqi cities were under barbaric siege and American veterans were stonewalled by VA hospitals. Just like reality TV—unscheduled, unscripted, and real, very real. Gulp! All the CEO had to do was agree to make the rounds with the progressive talking-TV-heads and plug Obama's drive to mandate the eradication of income inequality by raising the minimum wage. Starbucks would just wait in the wings and collect the disenfranchised employees of the out-of-business franchisees hobbled by the government-mandated pay increases.

Barista revolving door: Give the hourly retail-workers a few more dollars; offer online-degree tuition reimbursement to those too caffeinated to sleep anyway; deluge them with app-zapped, advance-pickup orders because the wait times in the walk-in and drive-thru lines aren't long enough; dump more time-consuming, cook-to-order, bonus-star products on the menu; monitor their customer-contact time by milliseconds; drive more customers in with free designer-drink coupons; GPS-track their every move in the "Starbucks Experience" mobile trucks; make food-handling baristas clean the toilets more often; redistribute their tips to street people who can't afford to buy a Starbucks anything; throw the coffee-crafters onto the ObamaCare exchange, then maybe, just maybe, the 100% annual turnover rate will self-correct. Income inequality AND clap-happy employees solved all by raising the minimum wage and making the baristas *really* work for a few more crumbs. What's not to love? A full-circle, liberal, corporate, crony-capitalist trifecta: Obama, Schultz, and Oprah—all winners! Are they addicted to caffeine, sugar, or celebrity? The shareholders were somewhat dismayed by Schultz adding millions of education dollars to the cost-side of the brewing-java equation. Within a couple of days, Schultz handily took care of that little detail—Starbucks announced they were raising their drink prices. Superfecta!

The following week, Obama strolled with his carnival sideshow to the close-enough-to-the-White-House-for-loads-of-pictures Chipotle Mexican Grill for sustainable, organic, family-farmed, local, gourmet burritos to feed the White

House's Summit on Working Families entourage. A photo op a day keeps the truth seekers at bay!

Stop & frisk: Funny thing how these model corporate-citizen establishments, Starbucks and Chipotle Mexican Grill, cater to their progressive customers' tiniest taste buds, yet forbid gun-toting, Second Amendment-exercising, coffee, tea, and organic foodies from mingling with the undefended stores' vulnerable anti-gun diners. It's just discriminatingly hilarious.

Enter at your own risk! Mexican wise guys on the loose! Chicago was no longer run by Mayor Emanuel. There was another "shorty" in town: Joaquin "El Chapo" Guzman. Leader of the venomous Sinaloa cartel, Guzman used Chicago as a hub to distribute drugs across the U.S.—*tu casa es mi casa*. Whatever the drug-partiers demanded—100% *Hecho en México cocaína*, methamphetamines, heroin, and *certificación orgánica marihuana*—El Chapo delivered. Guzman had cornered almost half the market of all drugs flowing into the U.S. The new Public Enemy No. 1 hid out in his rugged-mountain casita in western Mexico counting his $1 billion-plus fortune while Chicago street-gangs battled for bloodstained territory. February 2014, he was captured pre-dawn in his pajamas in a modest Mazatlán condominium. The $5 million bounty for El Chapo was a small price to pay to stave off the flow of drugs and the trail of corpses. Guzman probably donated that amount just in bribes and political-campaign contributions, north and south of the border.

Hey, Sinaloa cartel! Don't you know you're having a disproportionate adverse impact on members of a protected minority group? You haven't heard of "disparate impact" and you're a global cartel? On its face you appear to be giving equal lethal-treatment to all teenagers, but in practice you're killing fewer of the non-members of the protected group—"unintentionally," of course. That's illegal, *mang*. At least one black teenager is snuffed out by another black teenager every day in Chi-Town. Spread your guns, drugs, and carnage around! Even the score! Balance out the young black deaths with young white ones in the suburbs. It's only fair and, besides, it's the law, *amigo*! Call in the Consumer Financial Protection Bureau. If they can statistically find covert racism in home mortgages and auto lending, they can find it in the drug-trafficking underworld. Is Ally Bank still in business after the CFPB damaged their reputation and extorted $98 million from them on auto-loan discrimination allegations? El Chapo, you should have worked for the CFPB doing sting operations—that's where the real money is. Better still, working for former IRS official Lois Lerner to discriminate against and "intentionally" treat Tea Party groups fundamentally different would have given you tax-exempt privileges and Fifth Amendment immunity. It pays to have *compadres* in the highest of places—like the White House. Got any drug paraphernalia to scratch computer hard drives?

In neighboring St. Louis, the "Obama Boyz" gang must have read Quentin "Peace Out" Tarantino's reinventing-cowboys script. They became their own empowered-black-American-male-folkloric-western heroes and actually paid back blood-for-blood by shooting a pair of teenagers at 2:17 p.m. in a drive-by from the window of a Grand Prix. They had outgrown "flash robberies" that their black teenager bros in DC and Philadelphia occasionally enjoyed. Prisoners of their own culture, the Obama Boyz asserted oppression, restitution, and revenge. Hollywood-hero status, billion-dollar bling, and black retaliation are the new affirmative-action remedies.

Where was Polar Bears International as gangs of black men stalked "polar bears" in Brooklyn, Philadelphia, and other concrete-glaciered cities to test their hunting prowess with a killer "knockout" sucker punch? *Ursus maritimus* is one thing but your average *Homo sapiens*, well, that's a different story. For the environmental stewards, any human is a nuisance and doesn't deserve to live on their sustainable planet. A statement or donation from PBI to help those that died or suffered injuries would have delivered favorable headlines and probably donations. Arctic polar bears are easier to rescue than black urban gangsters.

Quick! It's 3 a.m.! Wake the president! There's a crisis going to waste! Black youth unemployment is close to 40% and trending higher! Repeat: 40% of black teenagers are not working but hanging out aimlessly! Overall the teen jobless rate hovers around 23%. The number keeps getting higher with each passing day Obama's in office. And he has their backs? Obama hobnobs with the bling-enrobed, heat-packing street poets and says he's taking care of the unemployed teenagers? What signal is he sending? The career options he's laying before these young people who idolize him are demoralizing on their face: depraved rapper, drug dealer, drug user, NBA basketball star, NFL football superhero, PGA golfer, slick community organizer, affirmative-action prostitute, or lifelong welfare good-for-nothing. Always myopically looking towards the next election, Obama abysmally failed the next generation. He taught them to trade their votes for everlasting entitlement slavery rather than prepare themselves for life's challenges and realistic success.

Obama as role model for young people—that's one for the ages.

Back to the Midwest madness. What pillars of Chicago society could have coached these underdogs from the first round, through the semifinals, straight to their own personal championships? No, not coach Phil "Zen Master" Jackson who was leading his own team of young men to NBA titles. Who on Chicago's South Side could have, should have, would have served as a role model for these self-destructing, homicidal homeboys? Barack Hussein "mmm mmm mmm" Obama had the chance in 1995 to inspire and elevate an entire generation of Chicago school children with the Chicago Annenberg Challenge. Alas, he chose to advance and promote himself, deserting the children and decimating the CAC. Another well-known black leader from the Chicago South Side is Reverend Jesse Jackson. Both he and Obama live in the tony Hyde Park section of the South Side, better known as the safe Demilitarized Zone. Obama was only five years old eating snow cones in Hawaii when, in 1966, MLK Jr. hand-picked Jackson to move to Chicago. With his Operation Breadbasket boycott-white-only-businesses brigade, Jackson focused full-time on the civil-rights movement. Jesse Jackson and his *legitimate* family have been in Chicago ever since.

Ostensibly crusading for black justice and equality, the in-your-face-and-your-wallet Jackson championed his own egocentric cause. For almost fifty years, the Reverend has made a living by extorting money from institutions that fear him publicly excoriating them as racists. For almost half a century, the Reverend has peddled bigotry, racism, and animosity as the rallying cries for the blacks' problems on the South Side. For five decades, the Reverend has bamboozled the black community into believing that he fights for jobs, housing, and schools. In the time it took Michael Jordan to emerge from his embryonic cocoon sporting Air Jordans, to blowing out fifty birthday candles worth a half billion dollars, the Rev. Jesse Jackson has perfected the art of leading the faithful from the Promised Land straight into South Side hell. Did you see Rev. JJ's encore performance in Ferguson, Missouri August 2014, inspiring the looters instead of calming the tensions with his very presence?

For all the largesse he commandeered during his lifetime, Jesse Jackson has not solved the problems on the South Side of Chicago. If the truth be known, the Reverend exacerbated the conditions by hollering racism, professing moral authority, and negating personal responsibility. Now he kisses the ground Obama walks on for having reignited the waning race-relations industry. Jackson's not the only liberal black mouthpiece smacking his lips. Civil-rights tourism is booming! Where's the Federal Trade Commission investigating this socially-engineered monopoly covetously guarded by the self-selected, liberal black leaders? How many billions of dollars underwrite this race-mongering, too-big-to-fail cartel? Atlanta recently squared-off against Jackson, Miss., Birmingham, Ala., Memphis, Tenn., and Greensboro, N.C. as the home of this cottage industry with its $103 million Center for Civil and Human Rights. The Smithsonian Institution in DC wants a piece of the action with their National Museum of African American History and Culture scheduled to open in 2016 as a farewell to Obama. Will non-black job applicants be offered equal opportunity to work at these black-legacy institutions?

To keep the shakedown franchise in the family, Jackson Sr. ushered Jackson Jr. to the U.S. Congress to represent their cherished South Side. Like father like son, Jesse Jr. benefitted greatly from daddy's affirmative-action scorched-earth tactics with Corporate America. The dynasty's bombastic wrath made them heroes in the hood. But, lo and behold, the Jackson Sr. fame-and-fortune template doesn't always work. Look what happened to Lil' Jesse.

Following in his father's valueless footsteps, Congressman Jesse Jackson Jr. enhanced his lifestyle with $750,000 of misappropriated campaign funds. Also following Sr.'s example, Jr. had an extramarital affair. When the white-political-machine-discriminated-against-me argument was obviously too obtuse, the black Chicago politician used the gastric-bypass-made-me-do-it defense. Guilty of actions unbecoming a preacher's son and an esteemed member of the U.S. Congress, Jesse Jr. pleaded bariatric surgery that begot depression that begot gastrointestinal issues which finally made him a bipolar basket case. Jr. was finally cured with two and a half years in prison followed by three years of monitored parole including 500 hours of presumed, apolitical, community service. To ease his pain and suffering, he pockets an $8,700 per month disability check with a partial federal pension of $45,000 per year at age 65. There went the safe, lucrative, black seat in the duped black ghetto, at least for a while.

In the spirit of converging scientific disciplines and paraphrasing the revered Nobel Prize theoretical physicist Max Planck: A color-blind society does not triumph by convincing its race-huckster opponents and making them see the light, but rather because the race baiters eventually die and a new generation grows up that is familiar with a world based on merit.

The lesson learned: Politicians are self-serving. Instead of community organizers and civil-rights activists, the South-Siders ought to look beyond the Magnificent Mile and the Gold Coast rainbows for inspiration and positive black role models. Dr. Benjamin Carson, world-renowned pediatric brain surgeon now retired, grew up poor, without a father, in inner-city Detroit. Yes, he's black, but who cares about his skin color. Talk about a moral-compass, true-north realignment! Check out his books and the Carson Scholars website. Here's a sample: "God has opened many doors of opportunity throughout my lifetime, but I believe the greatest of those doors was allowing me to be born in the United States of America." Too intellectual? Need another example of an accomplished brother that's kicking ass and taking names? Mike Tomlin, coach of the Pittsburgh Steelers, would bring some sanity to the gangstas' buzz-saw world with his words of wisdom: "Excuses are the tools of the incompetent." He walked the talk when he apologized profusely and paid a $100,000 forgive-me-for-I-have-sinned penalty for distractedly stepping into a restricted zone while a Baltimore kick returner sprinted on Tomlin's blindside. Time to man-up and get back to fundamental American values!

Been there, done that. Take heed of the illustrious words of Valerie Jarrett, Obama's consummate lapdog: "He's been bored to death his whole life. He's just too talented to do what ordinary people do. He would never be satisfied with what ordinary people do." Wise up South-Siders! Obama is just not that into you—after he's got your vote. He's got more important things to do, like kickin' it with Tiger Woods.

The Chicago political figures, especially Obama and Jackson Sr., have immersed themselves in Saul Alinsky's *Rules for Radicals.* Whether they picked it up in the drinking water or by osmosis, the dynamic duo's MO is undeniably Rule #11: "If you push a negative hard and deep enough, it will break through to its counterside." These supposed community organizers have pushed racism so hard and so deep that it has become their cause célèbre, their raison d'être, their lifeblood. Their ambition is to advance racism not eradicate it; divisively split the community not harmoniously organize it. It's difficult giving up the crutch of protected-class status. Jesse Jackson, who lives and breathes affirmative action, would be ineffective and impotent if racism didn't exist. His meal ticket depends upon it. His legacy to his children depends on it. He's the symbolic leader of the civil-rights establishment. Obama's entire career was built on it. Dispel the drumbeat of racism and affirmative action and they have nowhere to go. Community organizers know not how to create, only destroy.

Lights, camera, action! Jackson couldn't resist jumping into the *Duck Dynasty* fray December 2013. The A&E Network suspended the show's star Phil Robertson for honestly expressing his views that attracted millions of viewers—the largest audience of reality-show viewers in cable TV history. Unsheathing his "disrespecting Rosa Parks" boycott that he used against the movie *Barbershop* in 2002, Jackson demanded A&E executives and Robertson kneel to his royal extortion highness. Wrong! They blew him off as inconsequential.

Desperate to heal his inner cockroach after the A&E beatdown, the omnivorous Jackson decided it was time to feast on Silicon Valley's tech industry as his "next step in the civil rights movement." He set his sights on all the tech sweethearts: Facebook, Apple, eBay, Google, Pinterest, Yahoo, and others. Twitter felt the full force of Jackson's ravenous rage. As if goading the beast, Twitter announced record mobile advertising revenues the same day Jackson was conducting his roadshow to disparage the highflying company. The next day, the street showed Twitter their love and appreciation—TWTR stock skyrocketed. Tweety blue bird, welcome to the bricked-and-mortared, diversity-quotaed, prison camp. Meet the warden & chief enforcer—Reverend Jackson.

Ironically, the race hucksters have become white noise, droning on and on with the same tired invectives. They forgot that they were bound by Alinsky's Rule #7: "A tactic that drags on too long becomes a drag." While trying to sustain every last bit of power over liberal white-guilt and black-innocence, they were compelled to reimagine racism and affirmative action. Their peeps were getting bored and complacent. Again, Alinsky forced them to submit to Rule #2: "Never go outside the experience of your people." The masses easily understood racism, affirmative action, and equal opportunity. The new call to unite had to be as elementary on the surface, yet superior in its structural-change possibilities. Though rather benign and Stephen Covey-ish sounding, "beginning with the end in mind" could almost be considered uplifting and motivational. Think again. When **equal outcomes** replaced **equal opportunities** . . . kiss the Good Ol' U.S. of A. goodbye!

Where federally-decreed affirmative action should have obliterated entitlement assumptions while leveling the playing field, it has swung completely to the left and made a mockery of our system of meritocracy. To add insult to injury, equal outcomes have superseded equal opportunities. It's the equivalent of reverse engineering a merit-based culture to a collectivist society where everyone achieves the same goal, the same income, the same house, the same car regardless of individual hard work, sacrifice, aptitude, effort, character, excellence, and ability. Everyone gets the winner's trophy . . . just because. Gold stars all around, even for those working in the United States illegally.

Say the lofty equal-outcome goal is to have every worker in the U.S. making $100,000 annually. Start with that end in mind and work backwards, reverse engineer, to how a normal person achieves this level of take-home pay. All education requirements would have to be dramatically altered, relevant experience wouldn't matter, connections not important, talent unnecessary, imagination outlawed, dreams of making more than $100,000 would never happen. No need for equal opportunity because everyone would enjoy the equal outcome of making $100,000 regardless. Nice work if you can get it. In Obama's world, everyone will get it.

If expectations are lowered to achieve equal outcomes, what's the end result? How low can the expectations go? The choice has become meritocracy or mediocrity. Can expectations be set lower than mediocrity? What's lower than mediocrity? The ultimate ridiculous objective is to keep lowering, lowering, and lowering expectations until they disappear. Opportunity be damned! Everyone is equal and not expected to do anything but foolishly comply and do as commanded. This is all the political left offers because they don't know anything else. Period. End of discussion. Liberals are at the top of their game when they make you subservient and keep themselves in power. The implications are catastrophically communistic. To dumb down or not to dumb down? That is the question.

The biggest mistake in American history, worse than racial segregation, was voting Obama into the White House as proof that stigmatized whites were not racists. Those voters that inherently knew they *were not* and *never were* guilty of racism made more rational decisions with their ballots. Voters brandishing racism as their call to arms signified their own bigoted, intolerant selves.

Ever the wolf in sheep's clothing, Obama disdains the very institutions that afforded him the ability to ascend to the presidency. His mission has been to take down the underpinnings of a free American society—one by one, piece by piece, denounce, dismantle, demolish. And along the way, inflame racial hostility.

More precisely, Obama is transitioning the United States to a social democracy. He is moving the entire country from capitalism to collectivism. Pick your collectivist poison—communism, fascism, socialism—all centrally controlled by the progressive gods. That pernicious sick feeling we have every day is Obama nudging us from our capitalist roots to Euro-tested socialism. The more socially-acceptable, repackaged, reworked, no-hint-of-the-C-word term is "European progressivism." Still, the end result—a democratic welfare state. Thank you, Dr. Charles Krauthammer, for diagnosing the malady.

We can now rest easy knowing that the U.S. Constitution, the supreme law of the land, hasn't been replaced with communism, fascism, or even strict Karl Marx socialism. Instead, the reconstituted Commune of the United States is a pure, selfless, soft-and-cuddly, you-won't-even-notice-the-pain, social democracy. Washington politicians and bureaucrats now own every aspect of our lives! The fundamentally-transformed America is a dumbed-down, sedated, castrated, demoralized, hobbled, over-taxed, Europeanized, central-planned, democratic-welfare-collective of zombies. Socialize everything for the benefit of the welfare state—medicine, education, eating habits, banking, environmental standards, farming, manufacturing. 48 million Americans are on food stamps while "food insecurity" runs rampant! Yikes!

And the Final Solution: Death by debt. All U.S. citizens slowly garroted. The debt clock continues to click, click, click away. $17 trillion U.S. on-budget debt gone berserk! More exact: $31 trillion on-budget and off-budget U.S. obligations to payback, as promised, using your tax dollars! Impudent, lunatic anarchy to the nth degree! For those liberals that want America to be more like Europe, why not pack your bags and move to an organic olive farm in Tuscany or a seaside villa in Trieste? Rumor has it that the EU has already arranged a pied-à-terre in Brussels for Obama's new-world-order mischiefs post-presidency. Au revoir! *Dag*! *Kwaheri*! Good riddance!

Obama maxed out his level of competence October 29, 2012 when the Weatherman in Chief took to the airwaves warning all citizens on the East Coast to take cover from

Hurricane Sandy. Fresh from the White House Situation Room where he was briefed by his most senior hurricane-trackers, Obama appeared earnest, protective, and statesman-like. Millions of votes were on the line. With the contentious presidential election just one week away, Team Obama jerry-rigged a pseudo take-charge talking torso for the TV viewing audience. After all, Obama had to use the occasion to offset his gross incompetence witnessed by the world before, during, and after the **preventable** September 11, 2012 Benghazi massacre that left four U.S. citizens dead. The al Qaeda blitzkrieg with its precision mortar hits in Benghazi didn't even warrant a briefing in the Situation Room! Since then, Obama practically lives in the Situation Room with his photographer close by.

The only communication Obama had that fateful evening about the death and destruction at the U.S. consulate was a 30-minute telephone conversation at 5:00 p.m. EDT with Secretary of Defense Leon Panetta and the Chairman of the Joint Chiefs of Staff Martin Dempsey. The eight-hour attack had just occurred. Having performed his presidential duties with this regularly-scheduled half-hour chat and an aloof fade-to-black "stand down" order, Obama retired to the safety of the White House living quarters to enjoy a comfortable evening with his family. The passive Obama ate a sumptuous dinner, watched a little ESPN, played some NBA 2K, retired to his boudoir with his wife, then, peacefully went to sleep. The ghosts of Benghazi shouted: "Does anyone in the Obama administration know what the hell they're doing or even care?!" The Obama lackeys shouted back: "Dude, haven't we confused everyone enough already. It's been years since the slaughter. What difference does it make!" Sweet dreams.

If only President Obama had delivered on that which he was paid to do—first and foremost, protect Americans. Rather than campaigning all the time, we hired him to respect the office of the president by reforming government, fixing entitlements, lowering taxes, reducing dependency, creating an environment for the private sector to create jobs for the unemployed, and showing a little moral courage now and then. Almost deliberately defying American values, Obama never really came clean about his role in the Benghazi debacle; Fast and Furious guns killing Americans; his non-containment of a nuclear Iran ruse; his top-secret, racial-preferenced, inflated, Ivy League transcripts; his anti-American exceptionalism doctrine; the smidgen-less, "phony" IRS scandal. Only after Russian President Putin held his feet to the fire did Obama actually admit that America is exceptional—at least in his public talking points. The list goes on. Somehow Obama sidestepped the truth, honesty, and responsibility lessons while on his la-di-da, affirmative-action cakewalk through America's elite institutions.

Rule 1968
Spin the Myth and They Will Come

Martin Luther King Jr., civil-rights leader, was assassinated and race riots broke out in almost all major U.S. cities.

In an attempt to peaceably placate the raging violence, President Lyndon Johnson staged his second coup d'état by signing the Fair Housing Act of 1968, hawkishly fanned the flames by increasing Vietnam combat troops to 550,000, and asked for an additional 10% income tax on all Americans to pay for the war.

Eldridge Cleaver, Black Panther Party Minister of Information, was wounded in a deliberate ambush of the Oakland police.

Congress repealed the gold requirement to back U.S. currency, thereby collapsing the gold pools.

NASA launched Apollo 8, the first manned lunar orbiter in preparation to fulfill JFK's ambition to land an American on the moon before the end of the 1960s. While circumnavigating the moon ten times, the crew made a Christmas Eve TV broadcast in which they read the first ten verses from the Book of Genesis. The space mission was the most watched TV broadcast at the time.

Andy Warhol, artist and cultural icon, barely survived an attempted murder in his studio, The Factory.

Two days later, presidential candidate, Robert F. Kennedy, was slain in a Los Angeles hotel kitchen.

Student radicals shut down Howard University and Columbia University while protesting the escalation of the Vietnam War and the draft, dismissing the fact that 70% of Vietnam ground troops were volunteers.

Black Nationalists violently rioted, burned, looted, killed seven, and wounded fifteen Glenville/Cleveland police officers and civilians.

All this occurred shortly before the infamous 1968 Democratic National Convention in Chicago.

Thus was the Zeitgeist of 1968.

Antiwar factions of varying nihilist denominations descended on Chicago to ostensibly protest the Vietnam War. Those liberals nowhere near Southeast Asia decided the military effort was unwinnable, yet they themselves would fight to the death for their picture above the fold railing against their "lost war" phantasm. Where there are thousands of cameras, there will be thousands of anarchists to carpe diem. The antiwar madness commingled with the civil-rights chaos outside the International Amphitheatre on Chicago's South Side. The more long-term, consequential pandemonium, however, was inside the Democratic National Convention.

The Democratic Party that engaged in and escalated WW1, WW2, the Korean War, and the Vietnam War, struggled to find its inner pacifist-child. After much cajoling by the Leftists, an antiwar candidate was presented along with a peace platform. Both were rejected outright by the "dove" Democrats. Though much antiwar rhetoric was bantered about to pander to the disciples-of-Cronkite press corps, the Democrats were unwilling to change their warmongering attitudes. The liberal, war-as-usual candidate prevailed. By vowing to end the war if elected, the Republican candidate, Richard M. Nixon, became the peace candidate. He handily won the presidential election in November with 56% of the electoral votes and ended the Vietnam War—as promised.

With the media machine in overdrive, the Democrats were on display worldwide for their incompetence to control the carnage in Vietnam, the racial uproar across the country, the brutality in Chicago, and especially the bedlam at their own National Convention. The party of the progressives was fractiously fractured, the-blind-leading-the-blind leaderless, and up for grabs. Yet all was not lost.

The entire spectacle, fabricated and real, was recorded on reproducible film. Imagine the movie, TV, magazine, newspaper storyline possibilities! The liberals, known for their love of illusion, storytelling, and rewriting history, delivered a media marvel that fueled all sorts of legend-creating, myth-making, saleable scripts. In the spirit of a classic, money-making, liberal maxim: The spoils of any and all wars belong to the first photographer that captures and records them. Right on!

Another more compelling, self-serving canon of the left: Keep the revolutionary buzz swirling; make like we want to stamp out capitalism, then, capitalize on it. Burnish the brand, baby!

Abbie Hoffman and Jerry Rubin, the Yippie contingent from New York, used theatre as their organizing strategy at the Convention, staging the angry mob with their Youth International Party. To titillate the mass media, they concocted a gripping "stage play" about the mayhem about to unfold in Chicago. Their strategy failed, or did it? Neither was sentenced to prison for crossing state lines to incite a riot. And both of these Chicago Eight secured book deals. Hoffman, who was thirty-two during the '68 riot, wrote *Revolution for the Hell of It*. His final revolt was committing suicide at age fifty-two. Jerry Rubin, age thirty in 1968, wrote *Growing (Up) at 37*. Rubin impulsively committed suicide at age fifty-six by rebelliously jaywalking to his death on Wilshire Boulevard into six lanes of heavy traffic.

Bobby "bound and gagged" Seale, head of the Black Panthers, was the eighth man and sentenced to four years for contempt. Once released from prison, Seale wrote *Seize the Time* and ran for mayor of Oakland. Ben and Jerry's, Inc. hired Seale as an ice cream spokesman to promote vanilla without chunks. His personal website's tagline reads "From the Sixties to the Future …" where he advertises an upcoming movie along with his very own cookbook, *Barbecue'n with Bobby*. Don't mess with the brand, bro!

The Sixties counterculturists' political significance backfired through their stultifying conceit, atrocious hostility, and reckless hatred for America. Cultivating their capitalist chakras into "higher-consciousness" net worth and "spiritual-maturity" notoriety made the revolutionaries pseudo-cultural icons. More important in the annals of history, the Vietnam War Memorial is the most visited monument in Washington, DC.

Enter stage left: Barack Obama with Cool Rule 1968.

Schooled by Sixties radicals from his mother, to Frank Marshall Davis, to Columbia, to Harvard, to his black-liberation-theology pastor, to his anarchist neighbors and beyond, Obama entered the political scene looking, acting, and talking like your normal, consumer-cultured, Ivy League-educated, social climber. Though packaged as new and different, the reincarnated '60s radical attempted to fast-forward his rise to the top by promising to bring the entire country to a full stop and reverse fifty-plus years of progress. Desperate to find his very own civil-rights revolution, Obama was determined to relive the Sixties all over again. Hence his fascination with the overtly racist, retro NYC, high-efficiency, commercialized soap—*Mad Men.* He had seen the series, and yes, he could be the lead actor. Hell, even if he didn't really believe in the hippy-dippy-yippy counterculture, he stumbled into that 1968 drop-out zone and what a gusher of peace, love, and moola!

The Sixties radicals, deeply embedded in the establishment media and the entertainment industry, loved him. They welcomed Obama and liberally threw their sycophantic PR machines and bulging bank accounts into the

Obama project. Hey, man, it was entertainment and they longed for the good old days of psychedelia. Embraced and propelled by the media hubs of the left and northeast coasts, the Obama theatre of the absurd hypnotized the fly-over heartland States into believing they were meaningless, save for their tax dollars, then ushered them into a wicked alternate universe that once was their beloved America.

Not yet a trained political thespian, the unprepossessing Obama gaped from the peanut gallery as an unsophisticated Jesse "Viva Castro" Jackson unsuccessfully ran for president twice, 1984 and 1988. Jackson's inciteful theme song didn't help him much: I'm in a Hymietown state of mind. Lordy lordy, racism transcends race! Four years later and still on the sidelines, Obama gazed at then-Democratic Governor Bill Clinton as he won the White House in 1992 at age forty-six. Hot damn! If Bill can make a career out of running for public office on other people's money, so could Barack. In his inaugural address, President William Jefferson Clinton admonished Americans for their bad habit of expecting something for nothing from the government and each other. Obama was vexed by such heresy. The next election cycle would be different; it would be Obama's political call to arms. He would give the people whatever the pollsters tell him just to get their votes. Glacially transfixed on his future, Obama knew that one day the Democratic Party would be renamed—The Obama Party.

In 1996, the Democratic National Convention returned to Chicago after a twenty-eight year, cooling-off period. The delegates confidently ventured into the epicenter of black nationalism. Bill "I feel your pain" Clinton would be re-nominated and win the presidential race a second time. Now consider this: A thirty-five-year-old, ambitious, half black, Chicago upstart, working the streets, trolling Lake Shore Drive, beating the bushes for contacts and connections, witnesses a Lotharian, white politician honored with the moniker of the "first black president" by a well-respected, black, female, Nobel Prize recipient. Then, said politician comes to Chicago, Obama's adopted hometown, and walks away with a sure victory for the White House. Now it's easy to understand why Jackson wasn't a presidential contender but what did Clinton have that Obama didn't? Clinton swayed the stubborn black vote and he wasn't even a brother! It was clear from Obama's calculations that the Democratic Party was malleable, gullible, unprincipled, mercurial, and craving redemption. The Dems were there for the taking. Obama figured he would own them in due time.

Obama ousted a Democratic, black incumbent in 1996 on a technicality and became an Illinois state senator. He made a few enemies with that do-or-die move, but a win is a win. Extreme negative campaigning was the preferred lethal weapon for Obama and his hatchet men. His pseudo-autobiography was already unleashed in 1995, languishing but nonetheless it was one less hurdle to cross. Four years later Obama really, really wanted a position in the U.S. Congress and tried to unseat an entrenched Bobby Rush. Obama failed miserably. He then finagled his way into the Democratic National Convention at the Staples Center in Los Angeles to cheer on Al Gore in 2000. Realizing he was a penniless nobody beyond the confines of his protective home base, he rode his cancelled credit card back to Chicago to revive himself financially. At long last in 2004, the Democratic presidential candidate, then-junior Senator John Kerry, gave

Obama his big chance. The keynote address at the Democratic National Convention in Boston put Obama at center stage for the world to behold—not just the man but the benevolence of unbridled affirmative action.

The Democratic Party, the party of liberal white guilt, found their savior straight out of central casting. They had been waiting a long time. Malcolm X was gone. Martin Luther King Jr. regrettably didn't survive. Eldridge Cleaver was a turncoat Republican. Jesse Jackson was a hardball extortionist. Bobby Rush was too parochial. Finally, Barack Hussein Obama had arrived. By the way, what politically correlated algorithm generated that name?!

This wasn't just any stereotypical politician. Obama offered archetypal potential of mythical proportions. Granted his story wasn't the prisoner-to-president arc of Nelson Mandela but the lefties would substitute emotional enslavement by America's white establishment for the actual Robben Island torture. Yes, it would be gut-wrenching, teary-eyed believable. Not since 1968 had the liberals been given such a rich storyline. The traditional media decided to host a repeat performance of the Sixties and push the historical significance of Obama the same way they hyped the historical significance of the spoiled, rich, college kids throwing temper tantrums at authority figures in the Sixties. Think Bill Ayers's privileged upbringing. A fact that disproves the prevailing liberal factoid about the Sixties' protests: Only 0.025% of enrolled college students participated in the 1968 campus protests. Minority mayhem was unleashed by reporters looking for flamboyant stories.

The mainstream media had it made. These snide America-bashers discovered a presidential candidate that wasn't a proud, rock-solid American. Obama was their prototype, stereotype, and archetype narcissist all rolled into one—the holiest of the progressive holies. Their black—& white—swan. They would anoint him the pivotal being of the world center. His ego was even larger than Bill and Hillary combined. And he came to them fully equipped with his self-absorbed autobiography, shaded with enough fiction to stimulate even more fiction. As only Bob Dylan could, he poetically condensed Obama: "He's like a fictional character, but he's real." Get a grip! That was the full-steam-ahead signal to mass merchandise the fictional character—Obama of African "roots"—and sell beaucoup Obama-propaganda books along the way.

The magic carpet ride into the symbolic world of Obama mythology became front-row entertainment, especially for his friends in the media. There's nothing like a good myth to make foreboding evil look less threatening while gently distorting reality and obscuring the truth. And besides, a cleverly scripted fable can fulfill any desired truth. Why did the Pythia, the priestess at the Temple of Apollo, always deliver the right oracle at Delphi? She could never be proven wrong because her prophecies were interpreted by those seeking her advice. She also delivered the sacred oracles incoherently in a frenzy. How could anyone argue with her—they didn't even understand what she was saying! A few symbolic orations here, a couple of capricious speeches there, and Obama's big government designs weren't even noticed. In a feverish state with a lot of distracting drivel, Obama pandered to the true believers as if he were the Oracle of Delphi. Myths, like dreams, are subject to interpretation.

Obama, with his *Dreams* book, was subject to interpretation . . . by design.

The exemplary egotist, Obama stepped right into the wheeler-dealer role having been weaned on Chicago-style politics. Make Obama look like a superstar and he will reward with unprecedented access and open up the government coffers to all the special-interests' special interests. The left-leaners considered it a sweet swap, a superb exchange, a splendid tradeoff, a sophisticated form of barter that some might call a bribe by any other name. They loved the brilliant, cohesive, branding experience: simple, dramatic, focus-group tested, and priced just right for a top-tier influence peddler.

The Obama fanatics easily hyper-contributed to his election efforts in spite of campaign contribution limits imposed by the Federal Election Commission. Well versed in the IRS rules for *quid pro quo* charitable contributions, the nonprofiteers considered claiming Obamamania as an exclusive religious organization with intangible religious benefits. Granted, Obama gave them an irreverent thrill up their legs and private areas but the real turn-on was their lust for the tangible, greenback paybacks. Quid pro quo straight up! No obvious tax avoidance gimmes but mega pay dirt for sales of toady magazines, newspapers, books, DVDs, etc.

Light and breezy in public while privately wielding the big stick, cocky Obama delivered ample examples of his gritty schemes of quid pro quo, something for something, this for that, pay to play, tit for tat, give and take, you scratch my back and I'll scratch yours, a favor for a favor, an eye for an eye, in cahoots. Whatever turn of phrase, it's simply the Chicago way of paying for protection.

QPQ Act 1: Fogeyish bohemian hired-gun

Rolling Stone magazine made Obama their cover boy three times in seven months, a record first set with John Lennon. These first three covers, with several to follow, happened to run from March 2008 to October 30, 2008, right up to the 2008 presidential election. For an encore, another rolled-sleeve, manicured, blue-tied Obama front-pager was released October 26, 2012 just in time for another presidential election. Needless to say, Obama's pearly whites electrified the declining *Rolling Stone* readership while paying homage to the hippy counterculture and picking up hypothetically a million stoner votes.

The twenty-year-old, U.C. Berkeley drop-out that started the brash, music magazine in San Francisco in 1967, Jann Wenner, is still editor and publisher. He now lives and works in New York and, not surprisingly, donates exclusively to Democrats and their liberal causes. His progressive standard of living thrives on giving and taking favors, particularly publishing hit pieces on Obama's opposition or anyone that eclipses Obama's manliness.

Reinforcing their photogenic president's conquerer-of-global-terrorism image, Wenner splashed the Boston Marathon Bomber on the cover of the August 2013 *Rolling Stone* making like he was an angelic, harmless, polite, virginal, rock star. No way was Dzhokhar Tsarnaev a malicious, fratricidal, killing-machine terrorist! Impossible! Obama eradicated all terrorism off the face of the earth when he dropped into the Abbottabad compound in full SEAL-Team-Six body armor and personally shot bin Laden in the head. Obama's involvement in that historical inflection point has always been overblown. The *New York Times* ran the very same Tsarnaev selfie above the fold on the front cover of its Sunday May 5, 2013 edition. Liberal publishers love to rework the truth then replay, repeat, and recap it ad nauseam.

The world learned more about General Stanley A. McChrystal in the six-page smackdown, "The Runaway General," than anything *Rolling Stone* ever ventured to write about their treasured friend, Obama. The cynical staff produced a twisted biographical sketch of the four-star general and the liberal press still expects us to believe that *Dreams from My Father* is the real autobiography of Barack Hussein Obama!

McChrystal assumed command of NATO forces in Afghanistan June 10, 2009. He was promoted to a four-star general and commenced with Operation Khanjar, the largest offensive effort in the Afghanistan war. To put this in Army history perspective, there have only been 218 four-star generals. You may recognize a few of his peers: Ulysses S. Grant, William Tecumseh Sherman, George S. Patton, Creighton Abrams, Alexander M. Haig Jr., Norman Schwarzkopf Jr., Jack Keane, Tommy Franks, and David Petraeus.

After surveying the ground truth, General McChrystal submitted a report asking for more troops. Ambivalent Obama felt caught between a rock and a hard place. Should he act like Commander in Chief and help his loyal, military troops or indulge the anti-war liberals and have Afghanistan disappear off the map? He opted to perform his I'm-conflicted, can't-talk-about-it routine with an "Afghanistan where?" soft-shoe and decided to make the war vanish, victory aside.

Most believe McChrystal's death knell sounded because of his zealous nature to win the war with as few casualties as possible while diplomatically building a coalition with the Afghani power brokers and their people. Perhaps, but dig deeper. The omen that signaled McChrystal's demise was his very own real life story.

Graduated West Point. Attended Harvard Kennedy School of Government. Head of Joint Special Operations Command in charge of the Rangers, Navy SEALS, and Delta Force. This was just a sampler of McChrystal's illustrious career. While at West Point, he was the managing editor of *The Pointer* and legitimately wrote and published several short stories—on his own, he penned them, no ghost writer. The general ran 7-8 miles every day with but one meal and only four hours of sleep. He didn't smoke and was obviously tuned too precisely to do drugs. McChrystal was a highly disciplined, intelligent, articulate, brave leader who fearlessly spoke his mind and could easily, mano a mano, kick Obama's butt with one arm tied behind his back. McChrystal is what the world beyond Obama's orbit considers a real hero.

What was Obama to do? Just when he had the world convinced that "leading from behind" was a strategic military position, along comes a genuine leader who lives to be at the tip of the spear. At best, Obama considered the general mere pocket litter found in his golf shorts, an obnoxious vassal. McChrystal was Tier One, cream of the crop, an extremely valuable military asset who even wrote short stories—all without any affirmative-action booster shots. Green with envy and predisposed to being testy and spiteful, Obama signaled Wenner to put a hack-journalist contract out on McChrystal, *Rolling Stone*-style.

The craven hired-gun, Michael Hastings, did not have one single, solitary quote from McChrystal badmouthing Obama or his cronies. "The Runaway General" article ran online June 22, 2010 while McChrystal was in Afghanistan. The very next day—repeat, the very next day—Obama had a come-to-Allah meeting at the White House with McChrystal and "discussed" the general's resignation. One month later, July 23, General McChrystal officially retired from the Army after thirty-four years of distinguished service. Obama insisted that it wasn't personal, only business. By June 2013, the tell-it-like-it-is Hastings went totally gonzo by high-speed wrecking his car in Hollywood at 4:15 a.m. and going out in a burnt-beyond-recognition blaze of glory.

Why would a courageous man like McChrystal allow a cowardly scum *Rolling Stone* reporter interview him? Because the general lived his life every day looking evil in the eye like Abu Musab al-Zarqawi, leader of al Qaeda in Iraq. Certainly not one spineless, little punk impersonating a serious journalist could possibly intimidate him. People like McChrystal want the truth to be known, regardless of the consequences unlike liberal journalists who dream of the Watergate days and long for a young Robert Redford to play them in the motion picture version. President Nixon had ended the Vietnam War, signed Title IX into law which ended educational benefits discrimination, established the Environmental Protection Agency, doubled funding of the arts, instituted the Office of Management and Budget, shook hands with Mao Zedong on the Red China's soil presciently dividing China from Russia, sought international cooperation in space—the list goes on. Ho hum. Not enough "action" for the bored political journalists. Impeaching Nixon really got their adrenaline and fundraising going, yet he resigned instead. There's just no pleasing the thumb-sucking left-wing press. Go on, cry your eyes out.

Woodstock and Vietnam were history. The scribes hungered for the drama, the tension, the cynicism, the downfall. Debating "smarm vs. snark" wasn't selling newspapers nor winning Pulitzer Prizes for Public Service. Their next most puckish activity was to egregiously topple public servants of substance basis the left's definition of "using and abusing power." Think of all the gold medals begging to be awarded if the supine liberal press would shine some light on President Opacity's incessant abuse of power. What, lefty journalists aren't really fighting the good fight? Aren't they doing God's work? No, they really want to be on the silver screen but lack either superstar looks or backbone—or both.

With McChrystal out of the way and, dare we say, badly brain-damaged as evidenced by his cockeyed Lenin-Mao obligatory call to national public service, Obama's next high profile military target was another four-star prodigy—General David Petraeus. The *Rolling Stone* had badgered the general for many years and basically primed the pump for his takedown. Obama and his hit squad had to remove Petraeus from the political chessboard or risk eventually running the empty-suit Obama against a well-loved, well-respected, soldier, scholar, warrior, and intellectual.

Their chess game began by Obama pleading "we need you" then technically demoted Petraeus and sent him to the faraway Islamic Republic of Afghanistan to replace the disgraced McChrystal. In this medieval hinterland during the general's watch, the bomb-throwing Wikileaks released Afghan war logs. This forced Petraeus's hand to direct his forces to avoid civilian casualties at any cost, even if it meant sacrificing his own troops. A few months later, a NATO helicopter, under the general's command, unintentionally killed nine Afghan boys. His claim-to-fame counterinsurgency, of protecting the people rather than killing them, went up in flames. After apologizing to every tribal chieftain, every Afghan citizen, plus all of their karakul sheep in every corner of this godforsaken country, Petraeus relinquished command and retired from the Army.

Having captured most of Petraeus's chessmen, Obama deviously moved a queen diagonally to finally eliminate Petraeus from the world chess championship. Obama appointed him Director of the CIA, ever so carefully engineered the release of the disclosure of an FBI-known extramarital affair, and within a year, Petraeus was given the bum's rush with his reputation thoroughly besmirched. Obama, with the help of his spooks-in-high-places and a J. Edgar Hoover-ish attorney general, had checkmated another formidable political competitor.

QPQ Act 2: Struttin' down the GRAMMY red carpet

The National Academy of Recording Arts & Sciences has a long tradition of throwing their support to political candidates and causes. Though they present themselves as an organization that recognizes the best artists in the music industry, woe unto those that actually believe the GRAMMY is based solely on music excellence. The Grammy Awards may be peer-presented, but it is highly unlikely that they are apolitical, unsullied, and exclusively peer-reviewed.

Regardless of consumer-driven sales and popularity, many of the chosen Grammy winners actually have loyalties to The Academy beyond artistic achievement, technical proficiency, and overall excellence in the recording industry. For those of you that have been naively misled, The Academy's website explains their mission: "[T]o positively impact the lives of musicians, industry members and our society at large." That's a whole lot of wiggle room around what the music-loving, credit-card-swiping public considers music excellence. Sounds more like song-filled Don Quixotes flailing for social justice.

In 1997, The Academy awarded then-First Lady Hillary Clinton a Grammy for her audiobook, *It Takes a Village*. After HillaryCare was decisively defeated in 1994—may it RIP—the award helped Hillary give birth to its offspring and inbred cousin of ObamaCare, the Childrens' Health Insurance Program (CHIP). Successfully trading one gilded statuette for access to the White House, The Recording Academy established a mega musicians lobby in Washington, DC to advocate for the collectivistic world view of music. The GRAMMYs on the Hill Initiative included awards to honor senators, representatives, even presidents along with an advocacy day designed to endear the singing lobbyists to policymakers on Capitol Hill.

But that was the 1990s when the Clintons were the keeper-of-the-keys to the treasure chest that funded the arts. In the last decade, The Academy expanded its raison d'être. Of the seventy-eight different music awards, they parlayed one inconspicuous category into a huge, political-payback opportunity: Best Spoken Word Album. The favor-for-a-favor floodgates opened.

The Best Spoken Word Album appears to be reserved for influencing prominent politicians. Without any singing abilities, three U.S. presidents were awarded Grammys: Barack Obama, Bill Clinton, and Jimmy Carter. With equal inability to croon a tune, four U.S. senators likewise have won the award: Barack Obama, Everett Dirksen, Al Franken, and Hillary Clinton.

Imagine the behind-the-scenes, tit-for-tat outreach that rewarded these progressives with the BSWA gold gramophone:

2014 – Stephen Colbert

2013 – Janis Ian, a nod to LGBTQs; loser nominees included Michelle Obama, Bill Clinton, Rachel Maddow, and Ellen DeGeneres

2012 – Betty White; Tina Fey was a runner-up.

2011 – Jon Stewart and *The Daily Show* staff of 300 white liberal men; Woody Allen was a nominee.

2010 – Michael J. Fox; Jimmy Carter placed but didn't win.

2009 – Al Gore's *An Inconvenient Truth*; Stephen Colbert was nominated but lost.

2008 – Barack Obama blew away stellar performance artists including Maya Angelou, Bill Clinton, Jimmy Carter, and Alan Alda!

2007 – Jimmy Carter; losers included Bill Maher and Al Franken.

2006 – Barack Obama beat out Garrison

Keillor, Al Franken, Bob Dylan, and George Carlin!

2005 – Bill Clinton won for his memoir, *My Life*.

2004 – Al Franken

2003 – Maya Angelou

2002 – Quincy Jones

2001 – Sidney Poitier

2000 – LeVar Burton of *Star Trek* fame performing *The Autobiography of Martin Luther King Jr*.

Lefties celebrating lefties.

Obama holds the record in this category—two BSWA Grammys—with a cash value equal to two White House swag-bag exchanges. Under the rules of quid pro quo, The Academy put the squeeze on Obama: first, continue funding the National Endowment of the Arts using the $831 billion stimulus package; and second, cook up a Cabinet-level position for Secretary of the Arts, preferably with Quincy Jones in charge. Knowing how responsive Obama was to trading gifts, The Recording Academy organized a four-year schedule of headliners to perform at Staples Center East, 1600 Pennsylvania Avenue. Due to popular demand, the festivities were held over for another four years when Obama was re-elected in 2012.

If Obama wasn't on the golf course, chances are he was in the East Room hanging out with the musicians and their entourages. Christening the White House the "People's House," Obama institutionalized the redistribution of wealth while the taxpayers funded the gala events. If he could socially corral affluent, music-industry contributors and bless their activist activities, Obama figured he could leverage sweet-talking into other liberal fawn-fests.

The People's House became the unofficial DC chapter of not only the GRAMMY but also Emmy, Tony, The Oscars, World Series, Super Bowl, NBA Finals, MLS Cup, NCAA National Championships, and the Olympics. To show a little diversity, he expanded the high-roller hunt to include Obama-branded A-listers including reality TV personalities, misogynist poets, vegan hip-hop thugs, and the Bush-bashing Knight from Liverpool. The upper echelon of the 1%—big names, big wallets, big connections with Utopian dreams—Obama's ideal progressive partners. To think that all this started with just one Barack Obama audiobook.

With nothing left to prove after several years on the national football stage, several NFL players stuck to their principles and quietly refused invitations from His Highness. Pittsburgh Steelers James Harrison blazed the no-show trail in 2009, followed in 2013 by the '72 Dolphins Jim Langer, Bob Kuechenberg, and Manny Fernandez—all proud, ethical Hall-of-Famers in their own right who know when they're being suckered.

QPQ Act 3: Runaway runway politics in the Big Apple

Another pampered, rebellious child of the Sixties, Anna Wintour used women's style as her springboard onto the political landscape. The editor-in-chief of American *Vogue* was born in London into wealth and privilege. Unlike Barack Obama who went to high school and college to party, Anna dropped out of the North London version of Punahou

Academy for fun, clubbing, and fashion. Goodbye books! Way too tame for this jetsetter. With a license to be wild, Anna enjoyed the safety net afforded her by family money and connections in the publishing world. Indeed, her rise to the top of the fashion world was preordained.

Known for commanding fashion spreads and photo shoots like a drill sergeant, her reputation as a fashion industry panjandrum was undisputed. Wintour air-kissed her way into the crème de la crème of New York's Upper East Side. Why not? They have lots of money and consume tons of haute couture along with all the other habiliments to look beautiful. This most exclusive patch of Big Apple real estate was a very lucrative territory to hustle monthly magazine subscriptions door-to-door, museum-to-museum, or philanthropic-event-to-philanthropic-event. After all, this was center-of-the-universe Manhattan so it was no surprise that Wintour shrewdly leveraged her glossy rolodex into ad revenues that rivaled the Federal Reserve's underground vault deposits.

Having exhausted the celebrity-cover angle not to mention the gargantuan 832-page glam-a-rama edition, Wintour was looking for ways to expand readership and fend off the competition, internally and externally. She was also quite bored with the monthly grind of publishing a fashion advertising catalog with touches of soft *Penthouse*-porn. The perks were to die for, but telling women day after day the what, why, where, and how of wardrobes was becoming tedious. Sure, it was all about selling *Vogue* subscriptions and designer-label advertisements, yet her loyal followers needed more.

Anna's life had always been about fashion and creating fantasy worlds with photographic images. She knew nothing else. But within that illusory land of beautiful images, Wintour developed a talent for strong-arming designers, white-guilting trust-funded socialites, fundraising mega millions, and owning all the catwalks. She became a pay-to-play fashionista extraordinaire. So Wintour went about altering the runways into progressive tools to utopianize the world that she demanded and her customers craved. Finally, they would feel thin enough, rich enough, politically connected, and in control. Steeped in the New York media elites' power to grant power, Anna decreed herself kingmaker.

Bundling for Obama became Wintour's first big outside-the-rag-industry kingmaking project. She dabbled with a $2,000 donation in 2004 to John Kerry's presidential run and offered up $1,000 to Hillary Clinton's 2008 Senate campaign, even though government workers aren't very fashion forward. The aha moment came when Wintour, the grande dame of editing, saw Obama's photo proofs—utter eye candy! Bang! $10,000 to the Democratic White House Victory Fund. A few months later, she whipped out her checkbook again and, in a New York minute, befriended the Democratic National Committee with $30,400. The liberal media from coast to coast were going gaga for Barack.

Wintour's personal contributions to the Democrats eclipsed the $100,000 mark and counting. She hosted fundraisers specifically for Obama in New York, London, Paris, Milan, with Meryl Streep, Sarah Jessica Parker, Scarlett Johansson, Harvey Weinstein, Calvin Klein, Marc Jacobs, Donna Karan, Tom Ford, Kenzo, and David Plouffe, that famous Obama message designer from the AKPD house of fashion.

Combing through prospective benefactors' net worth statements as if casting a star-studded runway extravaganza, Anna hoped to capture that specific proportion of glitz, glamour, and guilt of a certain pedigree that would gratefully stuff the Obama donation basket with cash, jewels, or any in-kind gift. Examples of an in-kind gift with considerable venerable value were then-Federal Reserve Chairman Ben Bernanke's highly-accommodating QE money-printing, party-punch spiked with near-zero interest rates, and Saudi Arabia benevolently increasing oil production.

Obama and Wintour were cut from the same cloth. Both thrived in environments where they traded on their superficial attributes. Both adopted demure poses that masked their viciously competitive natures. Both crusaded for social justice as long as they could hide their high lives behind the opaque curtains of their aggressive and beholding media machines. Both enjoyed picking winners and losers. Both relished holding court. Anna, through haughty bossiness and size-000 ultimatums, became queen of the New York fashion society. She deigned to give Obama a hand up to help anoint him king of the progressives. As they held court in their respective magic kingdoms, Barack and Anna were a perfect win-win alliance—the quid pro quo twins.

Wintour's next attempt at head-of-state queenmaking wasn't nearly as successful.

Feeling like a bona fide member of the White House in-crowd, Wintour attempted Arab Spring diplomacy from the runway. If Obama could navigate the international scene from a bully pulpit with a teleprompter, Anna had full-color printing presses and international distribution at her beck and call. With a few more dress-rehearsed, money-raking soirees, maybe one day she would be the belle of the ball as the U.S. Ambassador to the U.K. Or better still, launch her own Condé Nast TV series based on the lives of the mysterious, the mischievous, and the miscreants. Anna Wintour was ready for her close-up.

The March 2011 *Vogue* "Power Issue" was unreserved hubris of the Obama magnitude. Yes, Asma al-Bashar was cover-ready thin and designer dressed. Yes, she used to be an investment banker at J.P. Morgan. Yes, she was British born and educated. Yes, she was married to the president of Syria, Bashar al-Assad and, perhaps, the White House thought it was a novel way to keep their favorite editor-in-chief collecting donor dough. But to proclaim Mrs. Assad "A Rose in the Desert," Wintour was guilty of the same ineptitude as Obama by supporting a repressive dictator masquerading as a reformer.

How long did it take to transfer considerable wealth from Syria, a country with economic sanctions, to a safe-haven, say Switzerland? Probably as much time as it took Obama to publicly say that "Assad must go." Wintour's official renunciation of the Assad regime came sixteen months after *Vogue*'s adoring profile of the first lady. As Obama gave the Syrian president cover by deflecting world outrage via the United Nation's Security Council, Assad proceeded to kill 162,000 Syrian citizens including women and children while forcing nine million to flee their homes, even their homeland. The best Obama could come up with, as he led from behind again, was a typical liberal tactic to avoid any responsibility—assemble a "working group" to study the matter. Seriously? Yes, a big bad working group. Obama's handpicked UN Ambassador Samantha Power, wife of his BFF Cass Sunstein, couldn't even find it in her bleeding heart to send a shipment of umbrellas as chlorine gas rained down on the Syrian villagers. Reason: Dead or alive, Syrians can't vote for Obama.

Several months later, the so-called U.S. Commander in Chief drew his pathetic weapons-of-mass-destruction "red line" then watched it fade away as he dithered. That was the go-ahead for the Assad regime to trial-balloon fourteen chemical weapon attacks throughout the Syrian Arab Republic. Taunting paper-tiger Obama, Assad celebrated the one-year ultimatum anniversary by wasting 1,429 Damascus civilians with jasmine-scented sarin gas. When the WMD jig was up, Assad used a more unobtrusive, no-gas-mask-required means of ethnic cleansing: starvation. Obama's namby-pamby response to the war crimes was to acquiesce to negotiations with Syria's protector, Russia. Why not just send one of those worthless liberal letters via cut-rate Priority Mail Flat Rate and save the taxpayers' money? Actually, that might be too extravagant since Obama's constant refrain is that the U.S. has no vital national interests in Syria.

Obama and his progressive numskulls made a deal with the Syrian devil essentially placating Assad's paymasters and puppeteers: Russia and Iran. The Assads have seen their destiny: either Egypt's Hosni Mubarak sporting a made-for-rock-pounding prison jumpsuit, or a tailored death suit designed exclusively for Libya's Muammar Gadhafi. By feigning concern yet doing nothing, Obama rescued Assad and emboldened the Russians and Iranians to fill the leadership void in the Middle East. By June 2014, his Excellency President Bashar al-Assad was positioned by Obama to win a third seven-year term with an 89% landslide vote. Phew,

Assad just skated by that one! Coincidentally, Saudi Arabia is keeping its distance from the United Nations Security Council and a watchful eye on nuclear Iran, chemical Syria, shifty Russia, and in-time-they'll-own-everyone China. Shakespeare nailed it: "Hell is empty and all the devils are here."

The dynamic duo, Obama and Wintour, no doubt viewed Mr. and Mrs. Assad as Western educated, modern progressives that should not be vilified and certainly not—horrors!—executed. The lovely couple, prone to acts of genocidal slaughter, gave rise to a Utopia in the desert and should serve as role models for the rest of the Middle East.

Lesson learned: The give-and-take in the kingmaking business can lead to your own embarrassing demise. Sometimes you make the king and sometimes the king uses you for a patsy.

Self-immolation alert! The Arab Spring was not crafted by the wily Obama as his Middle East foreign policy plan. Everyone knows that Obama's objective was to extricate the U.S. from the Middle East altogether, a promise he made to the Saudi king as he bowed before him. Assuming Obama was his closest ally, King Abdullah was stunned when Obama double-crossed him by elevating the ticking time bomb that was nuclear Iran. The king's public-relations machine immediately dispatched press releases letting the world know the Saudis had been duped and were seeking honest partners. Beware of Chicagoans bearing gifts. For the record, the Arab Spring fuse was lit by a publicly-humiliated, twenty-six-year-old Mohamed Bouazizi who set himself on fire in front of a Tunisian government building as an act of desperation after a slaphappy policewoman confiscated his fruit cart—his total means of supporting himself, his widowed mother, and six siblings. What's the Arabic word for government overreach, intimidation, and seizing personal property? Bouazizi's property was worth $225.

With Bouazizi burnt to a cinder and only a commemorative Tunisian postage stamp to speak for him, Obama conveniently expropriated the Arab Spring as his own personal property. Hey, Bouazizi was dead, buried, in the ground! So what? Obama could make better use of the graphic protest-suicide and claim it as the broader political movement that he, and he alone, inspired. Over the next sixty days, at least sixty-three more men and women in Yemen, Algeria, Syria, Egypt, Saudi Arabia, Tunisia, and Morocco were touched by Obama's soaring rhetoric and followed the Bouazizi-bonfire self-sacrifice.

QPQ Act 4: Nobel Penitent Prize

For the first nine months of his presidency, Obama traveled the globe confessing and apologizing for America's past sins. This appeasement tour tickled the fancy of Thorbjørn Jagland, the newly appointed chairman of the Norwegian Nobel Committee. An avowed socialist, career politician, and rumored source for the Soviet KGB, Jagland sensed an affinity with the U.S. orator, author, and fellow-dreamer. His own book, *My European Dream*, spelled out the same utopianesque themes that Obama espoused.

Like his newfound soul mate, the hair-shirted Jagland understood the need to repent for his mother-country's attacks on Muslims even though the Norwegian Crusade took place in the 12th century. Both fantasists were on their own greater and lesser jihads struggling for universal human rights, particularly for prophets of Islam. Remember Obama's pablum publicized as a landmark "New Beginning" speech in Cairo, June 2009? Talk about promoting the Five Pillars of Islam, Obama even slipped in a quick reference to *zakat*, the Muslims' word for eliminating inequality by redistributing wealth. The shout-out of all shout-outs!

Their shared and declared fatwa was to rid the world of bogus racism against Muslims and make the world safer with the adoption of sharia law, notwithstanding sharia intolerantly negates universal human rights and fundamental freedoms except as interpreted by Islamic jurisprudence. No matter. Jagland had a $1.4 million Nobel Prize as an inducement and a pliable U.S. politician with the world as his stage.

Machine-gun-to-your-head, life-saving trivia: The next time you find yourself in your local Kenyan-and-beyond, upscale, shopping mall and blood-thirsty, urban-safari, radical Islamists are killing every non-Muslim in sight, "Aminah bint Wahb" is the Prophet Muhammad's mother's name. Oh, and don't even try to hide your ivory tusks. Al-Shabaab will take it as a personal affront to their poaching trade and bang!—you're dead, along with 67 others. *Salam alaykum*. Obama dispatched his trusty U.S. drone brigade to protect his father's homeland . . . twelve months later. Hunker down!

All Nobel Prize nominations for that year were to be submitted by early February, just days after Obama was sworn in. The committee members reserve the right to submit a nomination well up to the point of announcing the award. Who actually recommended Obama for the distinction is classified for at least fifty years. It may have been Jagland himself. Apparently he uses the pompous award in clever ways, not always precisely as Alfred Nobel intended.

To wit, to further his dream of Norway joining the European Union, a hotly debated, suicide-claused issue within Norway since 1972, he awarded the Peace Prize to the EU. As Greece and Spain were at war with Germany over the austerity imposed on them for their profligate spending, Jagland praised the EU for six decades of building peace, economic prosperity, and decimating nationalism. He forgot to mention how the member states drove their euro to a credit-outlook downgrade needing life support. As he took his victory lap, he blamed Europe's economic crisis on the United States starting with Lehman Brothers. Sounds like he and Obama exchanged talking points. It also appears that Jagland was trying to rewrite history. Europe was reconstructed after WW2 by the Marshall Plan, the NATO Alliance, and American power, not the EU. Bottom line: Jagland, the consummate politician, doesn't much hide his quid-pro-quo wheeler-dealings.

Here is the official Nobel Peace Prize 2009 announcement as found on the web site:

The Norwegian Nobel Committee has decided that the Nobel Peace Prize for 2009 is to be awarded to President Barack Obama for his extraordinary efforts to strengthen international diplomacy and cooperation between peoples. The Committee has attached special importance to Obama's vision of and work for a world without nuclear weapons.

Obama has as President created a new climate in international politics. Multilateral diplomacy has regained a central position, with emphasis on the role that the United Nations and other international institutions can play. Dialogue and negotiations are preferred as instruments for resolving even the most difficult international conflicts. The vision of a world free from nuclear arms has powerfully stimulated disarmament and arms control negotiations. Thanks to Obama's initiative, the USA is now playing a more constructive role in meeting the great climatic challenges the world is confronting. Democracy and human rights are to be strengthened.

Only very rarely has a person to the same extent as Obama captured the world's attention and given its people hope for a better future. His diplomacy is founded in the concept that those who are to lead the world must do so on the basis of values and attitudes that are shared by the majority of the world's population.

For 108 years, the Norwegian Nobel Committee has sought to stimulate precisely that international policy and those attitudes for which Obama is now the world's leading spokesman. The Committee endorses Obama's appeal that "Now is the time for all of us to take our share of responsibility for a global response to global challenges."

Oslo, October 9, 2009

Does this sound like the Obama we know? Regrettably it does. No small wonder who helped Obama craft his agenda then dress-rehearsed "their Barack" for his future new-world-order gig: Monarch of the World based in Belgium. Hollywood may have even played a part in this absurd charade. Recall Dustin Hoffman's character in *Wag the Dog* recommended arranging the Noble Peace Prize for the president. Life imitating movie magic?

Four years later, Obama actually earned an award—an ignoble award. His ObamaCare "If you like your healthcare plan, you can keep it" mantra was honored as the 2013 Lie of the Year as tracked by the Pulitzer Prize winning PolitiFact.com. The liberal megaphone *Washington Post* crowned it the biggest whopping Pinocchio of 2013. High in the sky, the prideful and invincible Icarus soared so far so fast! As warned, the sun melted his wax wings and he plummeted shamefully back to earth.

A guilt-ridden Obama was now held accountable by the international progressives, not just the more tame domestic variety. His marching orders were crystal clear—throw the United States under the bus! Bury the U.S. Constitution and replace it with transnational law—the blame-and-shame, non-legally enforceable, norm-directed, softer side of state-enacted, state-enforced, and state-sanctioned laws. Negate all the embedded, irrevocable rights and privileges enumerated in the Constitutional Amendments and make Americans bow to European fraidy-cats. Reverse hundreds of years of human progress to establish a free world of self-directed voters for the sake of leveling the playing field and placating the acrimonious, thumb-sucking, mother-may-I, Euro-benchwarmers.

Seventy-five years ago the Continentals were unable to tell the good guys from the bad. A catastrophic, congenital blind spot they'll never admit. Sadly, they lacked the American Cowboy Code that recognizes evil and has the courage to terminate it. Cowboys even have the temerity to tear down walls of oppression. Many on mainland Europe still remain emotionally and mentally crippled by their ignoble and delusional surrender to the Third Reich. Guarding liberty never was, nor ever will be their strong suit. Why else would they choose a double-dealing Barack Obama to do their bidding? Off he went on another round of taxpayer-funded, forgive-us-please missions under penalty of, egad, elitist-inflicted humiliation. After all, there was a price to pay for his noble prize.

Norway, on behalf of the EU and possibly Russia, bought Obama's allegiance at the expense of the American citizens. Red alert! There's usually no more than three degrees of separation between Obama's foreign play pals and Russia. The world recognized that to honor Obama's ego is to be paid back in spades.

Ever speculate why President Obama has so many divergent views from the Illinois-centric, provincial Senator Obama? He got religion—the progressive, rule-the-peasants, European-imaged, transnational religion. Obama intimated his encore performance during the May 2014 Commencement Address at West Point. Envisioning his leader-of-the-pack ascension, he labeled international institutions like NATO, the United Nations, the World Bank, the IMF, and international law as force multipliers that command respect. Hold on EU—Obama's comin'! All roads—and Barack-talk—now lead to Brussels, Luxembourg, and Strasbourg.

QPQ Act 5: Hocus-pocus lifestyle focus

Access! Access! Read all about it! Michael Lewis, author and contributing editor for *Vanity Fair*, sent an email to Jay Carney, the White House press secretary at the time, with his proposed 2012 get-out-the vote propaganda piece. To give brother Obama that extra oomph in the presidential race, Lewis pitched an old-school journalism approach which required making like Obama's side-kick for six months.

Instantly, Lewis received "unprecedented" access. Of course he would. Anyone with a best-selling novelist's, screaming-liberal readership willing to perpetuate the Obama folklore goes to the head of the line. Lewis's old-school-journalism was really the lefties' new-school-journalism—complicitly bury the truth for all things celebrity.

Katie Holmes was the October 2012 cover girl, bright and beautiful. What, no glittery front cover for Barack? Even the fifty-year anniversary of James Bond 007 overshadowed the Obama report. Back on page 210, way after the Ralph Lauren ad and the dramatic HBO foldout, Obama appeared strolling towards the Oval Office with his new mouthpiece exchanging notes for the fourteen-page "Obama's Way" homage.

Another Condé Nast propaganda sheet, like *Vogue* and *The New Yorker*, *Vanity Fair* web-announced itself as a "cultural catalyst that drives popular dialogue globally." That's a clever catchall to include everything they can print that month to sell a magazine while casually avoiding any serious reporting in financial matters, the electoral system, and geo-political discourse. And never, ever any of that heavy historical perspective, that is, anything beyond the last issue. Yuck! How boring. Get it. All pop culture. In other words, a lifestyle magazine.

So when a financial journalist offered to do some hard-hitting journalism about Obama, the neutering process began with the quote approval. The White House insisted on signing off on all quotes before they were fit to print. By all morning TV show accounts, it really wasn't an unwelcome castration. The writer, a former bond trader, understood the poker game he agreed to play and was quite adept at trading securities, favors, even deceptions to score the legendary assignment. And under penalty of eternal censorship, *Vanity Fair* made a solemn pact to steer clear of any and all economic Armageddon, financial crises, exploding debt, squandering $831 billion to stimulate phantom projects, and unbridled government spending issues. After all, they had scruples.

Armed with his checklist of the nonnegotiable must-have topics, Lewis assumed the position and wrote a rather chatty account of 180 days in the life of the president. The reader didn't have to delve to deeply to tease out the pre-approved references: mention all the important voting blocks (military, veterans, seniors, students) and make like the president is humble, thoughtful, and cares about them; really stick it to the Republicans whenever and wherever; highlight all the important daily activities, you know, basketball with "44" on his high-tops, weight lifting, wake-up time, sleep time; Obama's unique two-thumbs texting on his smartphone; note somewhere Obama's use of at least one Apple product; hiding out with Michelle at night on the Truman Balcony (add the bullet hole for drama and empathy); redecorating by ditching the Bush-blue drapes and replacing with darker-skin-tone-friendly gold curtains (so much better for the cameras); reupholstering those greasy chairs that W left behind; blast and berate the Churchill bust dust-up regardless of its historical significance to the salvation of the free world; do tell about the MLK Jr. quote sewn into the Oval Office rug, though everyone knows that MLK Jr. would not have existed if it weren't for Churchill resisting Hitler and all; and don't forget the Lincoln Bedroom—the Clintons got a lot of bennies from that sleeping-with-the-Gettysburg-Address song and dance.

As the tit-for-tat became more chummy, they moved the story further with what might be reclassified as new-school journalism or raconteuring. Translation: Keep the intentionally fabricated, authentic-and-vulnerable-Obama story alive at any cost.

The storyteller resurrected the old myth that Obama actually wrote his own memoir, then proceeded to portray him as an ordinary, average, Joe Walsh-kinda guy. From his humble beginnings as a community organizer, Obama rose to become president of the United States. Loved by all, he fiercely defended the world 24x7x365 from the toxic terrorists of the Tea Party and cable news. (Do NOT mention Fox News by name; no free press for them.) The job of being president was so damn difficult and unnatural for one human being that even the progressive savior couldn't handle it. Day after day, decision after decision, Obama was overwhelmed by the reality of leading a country.

Virtually crushed by the responsibility, Obama shut down, became isolated, blocked out the noise. After his 10a-to-4p business hours, he roamed the halls of the White House retreating into ESPN and his new favorite British author, Julian Barnes. (He overused Shakespeare; had to find another must-read, liberal sweetheart to impress the New York cocktail crowd. What's that French economist's book of the century calling for a socialist global tax to correct income inequality, you know, the one that the *Times* thinks is so ooh-la-la, the *Das Kapital* companion book?) The world looked to him to solve all their problems. Are you kidding? He never even solved his own problems. But, in his quiet moments, in the dark of night, in his heart of hearts, Obama knew it wasn't his fault. No, not his fault! It was all Bush's. The crybaby should take responsibility, to some degree, for the negative tone in Washington, the financial collapse, high unemployment, death and destruction abroad. No, never! Big bad Bush made him do it, made him make all those damaging, wrong decisions.

Firmly absolved of any guilt, Obama rebranded himself. The role of President of the United States of America was just a pretext to what Obama really wanted. The former community organizer elected president became THE cognoscente of the fine art of public relations. To what end? Well, what every PR person wants—access. Obama wanted entrée to heads of governments, carte blanche to top-secret information, 24-hour protection, round-the-clock first-class travel accommodations, day-and-night use of the federal gyms, the keys to the gold stores, the right to fudge Labor Department employment statistics at will, and prostrate-yourself-before-me status, not only in the U.S. but all over the world. Obama and *Vanity Fair* parsed his words ever so precisely: "The question is: How do you shape public opinion and frame an issue so that it's hard for the opposition to say no." Sounds like one of those paradigm pivots designed for world domination. God forbid.

President as PR pundit suited his lawyerly sensibilities. In public-relations-land, he could sashay around the shades of gray. Diddle here, fiddle there, never any clarity—always tinkering with the message until the truth gets lost. But the objective was never to honor and uphold the truth. Obama's objective was to uphold and honor himself and, of course, outsmart everyone else. Which brings us to the subtext of "Obama's Way": justifying why the Nobel Peace Prize winner decided to bomb another Arab country March 2011.

France, Lebanon, and the United Kingdom proposed United Nations Resolution 1973 to establish a no-fly zone to contain Colonel Muammar Gadhafi from exterminating a million Libyan citizens. Muammar was partial to using aircraft to exterminate humans en masse. (Who could forget 270 souls wiped out in the 1988 midair destruction of the home-for-Christmas Pan Am Flight 103 over Lockerbie, Scotland?) Overlord Obama would have been forced to sheepishly follow his nemeses with fencing in the Libyan butcher. Needless to say, President Petulant took his frustration out on his senior advisors gathered tightly in the Situation Room and forced them to come up with a king-of-the-hill plan that he could shove up or down, no matter, the bodily orifices of David Cameron and Nicolas Sarkozy.

Not to be outdone especially on the world stage, Obama pump-faked, turned, and one-upped with his *unilaterally-modified* UN resolution to establish a full-throttle, U.S. air-powered, bombing zone smack-dab over Gadhafi as he made his way to Benghazi. He then strong-armed the NATO allies to commit to the bombing raids. Team America would perform the initial aerial raids and the Europeans and Arabs were responsible for the postmortems and the follow through. Obama blew right by the U.S. Congress, typical of his cavalier inability to form coalitions.

March 28, 2011, he explained it to the American people as such: “I said that America’s role would be limited; that we would not put ground troops into Libya; that we would focus our unique capabilities on the front end of the operation and that we would transfer responsibility to our allies and partners.” At that point, Obama took his U.S. firepower and went home. High-fiving his way to the victory parties, Obama bragged that it only took him 31 days to get Benghazi back in line. As an aside, he couldn't help but remind everyone that it took Clinton more than a year to protect Bosnia, as if chortling "I'm a better international community organizer than you, Billy Boy!"

Time to put the Libya invasion in perspective. The foolhardy U.S. president used American military power to throw his weight around Europe, the Middle East, the United Nations, and the Situation Room, humiliating all those in charge of their respective posts and countries, then contemptuously expected them to back his plan. Right? Well, perhaps initially.

The military intervention lasted from March 19 to October 31, 2011, a little more than seven months. U.S. forces were long gone, Gadhafi was dead, and NATO packed up and left, too. Was anyone in charge? Who filled the leadership vacuum? Who was protecting U.S. interests at the Embassy on "the shores of Tripoli"? How about the consulate in Benghazi sitting in the middle of that al Qaeda breeding ground, not adequately protected? Well, the Libyan police were there with bullet-less guns. The friendly next door Ansar al-Sharia neighbors hosted block parties. No need for those aggressive U.S. marine types—they're Neanderthals. Who forgot the Status of Forces Agreement? Like the hot-potato SOFA that Obama ditched in Iraq and the half-baked SOFA for Afghanistan that will never see the light of day? How about a rotational-force agreement like Australia's and Singapore's? For what?! Obama's military-hating, progressive, puppet masters would crucify him.

Obama vowed to the lefties and the Russians not to hang around Benghazi after they bombed it to smithereens. He promised a quick blast-and-bolt mission, destroying all forms of government and civil society with no intention of rebuilding. By the summer of 2014, President Pettish had his day in the militant-activist sun as Libya descended into hellish anarchy. Gadhafi smiled vengefully from the grave: "Do you miss me yet?"

Not even a year after all NATO presence disappeared, the U.S. "diplomatic facility" or "temporary way station" in Benghazi was demolished and the U.S. Ambassador and three U.S. diplomats were slaughtered. In the twelve months leading up to the attack, the consulate experienced 230 security incidents and was actually bombed in June, fortunately without any injuries. The U.K. consulate and the Red Cross recognized the danger and fled almost immediately. Two of the initial coalition forces that were brave enough to set up consulates in Benghazi, the Italian and Swedish offices with personnel were not targeted for annihilation. Al Qaeda wasn't on the run or on its heels. This syndicate of terror was celebrating the eleventh anniversary of September 11. Sure, GM was alive and bin Laden dead, but so were Ambassador Christopher Stevens, Sean Smith, Glen Doherty, and Tyrone Woods.

Conceivably, Obama learned his lesson about this self-inflicted tragedy. When Obama checkmated the NATO allies, abdicated responsibility for Benghazi, whitewashed the attack with an obscure video, and kowtowed to the progressive weenies, he sacrificed American lives on the altar of anti-American exceptionalism, mollification, and Obama narcissism. The president and his arch rival, then-Secretary of State Hillary Clinton, were *holding hands* in a show of Bobbsey Twins unity when the four caskets were delivered to

Andrews Air Force Base. Whoever staged the deceitful twosome surely wrote the hapless script for the video-made-them-slaughter excuse. The loyal diplomats saluted their useless leaders and were lulled into a false sense of soft-footprint security that someone was actually in charge and had their backs. Be warned when the Obama State Department offers the chance to rack up one million globe-hopping miles and visit 112 countries including a 30% danger-pay bonus . . . without any protection. To paraphrase Groucho Marx: Who are you going to believe, the Obama administration or your lying eyes?

Within four months of the Benghazi murders, both then-State Secretary Hillary Clinton and then-Defense Secretary Leon Panetta resigned their respective posts to pursue other interests outside the Obama administration. Both realized that Benghazi would eventually become their kryptonite when all the details of their mismanagement were revealed. The year before, when NATO took out Gadhafi and the U.S. troops left Libya, Obama, Clinton, and Panetta forgot to arrange a Status of Forces Agreement and diplomatic immunity for the Special Forces charged with protecting the diplomats in Libya. Obama won the November 2012 election in spite of the depth and breadth of the Benghazi tragedy—ducking and dodging, bobbing and weaving, elusively evading the truth.

So, what's the real real-life story here? Obama cabined the establishment media's message to control the national conversation while, once again, constructing a parallel universe too fantastic to believe. A "disgusting and reprehensible" YouTube video triggered the assassinations?! The president stood strong and steady in dealing with difficult challenges?! White House communication strategy: Ring around the rosy, pocketful of posies, ashes, ashes, we all fall down! Eventually the national heartbreak devolved into just another Obama-pigeonholed "phony scandal." As expected, the mainstream media strained to parrot Obama's talking points as the obedient *fourth branch,* while trying to steer their own version of the alternate reality by pretending to be the independent *fourth estate.* Neither is capable of processing reality let alone reporting it. When the president's messages are so ridiculous that infuriated and embarrassed voters reflexively reject them, blame Fox News and Rush Limbaugh. Who's zoomin' who?

QPQ Act 6: Smokin' in the *Men's Health* room

One month before Obama's election, *Men's Health* plastered Barack's casual self on the cover of their October 2008 edition titled "What Great Leaders Know." Obviously a presumptive close. Never mind Obama's only one-trick-pony ability was community organizing, let alone being great at it. Perhaps the purported twelve-million *MH* readers required only the most important facts, you know, how many fat grams are in an "eat this" protein bar vs. a "not that" candy bar.

Waiting in the wings was the special edition, "Obama's Success Strategies," featuring Obama's life condensed into "12 game-changers" including an Obama scripted how-to-become-a-health-god plan. You, too, can become this paragon of wisdom and virtue with a resumé so thin that only those with six-pack ambitions would believe. Obama found a complicit ally in twisting American values, one just south of fair-minded, journalistic ethics for peddling Obama's healthcare atrocity.

In the heat of the healthcare debate, Obama's arguments to nationalize the entire U.S. healthcare system weren't selling to the general public. Imagine: Taking away the right to manage your own health was unpopular. Who knew? Obama summoned his bartering team to bring in *MH*, the shouting-font artists that could airbrush Pee-wee Herman into Adonis.

Making like they were presenting the issues of ObamaCare as objective journalists, the editors of *MH* promised the White House kiss-butt stories about the incontrovertible benefits of ObamaCare in all their major publications. Once again, Obama made the cover with the "Exclusive Oval Office Interview." They even launched a new publication for the occasion, *Children's Health*, with Michelle Obama and "The Obama Diet" on the cover. To say the stories were slanted in Obama's favor doesn't do slobbering journalism any justice. The only genuinely verifiable fact was Obama admitting he had a nicotine-dependence, well, only on nail-biting occasions.

Marketing the president as the epitome of health that all should emulate, the magazine gave him a pass about smoking tobacco. Obama was obviously ashamed of it. He hid it. He blamed his grandparents for exposing him to cigarettes at an early age. He blamed his mother's weight problem for his weight-gaining phobia, thereby using cigarettes to squelch sugary-food cravings. Yet in Obama's postmodern, alternate universe, he justified his congenital nicotine habit as a metabolic accelerator to burn calories more efficiently for that extra competitive edge.

The moral indignation over this moral relativism is that Obama maintained his right to choose to smoke yet passed oppressive legislation against a job-providing industry that effectively took away your right to smoke as you see fit. Obama knows best. Obama alone dictates your health. As of June 2009, the Family Smoking Prevention and Tobacco Control Act became the law of the land. Obama invincibly decided that only he can bum a smoke when he wants to cut himself a little slack, certainly not you.

The Patient Protection and Affordable Care Act, better known as ObamaCare, was passed later that year with the same objective-reality-be-damned arrogance. After the October 2009 "Obama's Plan" issue, Obama's beaming grin and washboard abs have not appeared on an *MH* cover. Could it be that *MH* readers prefer movie-star and sports-celebrity advice rather than politics and policy?

The Obama brand offered a piece of the action for everyone that genuflected to the Obama publicity machine. They kept the "product launch" uncomplicated and exciting, after all this was more about Hollywood and Madison Avenue than Washington, DC. Advertising agencies, PR firms, fashion magazines, t-shirt printers, poster artists, mug makers all stayed on message. Even the self-appointed arbiters of cool stoked the fires of the trendy, cool chase. Their ten-second elevator pitch about Obama being the coolest of the cool ignited an excitement the likes of which had only been known in Silicon Valley with Apple, then Facebook.

Barack Obama, community organizer, and Facebook's Mark Zuckerberg, social-media organizer, rode the same contagious wave. Facebook was started as an online college dating site with no intentions of becoming a company. The Obama campaign became an extension of that dating website thanks to a co-founder of Facebook, Chris Hughes, who coded the social network framework for MyBO. Both sites captured the youthful exuberance and yearning to find the next new thing. Once Obama was in office, Hughes moved on and found his next new thing—social-networking his husband Sean Eldridge's run for New York's 19th Congressional District.

Neither Obama nor Zuckerberg had the credentials to lead a country or a multi-billion-dollar company, respectively. Obama hailing from Punahou, Columbia, and Harvard mastered disruptive partisan-politics; Zuckerberg spawned from Exeter and Harvard became a software-coding prodigy. Both understood their respective "code words" yet neither understood what they considered repugnant American business. They both offered an airy-fairy species of "hope and change" to build their respective brands—one billion voters, one billion users. The nerdy insecure Zuckerberg offered *hope* of finding dates from a voyeuristic perch using menacing, superficial parameters with the ability to remotely *change* to another "friend" when the first didn't work out. The hollow proselytizer Obama promised the *hope* of being part of his hip entourage, from a website-donation distance, to *change* the world into a liberal Utopia where life is spent digitally frolicking in Facebookland using other people's money. Recalcitrant, hysterical contagions like these are resolved when the drug-like euphoria wears off—devotees discover there's no there there, demand *quality* instead of *quantity*, there's no bang for the advertising buck, the stock price plunges, Unfavorable ratings outweigh Favorables, or

Facebook users are fundamentally transformed into "lab rats" by desensitized data-junkies.

Obama's campaign team and the institutional media joined forces to crowdfund Obama as a branded, consumer product. His consistently high "likability" ratings rescued him through every twist and turn of his presidency, as if the more "likes" he collected on Facebook the more competent, wise, and unstoppable he became. They built Obama into a mythical, cult figure that would specifically attract and take advantage of the youth. Consciously, unconsciously, and subconsciously, the mature bumptious white liberals with their esteemed guilt-complexes were also easy prey.

These shamed, left-leaning adults hijacked the eager Obama campaign and turned it into a media event as they had hijacked the '60s. Groovy, man! Much like they overplayed the significance of the counterculture radicals of 1968, the same media cabals overestimated the historical significance of the Obama presidency. Popping their Obama-lifestyle pills, they over-medicated with BO's elixir. Well, it wasn't as if they overdosed on LSD or some other Woodstock psychedelic drug. The Age of Aquarius was so yesterday; they had evolved. The Obama hallucinogen was soothing, blissful, and brought them redemption. His energetic being aligned their sacred chakras. The new New-Agers prescribed it as the acceptable, softer side of the forbidden drug culture that transported them to the highest state of progressive Nirvana.

Rather than spinning myths to suit a leftist head trip, why not have the courage to tell the truth. Even the doctor of dream therapy, Carl Jung, didn't blur the boundaries between reverie and reality the way Hollywood and New York does. Jung had ethical standards well before he became a practicing psychiatrist. Well-adjusted individuals rue the day when the Greek's inspirational Muses became incarnate—way beyond inspiration and avatars—for political consultants, advertising agencies, screenwriters, spiritual advisers, medical intuitives, college professors, and Pacific coast graduate schools.

Beware of words that resemble American values that come from Obama's mouth. Consider: Trying to make a case for community and national pride by claiming government imagined, built, and manages the entire U.S. social, educational, and economic infrastructures, Obama chastised arrogant, greedy business creators that "you didn't build that. Someone else made that happen." A few weeks later after the entire nation rallied against the idiocy, Obama did another repeat performance of his famous walking-it-back moonwalk. Obama actually defended his point by offering up regrets for his *syntax* but not the argument itself. Let that soak in . . . syntax, as in sentence structure. He said absolutely NOTHING with his feigned pang of guilt. This was not a Freudian slip; it was a defiant head fake to deceptively preserve the Obama brand.

Before the progressive historians insert themselves and reinterpret the history of the Obama years, let's recount a couple of really important events. Obama's healthcare debacle, aptly named ObamaCare, did not bend the healthcare cost curve as Team Obama alleges. Obama didn't make that happen, something else made that happen. The endless recession was the primary reason for the slower growth of healthcare spending during Obama's tenure as president. People lost their jobs and their health insurance leaving no money for doctor visits, surgeries, prescriptions, etc. The recession almost single-handedly bent the healthcare cost curve, not Obama. Yes, Obama mismanaged the recession recovery but he did not lower healthcare prices and spending. So, too, Obama did not drive the stock market to record levels—another Obama claim to fame. The Federal Reserve's massive money printing and systematic bond buying, known as quantitative easing, fueled the irrational exuberance with cash keeping interest rates low. The return on bonds of all types was so low that the only place for investors to make any money was the stock market. It was the only game in town! Again, Obama didn't make that happen. American resiliency, creativity, and self-reliance made that happen. And one other embellished trope that's become a constant refrain in the media that demands correcting: Obama was never a constitutional law *professor* at the University of Chicago Law School; he was a *part-time lecturer* occasionally teaching but one class. Whoop de doo!

Obama wiped out any legacy due him through his staunch anti-Americanism. All along, Obama overtly professed American values while covertly killing them with his *noble lies*, pretending to be an Everyman while wielding edicts as a philosopher-king. Over the past few years we have learned to watch what he does and not what he says. Categorically, Obama will say whatever he needs in order to have his will be done.

Rule 1978
Be Courteous, Smile, and No Sudden Moves

Whoooaaa, Nellie! Here we go again! Another group of learned, liberal, membership-restricted, tenured academics pushing another sweeping fatuous agenda bound to eventually impact every single American during the course of his and her life time. You know, one of those egomaniacal, aren't-we-the-most-intelligent-beings-on-the-planet, fiction-sold-as-fact, socially-engineered, paradigm shifts. Think of it as the psychopharmacological manifesto for eminent domain over every American's mental wellbeing. When we least expected it, DSM-5 appeared.

Because liberals live in a phantasmagoria where their reality is a continual dream state, they need the Diagnostic and Statistical Manual of Mental Disorders to survive their daily activities. Liberals choose to live in fantasies because coping in the factual biosphere is too grueling. They detest everyday life. They run from its pathetic earthiness and desperate tedium but can't escape the shackles of their own erratic passions and appetites. Now in its trendier number "5" edition, the DSM has been and continues to be the unstable lefties' life support for feigning normality in the truthful world.

The inside-baseball talk was that the DSM-5 project was ill conceived, poorly managed, and rushed to publication without proper real-world vetting. Many in the know say it was all about the publishing revenues. The creators sent it to print as a peer-reviewed checklist of categorized symptoms—no more, no less—with a negligible, insignificant, trifling impact on the rates of psychiatric diagnoses. Oh, to be sure! Who in their right-leaning mind believes that one?

Psychiatrists and other behavioral health professionals pay for their lifestyles with billable hours, similar to the lawyer-as-hourly-worker business model: obscure and confuse with word games that only the firm can decipher; scare the bejesus out of the client/patient; keep that insufferable math part kindergarten-simple; don't forget to elongate at every opportunity; and string it out, counselor! The more psychiatric diagnoses, the more counseling sessions, the more billable hours, the more cash money in the doctors' and the pretend-doctors' pockets. What better way to grow their analyst-couch calendars than to continually blur the distinction between psychopathology and normal psychology.

Some might call it predatory psychiatry, though it depends on how their practices are presented to their niche customers. Marketed properly, patients come to view their regimentally-timed sessions as a membership in an exclusive club or even a day at a boutique spa. Health-and-wealth seekers never miss a consultation with their self-identified life coaches. To enhance their brand identity, behaviorists differentiate their sessions with personalized take-home-meds gift bags to extend the experience. Some engrave the totes with "happiness" flowers while others brown bag them—not to be discreet but to keep the profit margins high. Others encourage their patients to use their affliction to differentiate themselves: the lefty cable-shock-jock Rachel Maddow's "cyclical depression," her existential emptiness used as a *Rolling Stone* read-me tease. Admitting "melancholy" was too get-a-grip old school. And for those high-fliers in need of a pep talk, there's the "phone session" app on their iPhones. Who said the intelligentsia abhors capitalism?!

This new version of diagnose-by-numbers empowers the provider to survey a patient and assign subjective impressions of the patient's ill psyche into simplistic, formulaic, DSM-5-coded symptoms. Just like the color-by-number books they used as kids, the psychiatrists learn to observe a patient then "color" said patient into the numbered box(es) they hazard best describes the patient's mental maladies. The symptoms are officially noted and the flow of psychotropic treatment begins. That getting to know the patient and learning who they are, what they've experienced, you know their "authentic selves," is so passé. Psychiatrists prefer not to touch a patient let alone talk to one! The psych industry has already cycled through the *introspection* craze, the *behavior* fad, and the *cognitive* hysteria. Neuroscience is the new rage. Dust off the 19th century phrenology charts and let the Obama $100 million-plus esoteric BRAIN-mapping Initiative begin!

Map it all—proteins, genomic changes, biochemical changes, electrical changes, structural changes. Look at the explosion of diseases uncorked and incubated by the Human

Genome Project. The brain is way more complex than reading out a few billion base-chemical DNA pairs. Imagine all the new disorders waiting to be discovered. Exploring for diseases is the fun part—treating and curing known terminal neurological afflictions is so blasé, so mind-numbing, so burdensome.

At long last, a way to elastically tie the concrete grey matter to the ethereal mind. Psychiatrist-ordered CAT, MRI, EEG, DBS, and PET scans will become the fashion with insurance reimbursements all around. Ka-ching! Talk therapy be damned. Imagine all the new therapeutic psychoactive drugs. A veritable cornucopia of pharmacopeia! We're talking synaptic liquid gold convertible to greenbacks in the researchers' and clinicians' bank accounts. DSM-5 will have to be segmented into volumes and volumes with its own Library for Looney Classification (LLC) system. Eureka!

The get-rich-quick guide was formally presented at the 2013 American Psychiatric Association Annual Meeting in San Francisco. Who better to give the keynote speech than the satyrical donor-magnet himself, President William Jefferson Clinton?

Perpetually in a state of trolling for tax-deductible alms to the Clinton Foundation, the Wizard of "Is" gravitated to this group of liberals for their appreciation of twisting, bending, stretching, and distorting ordinary words and human characteristics into abnormal mental conditions. Clinton's 2001 disbarment from the Supreme Court was viewed as a slap on the wrist for being puckish. Billy Boy could do no wrong. After all, he memorialized and monetarily rewarded the psych society's deviant penchant with insurance coverage by signing the Mental Health Parity Act of 1996. So when the inventive ideasthete invokes the word "is" thereby triggering, at will, the sensation of intimately sharing a cigar with a female intern in the Oval Office, the psych world celebrates the narcissistic Big Horndog as forward-looking. Continuing the 1996 crusade that all *mental diseases* are indeed *organic brain diseases* and on par with insurance-reimbursable physical medical illnesses, the new DSM-5 slipped furtively through the backdoor.

The DSM purportedly exists to teach, guide, and improve communications among clinicians. First and foremost, it provides them a common language because, for conceited liberals, it's all about their words. Correction: It's *only* about their words. A mere utterance from a progressive can transform reality! Never mind verifiable accomplishments. Witness the love affair libs have with Obama's soaring rhetoric while never holding him accountable for solving the problems he uses as fodder. Ah, but how eloquently he bespeaks! W on the other hand was labeled "Dumbya" by the libs; he was a hick that stumbled over the simplest phrases. Bush "embarrassed" them with his plain-spoken, down-home style and "VALUES" emblazoned on his forehead. Textbook progressive hypocrisy: Their erudite words rule.

On that note, only the lefties' version of "normal" is the definitive standard of behavior in their idyllic civilized society. Normalizing a population reduces everyone to their predetermined code of conduct: If you do not conform to the progressive norm, than you must have a mental/behavioral disorder. By the way, a mental disorder should never be misconstrued as a mental illness or a mental disease. Illness and/or disease signify a pathological, biological, physical condition having a known cause. Mental disorders are determined by observations made by psychiatrists subject to their own biases bolstered, perhaps, by a perfunctory blood analysis. The causes are never defined—metaphorically, symbolically, nor physically. None of the MD'ed mind readers have a clue! There is no "analysis" or serious scientific investigation before casting the disorder in the holy DSM bible. A mental disorder is fabricated on societal expectations and social controls, essentially the whims and fancies of the mental professionals that perch at the top of the cuckoos' nests.

A mental disorder is behavior that's not normal—not abnormal, not deviant, just not normal. An uncommon collection of otherwise normal traits is deemed a syndrome. On an off day, a syndrome could morph into a disorder. Only the shrinks decide what's normal and what's not. In the mental health cosmos, everyone is a little crazy—psychiatrists included. It's worth noting that an implicit psychiatrist credential is "it takes one to know one." It's also worth noting how twisted their terminological knickers are! Realizing that they are in over their heads about finding the true cause of all human non-normality, the head doctors proceeded to perform their interpretive dance and make life as we know it even crazier.

Sidelining their "First, do no harm" motto, the DSM-5 task force set out to modernize the practice of behavior health. Clinical diagnosis: The soft scientists became conscious of losing market share to even softer pseudo-scientists. It was time to circle the wagons and put more censorship teeth into the occupational licensing laws. Once and for all the psych fraternity would show the world that they, and they alone, are the only permitted purveyors of therapeutic advice. And while they were at it, the business development whizzes added Section 3 with turf-protecting, self-assessment tools as a preemptive strike against the enviably popular Myers-Briggs Type Indicator (MBTI) and all the other DIY-naval-gazing charlatans. The sage social scholars tend to cut the population into XX *v.* XY chromosome battles. If they ever deign to get their heads out of other people's crotches, they'd understand how ground-breaking the non-gendered MBTI really is!

Psychologists found themselves in a rancorous tug o' war with behavioral scientists over who owned the rights to interpreting human behavior. Behavioral scientists pass themselves off as "behavioral economists" often without any economics or psychology credentials. Another case of liberals contorting the boundaries of credibility. Through the haze of factual-looking numbers, percentages, and ratios, the behavioral economists make their opinions look more analytical, less subjective then they really are. Subjective vs. objective, "ought" vs. "is", normative vs. empirical, my government grants are bigger than yours—life in the social sciences was becoming more and more fuzzy. The shrinks drew a line in the sand with their throw-this-against-the-wall "affluenza" defense and took control of the courts. The behavioral economists marked their territory in Obama's government with libertarian paternalism. Exhibit A: ObamaCare.

Rather than narrowing their guidebook's focus, the degreed drug-dispensers opted to think big, as in billionaire big. ObamaCare alone will deliver 62 million mental-health patients—that's 20% of the U.S. population!—to their open arms and electronic prescriptions. And that's with a mandated 10-minute maximum doctor's office visit. When they couldn't legitimately stuff anymore categories into the grayly shaded manual, the task force doctored it with boundless words to infinitely expand varying degrees of abnormality: spectrum, continuum, clusters, developmental lifespan, and the earlier the better. Next, the mind-melders reshuffled the deck and cut the disorders by the usual cultural diversity must-haves: age, gender, race, ethnicity, language, religion, social custom, geographic region and origin. Factor in endless therapy sessions and they scatter-graphed their very own off-the-charts, cash-cow matrix. Move over Boston Consulting Group.

Pangs of ugly, money-grubbing guilt overwhelmed the talk-docs. The mind-blowing realization of their patient-centered Hippocratic duties sent them over the edge. Quick, dial 9-1-1! Warn the shrink syndicate! We have board-certified 5150s on the prowl! Not only could they not prevent disease whenever they could, they couldn't even say the word "cure" with a straight face. Their only way out was to smoke-and-mirror mental disorders for all. Progressively rational, if everyone has a mental disorder then no one is responsible and accountable for their actions. The psychobabblers democratically lowered the bar for pleasure-seeking impulses acted upon willy-nilly. The price of admission to the social-conformity club was reckless behavior—excused, condoned, even applauded.

Mental misery became the go-to excuse for compulsive overeating, binge drinking, drug addiction, caffeine addiction, caffeine withdrawal, obsessive sex, overreacting, underreacting, excessive expressing, disproportionate brilliance, grave lethargy, too kinetically energized, killing innocent people, mutilating multiple mortals, abusing teenage girls as sex slaves in a Cleveland house of horrors, and general self-indulgence; along with the run-of-the-mill headache, fatigue, insomnia, blue mood, and unexplained muscle pain. What about the woes of workplace violence? The "infidels made me do it" alibi was intensely rich for a radical-Islamist, card-carrying member of psychiatry, self-assigned to the "Soldier of Allah" unit at Fort Hood, caught bloody-red-handed with a Five-seveN semi-automatic gleefully screaming "Allahu akbar"—slaughtering thirteen and maiming thirty-two while lusting after 72 virgins. Stressed out: Don't forget the cognitive-enhancing jolt for ADHD system-gamers that need more time to take the SAT/ACT college admission exams.

Flip a coin—recreational or medicinal? Wading in the weed, the late wealthy progressive hedonist, Peter Lewis, financed multi-million dollar campaigns to legalize marijuana with the same intensity he funded MoveOn.org, Media Matters, and the Center for American Progress. His Progressive eHealthInsurance had their enviable advertising machine ready to roll as soon as Obama inked the federally-subsidized insurance gusher—ObamaCare. Who said Progressive was all about automobile insurance! Progressive was poised to resell all the major health insurers' plans including those companies that made the risk-free, no-loss, profit-popping meetings at the White House. Flo baby, don't bogart that joint! Undeterred by the proven health risks of consuming weed, the mental health counselors viewed pot as a calming substance to help their clients relax and self-actualize. So the shrinks, acting as clever little entrepreneurs, expanded their hours and mellowed out in guaranteed-reimbursable therapy sessions.

Happy day for the sex addicts! DSM-5 gave up trying to establish a separate criterion for *hypersexuality*. Apparently, acute horniness is not a consistently linear activity and defies classification. However, male *hyposexuality* is consistently linear and uniform which qualifies for placement in the annals of abnormality. Liberal *linear* logic: Any man that is not humping like a crazed rabbit—whenever, wherever, with another, with multiple others, or by himself—has to have his head examined. Liberal *circular bidirectional* logic: Male excessive sex is emphatically normal and a First Amendment right protected by the U.S. Constitution! Pray tell, family-jeweled colleagues, what other mental-emotional-physical activity is consistently linear and, therefore, abnormal? Exposing their chauvinism: Female Orgasmic Disorder is uniform, one-dimensional, and a no-brainer abnormal. Aren't learned lefties supposed to be equal-opportunity, pro-choice, open-minded, vagina advocates? Waging their own war on women, the progressive penis-protectors flashed their dysfunctional gender bias in the dicey Sexual Dysfunction section.

Doesn't this convenient, relativistic rationale negate the entire mental health profession? Sexting nude photos while running for NYC mayor isn't deviant behavior? No, because it's so porno-artsy, freakin' Freudian, and chutzpah gone mad! But really, what's the harm? It's the liberals' perfect infantile land of relative make-believe. Drum roll, please . . . and the winner of the most infantile place to live in the United States is . . . California! And the runner-up is . . . New York City!

White Coats, start your engines! The endurance race to detect mental distress, disturbance, disability, dysfunction, dysphoria, and disorder went full throttle. "Diagnose everyone with something" became the dystopian rallying cry. Lionel Trilling, an English professor at Columbia since 1932, fellow traveler, and member of the New York Intellectuals, predicted this descent into dystopia. The cynical left's Utopia would disintegrate into anarchistic authoritarianism, just as Lionel imagined in his liberal mind. Committed to enfeebling and imposing order on society, the psychotherapists' conscious and subconscious aim was to make gobs of money while protecting themselves from their clients' defended conflicts. Of course, the best defense is a strong offense: whip out the checkered flags for Ritalin, Adderall, Vyvanse, naltrexone, methadone, oxycodone, and the bipolar-Rx bioengineered with male breast enhancement—Risperdal. The patrons of pill-poppers could also shield themselves from their equally greedy legal brethren by co-opting them with a plethora of bizarre defense arguments, scripted for sensational court TV.

The majority of twenty-first-century medical practitioners diligently segment disease categories, like cancer, to offer more precise diagnoses for individual patients. Not the behavioral health experts. They delight in more latitude, more wiggle room when judging head cases. In their efforts to ensnare everyone, the DSM took to broadening uncontested categories on a continuum of normality. Schizophrenia is an extremely serious, undisputed, life-altering disorder. Any behavior that's not classified as schizophrenia could and would be filed under a new category called "Unspecified Schizophrenia Spectrum Disorder." The same goes for "Unspecified Attention-Deficit/Hyperactivity Disorder" (ADHD). When the esteemed psych doctors can't figure out what's wrong with someone, they toss them into the "unspecified" bin. Once again, this absurd, criteria-free, anything-goes, no-objective-standard method of taking care of sick patients nullifies the very profession dispensing the expensive and scarlet-letter diagnoses. Fiddlesticks! They forgot to add "gluten sensitivity" as the newest mental debilitator. It's selling like GF hotcakes at the transcendent, hippy, health-food store—Whole Foods Market.

President Obama recognized the error in their mental-health community organizing. The small-minded introspectives were going about it the wrong way and losing credibility. Psychics and palm readers were more revered. Reaching into the dark recesses of his primal psyche, Dr. Obama had a mind-expanding breakthrough. Sure, Obama demonized his opponents all the time using sacrosanct DSM terminology to label conservatives paranoid, delusional, lunatics with suntan fetishes. *All* die-hard progressives used Alinsky's Rule #5: "Ridicule is man's most potent weapon." It was a standard-issue firearm for lefties. Upgrading for twenty-first-century liberal warfare demanded a broad, low-profile, and highly efficient approach.

Rather than amplifying already existing categories and adding wastebasket diagnoses, Obama weaponized the DSM. First, his highness did hereby proclaim May 2013 National Mental Health Awareness Month. Then on June 3, 2013, Obama waved his imperial scepter and outflowed MentalHealth.gov. Now liberal loonies could cast about "normalizing" all U.S. citizens, using celebrities and pop culture to institutionalize progressive policies. House Minority Leader Nancy Pelosi pledged to watch the normalizers' backs by sabotaging any efforts on Capitol Hill to reform the mental-health system which would rout the liberal orthodoxy that guns kill people. Ready, aim, fire on any and all bipartisan bills to help save the mentally impaired!

By showing the behavioral-health healers some love with their very own White House-sponsored website, Obama lured them back into his pocket for future get-out-the-vote favors—Clinton projects prohibited. When it came to sizing up the paranoid, delusional, and puerile liberal mind, his cerebral majesty believed he was light years beyond these mental midgets. The mind-probers just published one of the most powerful means to harness all bona fide liberals along with naive entitlees. Not only did they make maladaptive choices while shaping their instruction manual, they blew it! Obama let loose a primal scream! Only two categories matter when exploring the aberrant mindset of the left: Liberal Adolescent Forever Syndrome (LAFS) which, when fully manifested, becomes Progressive Utopia Disorder (PUD). After years and years of self-absorption, the superficial liberals still don't know themselves.

Obama recognized the subjugation possibilities immediately. These two categories capture the entire liberal universe. If the mental health professionals wanted to be more relevant and grow their businesses, all they had to do was redesign the DSM around LAFS and PUD. In one fell swoop, they would capture at least 20% of the U.S. voting population with heavy emphasis on Hollywood, San Francisco, Manhattan, mainstream media, environmentalists, sustainabelievers, trust-funded socialites, nonprofits, teachers, professors, public unions, community organizers, LGBTs, smug $7,500-tax-credited Tesla owners, jealous $2,500-tax-credited Prius owners, kale junkies, and a boatload of crazies at the University of California's ten campuses plus the mother-ship asylum in Oakland, a.k.a. Amsterdam USA.

The DSM dispenses liberal adulthood by proxy—lefties never have to grow up. Boys and girls forever! Their self-destructive behavior is forgiven by their printed-and-bound surrogate parent. Sounds eerily familiar: Hillary Clinton's *village* takes charge of raising the lefts' children, absolving the parents of any decision-making obligations. The liberal parent bows to the village collective; the liberal adult bends to the collective weight of the DSM. No one is ever solely answerable for his choices—all the freedoms without the responsibilities. Progressive Utopia energized, fortified, and garrisoned by the DSM.

Obama now had a potent unifier with his fundamentally transformed version of the DSM. Having had a shapeless personality himself before he adopted the progressive pose, he understood his liberalites and what motivated them. He himself began as an empty, amoral vessel. Easier to espouse touchy-feely liberalism than the more "make things happen" conservatism, the practiced chameleon adopted the liberals' bleeding-heart causes. Still an empty vessel, he perfected their art of never making a value judgment because they didn't know what a "value" was. He instantly gained popularity, their votes, and their money.

The progressives' psychological profile mirrored Obama's:

- Intense self-hatred overcompensated with extreme narcissism
- Spiraling into inane infantilism in pursuit of their inner child
- Confused, lost, and helpless in their "surreal" world

- Seek safe haven in large congested areas where their sickness is the norm
- Self-gratification dominates their every waking thought and action
- Cultish desire to belong to centrally-controlled institutions with celebrated logos
- Cynical doomsday view of the world where misery loves company
- Lacking core values that manifests as moral ambivalence
- Peculiar habit of framing their egotistical tantrums as social-justice struggles
- Righteously indignant for no apparent reason as they wilt under competitive pressure
- Difficulty accepting factual information; yearn for abstractions and faux knowledge
- Believe they inhabit an "authentic" world made exclusively for them and theirs
- Fancy themselves cultured and compassionate, yet savagely kill unborn children
- Use abortion to drop a few pounds—theirs and their babies'
- Canny ability to suspend reality 24x7x365 and retreat into their mystical worlds
- Spoon-fed, hand-held, mind-numbed at a very early age leaving them juvenile, disruptive, and jaded
- Powerless to protect themselves unless it's for their "right to party"
- Vague sense of history since they are certain the world began on their birthdates
- Unable to make decisions therefore paralyzed to judge right versus wrong

- Flummoxed by the truth consequently incapable of discerning evil
- Haughty, degree fetish with delusions of tenure-secured grandeur or, even better, never working
- Mesmerized by technology capable of only thriving in self-important houses of mirrors
- Deranged thinking when confronted with opposing perspectives
- Fear of risk thus prone to conformity
- Storybook notion that money grows on crayon-colored trees—inherited or government-endowed
- Supercilious disdain for the elderly mixed with an incongruent delight over granny's money while muttering "When's the funeral?"
- Unrecognizable speech patterns when asked about anything that resembles business, finances, accountability, or responsibility
- Clingingly obedient to an impairing herd mentality
- The mere mention of "autonomy" causes life-threatening convulsions
- The "hypocrisy" gene irreversibly embedded in their DNA and expressed constantly and carelessly as if it were their god-given right
- In general, insecure, petulant, greedy, intolerant, entitled, authoritarian, disingenuous, elitist, and guilt-stricken

Obama and the libs were simpatico on so many levels. Born in the greatest country on earth, the progressives don't have to lift a finger to enjoy all the Creator-endowed freedoms. Life-on-the-line "events" have been taken care of by the brave and unafraid, qualities rarely attributed to liberals. All the heavy lifting was done by our ancestors usually portrayed by the left as greedy, slave-owning, land-grabbing, extremist, conservative terrorists. The original settlers won their hard-fought independence from the motherland, penned the U.S. Constitution, codified the rule of law, negotiated States' boundaries, built towns and cities, established universities. With great sacrifice, succeeding generations continued to build on that foundation to secure peace, stability, economic prosperity, and a just society. Does D-Day, all 43 gruesome days of ferocious warfare to liberate Gai Paris, ring a bell? Dude, that was 70 years ago!

What's left for the flaneurs to do? Just kick back, enjoy the fruits of others' labor, and take their independence for granted. It's not the Euro-chic *balanced lifestyle* but it'll do. Not everyone is entitled to live in Brussels—Belgian chocolate, beer, the de facto capital of the European Union. Ukrainian fine chocolate? Ptooey! Ukraine doesn't have the pedigree to be part of the EU so why bother with their bitter, carcinogenic, garbage especially now that Petro "Chocolate King" Poroshenko is their new president! Better Willy Wonka than a prosperous, enterprising capitalist. The liberal loafers settle for the sublime high from eating half of all the world's cocoa candies with their European chocoholic comrades, liberating their spirits though tragically imprisoned in the Euro-Union colonies—Madison, Boulder, Berkeley, Santa Monica, Cambridge, Manhattan's Upper West Side, Ann Arbor, Austin, Tempe, and other university enclaves. In the not too distant future, the lefties may have to get their chocolate fix by emigrating to India or China with those two countries inhaling cocoa as voraciously as they devour carbon-rich coal. Life is full of trade-offs.

And boy, those unalienable Rights! How do they love them? Just count the ways. Not satisfied with Life, Liberty and the pursuit of Happiness, the progressives dismiss personal responsibility and obligate government, that is, taxpayers to foot the bill for their expansive Lifestyles, lawless Liberty, and insatiable Happiness. Taking liberties with the words "unalienable Rights," the left reinterprets them to be whatever their little hearts desire. Skipping merrily down the yellow brick road, the liberals collect a rainbow of social goodies like Munchkins in Lollypopland. Ding! Dong! Straight to their Wiz in the White House they go. Behind the curtain where he does wonderful extralegal things, Obama converts them into land-of-liberal rights. Any special demands the progressives make are "morally, ethically, spiritually, physically, positively, absolutely, undeniably, and reliably" deemed a righteous right. Close your eyes and listen closely to Obama's ruby-slippers incantation: *My words are magical. My words are transformative. My words can change the world. Follow, follow, follow, follow, follow me to Utopia.*

Another golden oldie the left loves to remix is "The Star-Spangled Banner," the national anthem's "land of the free." With no balanced perspective of history save that which they're fed by the mainstream media and suffering from a long list of the aforementioned psychoses, liberals dismiss intrinsically "free" and hallucinate it as literally F-R-E-E. Disoriented, they relegate America's celebrated "free market" to their shopping mall for free stuff, no currency required. The hysteria over Oprah Winfrey's "Ultimate Favorite Things" two-part episode comes to mind. Humongous ratings and liberal sheeple are easily bought.

Did you hear the one about Oprah the Bitter Scold berating the American public for being racist Obama-haters from her privileged $3 billion "Made in the USA" perch paid for by her mostly white, female, true-believer audience? This happened just days before she sashayed to the White House to pay her respects to the Office of the President. Obama, in turn, paid respects to her megawatt bankroll and star power by hanging the 2013 Presidential Medal of Freedom around her once-color-blind neck. At last, the Harpo harpy shed her sanctimonious, big-buck-advertiser-friendly façade to show her true colors.

Let's take a moment here: Freedom to express yourself, freedom to be whatever you want to be, freedom to live wherever you want, freedom to choose just about whatever, means absolutely nothing to the lefties. It's just so 18th century. "Land of the free" in the progressive universe means the taxpayer-funded government says "yes" to everything the left wants, then obligingly shells out the cash via subsidies, grants, tax credits, food stamps digitized as JPMorgan Chase debit cards, government jobs, gifts, bonuses, promotions, luxurious conferences, etc. The lefts' nonnegotiable freebies include universal healthcare, birth control with carte-blanche abortions, better pay with shorter work weeks, mandatory multi-month vacations, education, phones, computers, autos, appliances, child care, and child support. Whew! It's the androgynous, cradle-to-grave "Life of Julia" on steroids.

Feed the liberal junkies a good story and they'll be hooked forever. Their entire world revolves around smoking, swallowing, snorting, inhaling, chewing, and injecting their lawful designer drug—WORDS. Numbers, arithmetic, mathematics, algebra, geometry, statistics, facts & figures are nasty, sobering buzzkill! Nothing else matters save impeccable words delivered at the precise moment in a resonant tone evoking an enlightening human experience through the arc of a private story. The industries they dominate float on such verbal abstractions: advertising, print, film, music, academia, law, community organizing. The professions they choose rely on theatrical verbiage with success measured by one's ability to elicit human drama—the more exaggerated the better. Only progressive throwbacks would call Obama the greatest orator in their lifetimes.

Storytelling is so treasured by the progressives that they award Nobel Peace Prizes for the most ingenious fabrications. Al Gore, former presidential-campaign-loser turned stand-up PowerPoint comic, sucked up to the left-leaning, investment-hungry TED crowd warning the world about the sensational perils of global warming. But not just any old global warming. He cautioned them about anthropogenic global warming—increases in the planet's temperature caused by the dirty-rotten-bastard Americans that inhabit Mother Earth. China's and India's carbon emissions were ignored. Abrupt-rebranding note: Global warming proved to be a grossly false narrative so the left dreamed up another more amorphous phrase—global climate change. Nah, scrub that. "Global climate disruption" #trends better. The Technology, Entertainment, Design pack lapped it up then began the hyped-up hunt for green government subsidies steering clear of the environmental truth-seekers at the *Wall Street Journal* ECO:nomics conferences. TED groupies even burned their invitations to protest open dialogue about making money off sustainable alpha markets declaring they had a lock on the U.S. energy policy hidden in Obama's pocket.

Within a year, windbag Gore had the Nobel Prize and an open mic in Oslo. He presented his doom-and-gloom prognostications in his stiff, convoluted style that portended his eventual debunking. His bank account, however, saw a meteoric rise through his lobbying efforts for the venture-capital group Kleiner Perkins Caufield and Byers's green investments that would be handsomely augmented when their carbon credits trade on the Goldman Sachs-funded Chicago Climate Exchange like pork bellies. June 2014, former chairmen and CEOs of Goldman Sachs and later former U.S. Treasury Secretaries Hank Paulson and Robert Rubin [Old Boy's Club in the flesh!] released their "Risky Business: The Economic Risks of Climate Change to the United States" report touting the latest reinvention of global warming: Climate change is a huge economic risk to U.S. businesses. Their solution: Put a price on CO_2 emissions—a carbon tax. Their obvious Wall Street play was to boost Goldman Sachs waning stock price by hawking the urgency of trading carbon credits on the CCE. Hank, this "climate bubble," does it have the same 24-hour burst pressure that the 2008 "financial bubble" had? By the way, do the environmentalists know they're being used as cat's-paws by the closet-crony-capitalists? Billionaire environmentalist Tom Steyer knows it and loves it!

A Gore friend and supporter, Rob "Meathead" Reiner has won two Emmys and an Oscar nomination. The actor, MoveOn.org director, producer, and liberal activist explained his inverted reality: "I like writing because you can make things happen and turn out the way they never do in real life."

Might this truth-as-bendable-art mindset have instigated an animated narrative like the one where an inanimate YouTube video spontaneously provoked the murder of four American diplomats at the U.S. consulate in Benghazi, Libya on the anniversary of 9/11—no targeted animus intended? Just sayin'. Always the model pompous progressive, Reiner thinks Washington, DC is "Hollywood for ugly people" and staunchly trades dead babies for lefty female flattery. All Rob Reiner roads in his liberal loveland lead to unfettered access to unconditional, uninhibited sex modishly coined as "hooking up." Get rid of the fetuses, the potential rugrats. New Hollywood is stuck in a time warp known as the sexually-liberated Age of Aquarius. 3D/4D ultrasound images of the fetus in the womb kill the mood quicker than any condom. What a bummer!

John Lithgow, a proud Democrat contributor with a laundry list of liberal darling awards on his resumé, praised the thespians' proclivity: "We actors are all after the suspension of disbelief." Come again? A liberal speaking the truth? Perhaps Lithgow deserved the Oscar for his transsexual ex-football player role in *The World According to Garp*, but what's with writing children's books after playing the bizarre serial killer Trinity in *Dexter*? Atonement? Catharsis? Probably not in the Harvard grad's vocabulary. Silly me! Lithgow is just stretching the limits of his own duality—hopefully into oblivion.

Another Occidental College alumnus who played John Wilkes Booth in the "Killing Lincoln" docudrama, Jesse Johnson clarifies the pitfalls of fame-obsessed fabulists: "[An actor's] interpretation of reality is curiously dramatic." Methinks it becomes even more dramatic as the actor's wealth increases. And the other Oxy grad who successfully peddled fabulist fiction all the way to the White House was, of course, Barack Obama.

Breaking News from the Heritage Foundation! Martin Kaplan, the director of the University of Southern California's Norman Lear Center, sees entertainment as THE driving force, the intellectual framework in our culture. When Obama doled out half a million taxpayer dollars to Hollywood scriptwriters to strategically place the floundering ObamaCare product into television stories, Kaplan acknowledged the wisdom of such cronyism: "We know from research that when people watch entertainment television, even if they know it's fiction, they tend to believe that the [information] is actually factual." The Lear Center is funded by gift givers such as the Bill & Melinda Gates Foundation along with the ObamaCare kitty laundered through the California Endowment—even the Center for Disease Control and Prevention throws in. Kudos to the brave USC College Republicans for inviting the fearless and outspoken Ann Coulter to the everything-is-entertainment campus for a book-signing.

Mr. Lear, how does your virtuous, anti-religious-right, Born-Again-American crusade square with promoting ObamaCare that prohibits by law Americans' right to choose how they wish to purchase healthcare? Cedars-Sinai Medical Center, the nexus for Hollywood healthcare, is an excellent example of ObamaCare stunting the free market made up of freedom-loving Americans—one choice only, Health Net, take it or leave it! Well, unless you're part of the Beverly Hills jet setters and can easily afford VIP concierge medical care. Mr. Lear, didn't you implore all progressives, including Obama, to follow your lead with "straight talk mixed with common sense" or were you just pontificating for posterity? But we digress.

Even the liberal headshrinkers encourage weaving a tantalizing, saleable life story with numerous sub plots which make for many office visits, many chapters, and many HBO episodes. It's called the psycho-blather multiplier effect. Was the NYC psychiatrist's complicit fabrication of Sybil's sixteen personalities that sold six million books and launched a star-studded TV special that uncommon? The psychoanalyst's couch has become the progressives' gold mine for titillating spellbinders set to words. What left-leaning film production doesn't portray, focus on, or make reference to an analyst? If it's a liberal script, it's got to have a psychotic component.

Where once troubled clients would visit a mental health provider to help resolve psychic suffering, they now book sessions to stimulate creativity. Even if a patient is perfectly healthy, a Rorschach test or a free-association game might spark that once-in-a-lifetime script. Psychiatrists even encourage apophenia to help connect the dots to a future smash-hit film. Only the most talented shamanic therapists, or LSD if you're in a hurry, are capable of guiding novice clairvoyants to intentional paranoid schizophrenia hoping to see ominous screenplays where none exist. We're talking Hitchcock-, Kubrick-, and Fellini-caliber patternicity. A good many libs are drawn to the 100% tax-deductible flame of The Moth storySLAM to hone their naked-soul techniques and perhaps light on a PBS talkathon. But nothing compares to the fervor propelled by the preeminent catalyst for epic storytelling, the granddaddy for raconteurs, the architect of archetypes, Mr. Mythology, Dr. Dream himself, revered Swiss psychiatrist Carl Jung.

Jung got the storytelling party started when he meticulously explored the religiousness of the human psyche. The taletellers' treasure trove he created included fertile concepts like collective unconscious, archetypes, individuation, spontaneous mandalas, synchronicity, and psychological types. Though a medical scientist first, Jung was open minded and explored other specialties that would lend credence to his main pursuit of helping his patients become integrated, whole human beings.

His contributions to analytical psychology were vast though in a nutshell go something like this: The human psyche is an expression of man's instinct system, the inherited biology common to all mankind—Jung called this the *collective unconscious*; all of the organs in the body contribute to this inherited, biological instinct; the *personal unconscious* is specific to each individual thus biographical and socially determined; dreams, myths, and archetypes are revelations of a divine life in man; when properly understood they serve to bring the sometimes misdirected, outward-oriented consciousness back in alignment with the circumspect, inner-oriented self; confronting and synthesizing pairs of opposites—good and evil, light and dark, extrovert and introvert, personal responsibility and surrendering to the collective—when exposed through dreams and myths leads to the wholeness of the self. Jung's gift to his patients was helping them reconnect their outward self with their inward self.

Unlike his contemporary Sigmund "sex is everything" Freud who viewed the world negatively and through a repressed-childhood-incest monocle, Jung's philosophies were positive and life affirming. From an historical and universal perspective, he believed that man and his inward self could only be articulated through mythology. He quietly reflected: "It is not we who invent myth, rather it speaks to us as a Word of God." In Jung's writings, he knew he could equally well interchange "the unconscious" with "God" and still be true to himself.

To understand how Jung plays into the left's melodrama fixation, we have to also consider Joseph Campbell, one of the earliest disciples of Jung the Myth Master. A charming, brilliant, independent-minded professor, Campbell was intrigued by mythology from a young age. When he discovered how Jung conceived archetypes and used them as groundbreaking psychotherapy with his patients, Campbell set off on his own explorations. His pioneering work focused on comparing the various world religions and their mythologies, all brimming with common archetypes. The intrepid Campbell made many discoveries and is widely known for: "All religions are true, but none are literal." In other words, all religions manifest the same essential universal truth though express themselves uniquely to their history and culture. Campbell so admired Jung that every year on his birthday he would make a cross-country pilgrimage to a Big Sur retreat to refresh his own myth with a Jungian immersion.

Jung and Campbell are inextricably linked by their fearless pursuit of the truth. To label them mythologists trivializes both men and their life's work. Though each studied mythology, it was in light of what myths meant to the human spirit and society. They both concluded that mankind is nourished by myths. Mythology depicts how people live in harmony with each other, themselves, and the universe. The psychiatrist and the literature professor mutually believed that the myth offers inner direction that readies the youth for responsibility, to eventually leave the myth and function as an equipped adult. Mythology is meant for children and the child-like psyche that needs to be shown the way to maturity.

Well-grounded in empirical research, Jung confidently weighed in that: "No science will ever replace myth, and a myth cannot be made out of any science." Campbell equally self-assured from his anthropological studies asserted that: "[Myths] are not entertainment stories. The folk tale is for entertainment. The myth is for spiritual instruction." With great respect for the human struggle and the belief systems that are fashioned to guide the human psyche through life's twists and turns, Carl Jung and Joseph Campbell protected the integrity of the link between religion and mythology. Because of their elucidations, the myth achieved its rightful place in the development of mankind—imparting wisdom through stories.

Then blasted from its religious and spiritual underpinnings, the myth was catapulted into relativism orbit. The Bay Area, Modesto-phobic, hirsute hippy, sugary-munchie-spiked-self-inflicted-Type-2-diabetic, draft-dodger, and technical cameraman, George Lucas was sitting atop a galactic empire worth a half billion dollars. His *Star Wars* cult had lost its mojo, as had Lucas himself. What would Buddha do, karmic blowback aside? From his Death Star lair in Marin County, Lucas planned a heist of breathtaking proportion. Like Darth Vader in sheep's clothing, he invited the retired professor turned popular traveling-teacher Joseph Campbell to ostensibly lecture at Skywalker Ranch, the docking station for New Hollywood digital film production. Lucas hoped to hitch his retreaded-trilogy wagon to the shining stars of Joseph

Campbell and Carl Jung by inserting himself into the Sacred Trinity of mythologists. Lucas would hijack elegant mythological storytelling and reinterpret it as bang!-bang!-shoot-'em-up laser light shows.

When the science-fiction comic book called *Star Wars* was originally launched, there were those that couldn't believe that anyone would have made a movie that was so juvenile and artificial, not counting *American Graffiti*. To defend the toys-in-flight flick with some semblance of forethought beyond rapidly rolling cameras, the *Star Wars* zealots improvised a tall tale that elevated the "Force" beyond filling the empty dialogue to morality-play status. Lucas didn't seem to mind the imaginative face-saving and proceeded to embellish it with references to having read Joseph Campbell's epochal *The Hero with a Thousand Faces*. So somewhere in between chasing fast-moving objects through a camera lens, Lucas would have the world believe that he was a serious reader, talented writer, and astute intellectual. Carl Jung would have sussed Lucas's *hubris of consciousness* immediately—nothing in the celestial sphere is greater than George Lucas and his high-velocity, mind-blowing, eardrum-shattering animations. Lucky for Lucas, Campbell was in his twilight years and receptive to spreading the gospel of culture-nurturing mythology spawned from religion even if it was in George's den of secularity.

The Q&A session was staged on Lucas's turf, all the better to pick Campbell's brain. The far-left PBS interviewer was courteous and deferential, smiled without fawning, and ever so gently posed his leading questions—a liberal liar's, don't-tip-your-hand technique. Ethical journalists would never intentionally hoodwink with prodding questions but this was the hallowed, double-dipping, pay-no-taxes nonprofit, and taxpayer-funded PBS in cahoots with a mega-wealthy movie producer not to mention an Oscar-winning editor. And they were, after all, precisely in the middle of the editing universe—Skywalker Ranch! With their digital tools they could turn Joseph Campbell into Zeus incarnate with a montage of Norse and Roman gods feeding him honey set to mystical music. If George could imagine it, they could shape a point of view that made the mythic themes in the *Star Wars* original trilogy seem "obvious" and "intentional." The final cut was all that mattered. Well, sort of. What mattered more was adding many more millions to Lucas's bank account.

If George Lucas were genuinely "Joe's mentee," he would not have manipulated the humble storyteller the way he did. In regions beyond California fantasyland, we call it human decency. Also, if Lucas truly studied mythology at the foot of the Master, how did the movie mogul miss some of the most profound truths, those truths that constantly elude the movie industry? For starters, in *Myths to Live By* Campbell recognizes that most contemporary "mythological themes" are not mythological at all but "infantile biographical associations . . . are allegorical merely of childhood desires frustrated by actual or imagined parental prohibitions and threats." Symbolic of childish temper tantrums. Hmmm. Sounds a lot like *Star Wars*—nowhere near the supernatural mythic level that serves to explain man and the world he inhabits.

Then there's a guiding-light passage in *An Open Life*: "Ethics and religion are not the same. Religion has a mystical dimension, and that's what it's really all about. Ethics has to do with social values and religion has to do with personal, inward realizations. Those are different things! And living in a society defines your realization of the inward values through the ethics of society. That's the trick, I might say, of being alive in the world." George, was Campbell really your mentor? Fess up.

Progressives are known to be metaphysically repressed and socially backward when discussing spirituality. They have a phobic fixation about religion: Keep the church out of the state. It's an automatic reflex. Liberals conveniently dismiss the fact that the First Amendment of the U.S. Constitution says: "Congress shall make no law respecting an establishment of religion, or prohibiting the free exercise thereof." Translation to enlighten the lefties: Keep the damn state out of all the churches, regardless of the denomination! Facts are fluffy, superfluous nuisances for the progressives. They continue to plod along making like they are enlightened and engaged in the mystery of life. It may be expecting too much for them to fully understand the error of their secular ways. *Mea culpa, mea culpa, mea maxima culpa.*

Details. Details. Who cares about the truth and what Joe actually meant! Lucas and his co-conspirators smelled a blockbuster, mass-audience, wide-release, movie bonanza, and seized the opportunity to capitalize on Campbell's colorful work. High-concept, low-concept, whatever! George's motion picture gravitational force was held together by eat-my-dust fast cars, intravenous sugar highs, and profits—billions and billions of out-of-this-world profits!

Once the progressive profiteer milked the magical Campbell relationship and usurped Joe's examined religious insights to spin the god-like illusion of *Star Wars* in the big-screen temple, the liberal Lucas came about as clean as any rapacious secularite dare: "I don't see *Star Wars* as profoundly religious. I see *Star Wars* as taking all of the issues that religion represents and trying to distill them down to a more modern, more easily accessible construct that people can grab onto to accept the fact that there is a greater mystery out there." At long last, in a frankly-don't-give-a-damn moment, the synthetic $7.3 billionaire George Lucas unplugged and bit the hand that fed him royalties. Loyal progressives must always denigrate everyone else's religion—it's the progressive anti-ecumenical doctrine. Six months earlier, GL confessed that he had embedded political undertones into *Star Wars* that subliminally messaged a corrupt, dysfunctional government. Yeah, that's what *Star Wars* was about! Yeah, that's the make-it-up-as-you-go ticket! Jon Lovitz may even induct the relativistic SanFran-Sixties capitalist into his pantheon of Pathological Liars.

The Power of Myth six-hour PBS special aired in 1988, shortly after Campbell's death. That same year the companion book was published through the power of Doubleday editor Jacqueline Kennedy Onassis, the stylizer of the JFK Camelot myth. The gods must have orchestrated this vortical confluence of a liberal publisher, a liberal producer, a liberal filmmaker, and the liberals' beloved academic—a media jackpot for Lucas who needed Campbell's imprimatur to breathe irreligious life into his lackluster *Star Wars* franchise. Eventually *Star Wars* worldwide licensing revenues grew to $27 billion. The double-dealing vexed sincere, principled individuals seeking intelligent entertainment. They recognized a degradation of the nation's values when they saw it. Lucas made a pact with the Devil: monetize the myth and coarsen the culture. Dumbing-down movie-viewing Americans was a satanic signing bonus.

The unscrupulous technology nerd bastardized Campbell and Jung. Nothing new—that's how Lucas rolled. The suck-the-life-out-of-his-mentors Lucas stripped away the sacred side of myths and used the unspiritual story shell for his tony-the-tiger, snap-crackle-pop, space cartoons. Joseph Campbell's comparative religion groundwork was overshadowed by the twerpy progressive's greed for money and power. Jedi moral relativism: With the wave of a lightsaber, the wisdom of life was relegated to whiz-bang animation. Doesn't much matter—just tell the libs a good story. Popcorn! Popcorn! Get your popcorn and life role models topped with a glob of hot-buttered ethos! Hollywood's new conceit: money-making mythology.

The best rubbernecking entertainment is watching liberals getting twisted up in finding the next best "myth" or "mythic being" knowing they will never achieve it. It will never happen. *The progressives eliminated religion, God, and the spiritual from the mystery of life, effectively destroying the centrality of the psyche from the culture.* No Lucasfilm Expanded Universe technology, nor Disney, awash in billions of advertising dollars can manufacture the myth.

Were you invited to the swanky June wedding? When George Lucas married Mellody Hobson in 2013, he invited a few close effete friends to the liberal lovefest. Only star-struck politicians, sycophantic TV news personalities, and bootlicking moviemakers were permitted. Eighteen months prior in a PBS interview with Charlie Rose, Lucas expressed his ardent belief that rich capitalists should not be able to sway the democracy. Cut! Unless it's GL and it's GL's version of 1960 San Francisco democracy, and it's GL's definition of patriotism, and it's GL's sound bite to promote his latest movie, and it's GL's big bash.

The Skywalker Ranch festivities followed by the Chicago lakeside get-together included several recognizable names: Chicago Mayor Rahm Emanuel, jack-of-all-race-mongering-trades Jesse Jackson, former Chicago Mayor Richard Daley, former Obama White House Chief of Staff Bill Daley, former Obama Social Secretary Desiree Rogers, MSNBC host Al Sharpton, former New Jersey Senator Bill Bradley, CNN contributor Paul Begala, CBS co-anchor & Oprah's gal pal Gayle King, then-editor-in-chief of *The Daily Beast* Tina Brown, and *Vanity Fair* editor Graydon Carter. The list of lefty political entertainers with deep, exquisitely tailored pockets was to die for. The new Mrs. George Lucas is herself a CBS contributor and chairman of Dreamworks Animation. The wait staff was screened for any conservative credentials; all their cameras were impounded. The photo-elusive Lucas awarded his exclusive wedding photo to the *Huffington Post*. Apparently, Obama made a special videoconferencing appearance on everyone's hand-held mobile devices.

Alas, Joseph Campbell and Carl Jung have departed. Honest introspection holds no value. Who needs religion? Spirituality be damned! Look to Big Government, look to Barack "The Messiah" Obama to fill the void!

Barack Obama was but eleven years old when in 1972 Joseph Campbell retired from his professorship at Sarah Lawrence College and moved to Honolulu with his wife. Would the pubescent Barry have bodysurfed with Joe? Probably not. Maybe they munched on *manapua* together?

Not likely. Did the Campbells socialize with the Dunhams? Don't think so. Has Obama ever visited Campbell's grave at the Oahu Cemetery during his many extravagant vacations? Not a chance. Is Obama's alleged post-presidency $35 million palace in the BHO-anointed, 15th Amendment-ignored, sovereign Kingdom of Hawaii near the Campbells' university-pensioned homestead? Not within miles. Joseph Campbell and Barack Obama never met in Hawaii. The intersection of their lives occurred through a profound Lucasian social construct of greater mystery formed in a far-away galaxy by cosmic energy. A new hang-onto-anything-except-religion hope for America would eventually emerge, forged by intense campaign contributions. Where Campbell's spellbinding spiritual storytelling took a lifetime to perfect, Barack had mastered a glacially detached, insensate, robotic, I-centric style before graduating high school.

Obama didn't need to be present while Lucas and highbrow PBS ripped off Joseph Campbell's body of work. In liberal circles, such fleecing is common practice—it's part of the progressive credo. Just make sure the swindling is done with a soothing, nonthreatening voice, as if lulling an infant to sleep. Obama understood this; he embodied it. The Obama Cool Rule 1978 would sustain him throughout his career, even usher him to the White House.

All Obama had to do was be courteous, smile, and make no sudden moves. It worked on his mom every time. Obama knew how to gain white cred. By 1978 at age seventeen, he had perfected his "trick" and shared it with the world in *Dreams*: be courteous, smile and make no sudden moves; give them a reassuring smile, pat their hands, and tell them not to worry; white people loved "a well-mannered young black man who didn't seem angry all the time." Gnarly insouciance.

The Democratic faithful saw Obama as their measured and prudent champion, someone who saw the world as they wished it to be—purged of the evil uncouth Bush & Cheney tag team. Obama's calm-guy veneer though would never reach the venerated John Wayne's standards: "Talk low, talk slow and don't say too much." Even so, adopting the famous Marion Mitchell Morrison swagger helped convince certain naïve independents to also vote for the con artist. Liberals are tone-deaf to words delivered by people of integrity like the Duke, yet are mesmerized by progressive utopian promises—the more unfathomable and duplicitous, the more enticing. Just like their mild-mannered loquacious wordsmith, Barack Obama.

Who's your daddy? Obama had the liberals eating out of his slow and steady hand. His soi-disant normalcy and understated demeanor were catnip for the lefties. Just don't tell them any scary bedtime stories! You mean like the one where Obama's mother asked her son the lawyer to help her with her disability claim while she was dying of cancer, but he was too busy pressing the flesh in Chicago to get to the crazy hard paperwork because it was too much like work, and besides she was a 52-year-old bohemian flake that abandoned him way too many times; so she died in Honolulu still waiting to hear if her dear boy did indeed fight to save her from the big bad insurance company, though he too believed that she had become a sickly senior sucking money out of the healthcare system that really should be going to young guns like himself that deserved the resources since they had their whole lives ahead of them, and that if they had ObamaCare at the time he could force her against her will into Medicaid, because it was her time to go and get off his back! But wait. Obama did show up several days later to spread her ashes in the ocean. What a generous young man!

Riddle me this: a) Was Obama avenging his mother's death by taking revenge on the insurance companies with ObamaCare; b) Trying to make amends to his mother by impounding the entire U.S. healthcare system into one-stop-shop.gov paperless website to make it easier for all; or c) Believed that young people offer more value to society than the older people even though the seniors have built the country that provides the lifestyles that the young have become accustomed to?

Progressive paternalism, personified in Obama, was the answer to all of the lefties' problems. Obama would protect them and keep them safe. Where once they neurotically hid out in anything-but-country-music stories afraid of the boogeyman, now they were free to pursue their passion, mainline drama, follow their bliss, and fulfill their happiness. Liberal lemmings love to be controlled by their elitist leaders, even sadistically demand it. So what if they have to give up individual liberties to the common cause. Tax, spend, and regulate them to death, just make sure to legislate their progressive lifestyles into the living U.S. Constitution. Big government will make all the tough decisions and free them to romp in no-responsibility-land. Luxuriating lefties can live happily ever after.

Prone to sinking too far into their fantasies and dream tending, liberals often need rescued from their fictional lives. Progressives don't talk much about their inability to self-reflect and face the truth. They leave that painful, back-to-reality demythologizing to their therapists. Occasionally their anarchistic madness escapes the confines of civility and they unload their vitriol on respectable citizens and civil servants. Scenes of fanatical City University of New York students haranguing retired General David Petraeus on his way to teach a class spurred on by their inferiority-complexed professors come to mind. Jump back! This was just the natural duality of the passive, low-stressed, tenured-professorial, shady **yin** interconnected and interrelated yet, at the same time, intimidated by the solid, focused, fiery, sunny **yang**. Ommmmmm. Trigger warning: run-amok liberal cant inflicting emotional harm on the rest of us. Double-take: How did "trigger warning" make it through the schools' censor squads when Pop-Tart pistols are marked as killing machines? There's just no end to liberal peevishness.

Not to be upstaged in political theatre, intolerant Brown University students heckled then-New York City Police Commissioner Ray Kelly to silence him with their superior free-speech rights bolstered by a pathetic Ivy League president. And let's not overlook the subjugated demonstrators at White Supremacy U., formerly known as Dartmouth College. The squatters that took the administration hostage delivered a 72-point manifesto to force the dean to protect them from "further physical and emotional violence enacted against us by the racist, classist, sexist, heterosexist, transphobic, xenophobic, and ableist structures at Dartmouth." Was this a victimology practicum? A professor at another liberal, hoity-toity, NYC college, Joseph Campbell witnessed the same chaotic behavior from students and teachers on campus and called their scornful nihilism "a lunatic asylum without walls." Liberalism hasn't evolved much in fifty years.

What's tattooed on every progressive's backside? "We ♥ Big Government". Such exhibitionistic message discipline was even better than Obama's tedious, teleprompted repetitions. Initially jealous of their visceral devotion to a cause not to mention the carnal appeal of native booty advertising, he decided to leverage it. Obama used liberals as both his fools and his foils. Does that make them foolish foils or foilish fools? Either way, the melodramatic, liberal dolts were primed for the nudge.

The night before his 2009 inauguration, Barack Obama accepted the AFC championship game ball from the Pittsburgh Steelers chairman and owner Dan Rooney. Certainly the football was a prized possession as was the black and gold Terrible Towel that Rooney, Jerome Bettis, and Franco Harris used to campaign for Obama throughout Steelers Nation. Rooney and Cleveland's Jim Brown got out the Obama vote in northern Ohio waving the knock-off Dawg Pound towel. But what really excited Obama was the *Official Playing Rules of the National Football League* and the *Steel Curtain Playbook* app that Rooney slipped him when no one was looking. The flea-flicker deal was sealed. When the Steelers won the Super Bowl a few weeks later, Rooney gave a peculiar-for-a-lifelong-Republican, jubilant shout-out to President Obama. By St. Patrick's Day, U.S. Ambassador Rooney and family were packed and moving to Dublin, Ireland.

The NFL Rulebook gave Obama a template for redesigning Washington, framing the game as he saw it in his mind's eye. Any run-of-the-mill redistributive progressive could do tax-and-spend plays all day. He felt way too stifled as a "traditional" president with so many princes and princesses in Congress stealing his limelight for what, bi-partisan compromise? Obama would have none of that. He fancied himself more like the Commissioner of the League of States where he could make the rules and have final ruling on the rules when an interpretation is required. He would harness even more power than the $44-million-a-year NFL Commissioner. If the-once-a-yearlong-intern-never-an-NFL-player turned Commissioner Roger Goodell can subordinate the sacred game of American football to global-TV-advertising prostitution labeling whatever he can get his hands on with an "NFL Shield" hologram sticker, Barack Obama can subjugate a nation of 317 million sets of trusting eyeballs to his progressive rules and regulations. In Obama's new world, there would never be any disputes. His rules are final. Those that don't comply will be punished. No more archaic U.S. Constitution. The NFL Constitution and Bylaws were more suited to contemporary times—more Obama metrosexual, suck-up footsyball; less Bush cowboy, rock 'em sock 'em, muscular football. And to boot, the NFL is a 501(c)6 nonprofit industry association—red meat for Obama and his ambulance chasers. Instant replay: "Illegal" in the NFL Playbook is regarded as "an institutional term of art." Obamaspeak is everywhere!

The *Steel Curtain Playbook* app opened up a more adventurous and mischievous world than any law-book weenie could imagine. Obama's constitutional-law collaborator, Jonathan Turley, suggested a new title to make it more #EmperorObama trendable: "Uber-presidency." Thanks, JT, you legal-devil you! The digital tool gave Obama instant ability to concentrate all the power of the Office into his presidential-sealed iPad. Every morning he worked out in a different muscle shirt printed with the name and number of the fiercest defensive line that ever lived: 75 Greene, 68 Greenwood, 63 Holmes, and 78 White. "Mean Barack" became Obama's daily visualization. Not quite sure how to best use his defense-is-the-new-offense gizmo, he started practicing by moving the icons around doing what he knew best—wussy community-organizing plays. These scrambles worked to get him elected but he needed to up his game. The quarterback sneak—O's signature maneuver—lost its furtiveness having been used every day. Right, President QB?

Obama was frantic to avoid getting sacked in the quarterback's pocket. Imagine the humiliation of being tackled by that right-wing then-Secretary of Defense Robert Gates after he, the President, the Commander in Chief, gave him an order! Ain't gonna happen, not now, not never! Still a novice scatback when it came to national and international politics, he was in desperate need of experienced playahs that understood hard-core, political-bulldozing, no-huddle offense. Only unsportsmanlike-conduct specialists need apply.

During his first few months in office, Obama sent out an SOS to billionaire investor Warren Buffett for some coachin' up on a strange new concept for the rookie president: the U.S. economy. Yes, Barry, the United States' GDP dwarfs every country that produces goods and services . . . and you're now in charge. A little global perspective: It takes all 28 countries in Europe's Economic & Monetary Union (EMU) to even come close to the productivity of the revolutionary upstart across the pond. What TF! *American exceptionalism* qualitatively quantified? How can this be? Leveler Obama declared the U.S. as just another member of the international community, the global village just like, say, Greece.

Obama's liberal default position was to trash talk America. With every negative word out of his mouth, Obama drove the economy further and further to his nefarious goal of inflaming "the deepest recession since the Great Depression." Ricochet Rabbit: Obama wrestled the CYA-as-the-Keynesian-economy-tanks title from that horrid 1973-75 "Great Recession" only to have the distinction boomerang. July 2014, a Quinnipiac University national poll ranked him the worst president since World War II.

At first, Buffett thought Obama had gone off the deep end, taking the economy with him. With closer observation, Warren soon realized that Obama was an unbelievably, disturbed, shape-shifting pessimist and his dark statements about everything except himself came natural to him. Over a cozy lesson in beginners' bridge, they had a father-son, facts-of-life discussion: Put a muzzle on the muddled messages! Not only was Obama confusing Warren with his obvious lack of basic finance but Barack's fumbling was also driving the markets insane. Since Obama didn't have a clue what he was talking about, Buffett suggested he focus on happy talk interlaced with stand-up comedy that made all the sycophants laugh. For daily joke-writing assistance, he gave Obama a GEICO gecko bobblehead and suggested he work on his British accent if all else fails. And, son, lose the friggin' "political football" analogies! This sage advice from the Oracle of Omaha helped Obama make it through his first four years.

For Obama's second term in office, Warren gave him a business dictionary so he could at least master a few business-friendly words that made him appear as if he had a smidgen of practical commercial knowledge. Even with a quick immersion course, Obama kept getting all the business issues reversed. Upside down! It was like a Monty Python skit where every significant business-impacting decree had the opposite effect. In the business world, nothing Obama was saying or doing was making any sense at all. Buffett was stunned; he had made a really expensive mistake.

The Oracle's ballyhooed "institutional imperative" was playing out in the Oval Office. Obama became the poster child of narrowly focusing on only his ideology, squandering any and all available taxpayer funds, playing hide-and-seek with factual data, and imitating previous progressive presidents. Warren was mortified. The famous soothsayer's druthers were to not have to make operational improvements in his majority-shareholding companies nor his pocketed politicians. Nonetheless, Buffett acquiesced with an Ollie Ollie in come free.

While romancing Obama with remedial dos and don'ts of business administration, Buffett was placing buy orders for 100% stake in the Burlington Northern Santa Fe railroad. Where once they were hauling coal, BNSF and Buffett read between the lines of Obama's energy hieroglyphics and had his railcar supplier retrofit the tank cars with splash-proof canopies and crude-oil spigots. Well versed in transferring risk in make-or-break insurance computations, Warren strongly suggested the railcar manufacturers weld steel plates all over the trains in case of explosive derailments. Holy smoke! That giant fireball wasn't supposed to happen when the BNSF grain train collided with the mile-long BNSF crude oil trolley in Casselton, North Dakota December 30, 2013. At least they kept it in the family where they could weep in private about the subsequent first-quarter profit nosedive.

Drawing only a $100,000 annual salary as a distraction from his irresistible "wealth accumulation" compulsion, Buffett felt above reproach in lending his support to Obama's tax increase on "millionaires and billionaires" with pre-tax income starting at $200,000. Warren realized then the extent of Obama's cluelessness when it came to just basic numbers. The president was pressuring him to demonize "thousandaires." Jeepers creepers! He was aghast but his white guilt got the better of him. Obama knew Buffett worked really hard to help him. To show his gratitude Obama made sure that the unobtrusive, State Department-stamped environmentally-safe, Keystone XL oil pipeline originating in Alberta, Canada would never become a U.S. job-creating, energy-independence project. All Buffett had to do to mend relations with the Canucks was to send them Burger King Worldwide headquarters and tax-inverted Whoppers in exchange for a side of preferred-stock tax advantages.

Once again, Obama was making another one of those opposite-what's-good-for-America decisions; however, Warren saw it as a magnificent boost to the valuation of his Berkshire Hathaway stock. Believing that one good turn deserves another, Buffett advanced the giving-back pledge and sent the environmentalists opposed to the XL pipeline 50-pound boxes of See's chocolate walnut fudge (Warren's favorite), a lifetime supply of Dairy Queen Blizzards, and gallons of Brazilianized Heinz 57. He wrote a personal note to San Francisco anti-Keystone billionaire and follow-the-government-green-grants opportunist Tom Steyer encouraging him to drop $100 million more on additional inflammatory "sucker punch" ads against the pipeline and to ignore the *Washington Post*'s Four Pinocchios. And Steyer baiting the Senate Democrats with an additional $100 million to an all-nighter talkathon on climate change, was classic "money talks"—literally! While under the cloak of media darkness, the National Oceanic and Atmospheric Administration (NOAA) hoped no one would notice that they swapped their fungible hottest month on record in the U.S. from July 2012 back to the original July 1936.

Obama high-fived Buffett for his bodacious Berkshire branding! They agreed there was no limit to what the two could do together—Obama's fun-money tax credits and Warren's lust for Obama's fun-money tax credits. What about having the Chinese build electric buses in Los Angeles, discounted 80% with federal subsidies? Berkshire Buses. That's kookie, man! Throw in $15 billion on a bunch of wind farms and solar fields, too. Both chuckled about never having really built anything, that somebody else built everything . . . they were just greasing the skids for their own selfish purposes. Keystone blue-collar and white-collar construction professionals (also known as people that actually build things) go find your own sugar daddy . . . all 43,000 of you!

To further divert attention from his black gold choo-choos, Buffett made headlines with his bread-and-circuses offer of $1 billion for anyone that could fill out a *perfect* March Madness basketball bracket. Again, Obama was blown away by the billionaire's ability to control the message and the frivolous, greedy masses. [Note to O's smooth self: Got to use this "Buffett $1 billion" hype to rally my greenie gofers to support my toadies' social-impact investments—Climate Resilience Fund—yea, they'll buy it hook, line, and sinker!]

With his special relationship and many years of practice filling out the NCAA Tournament bracket christened Barack-etology by ESPN, Obama reckoned he had a pretty good chance of winning. It would be like cashing in the lottery. He couldn't wait to get one of those Johnny Paycheck cowboy hats and flip-off the American people with "take this job and shove it!" Warren as usual was ten million steps ahead of Obama. Buffett knew the odds of winning were incalculable, yet gladly pocketed the reinsurance fee from Quicken Loans. After only two days into the tournament, Warren beat the houses of the *imperfect* brackets. His Reinsurance Group wasn't one of BH's most profitable ventures by betting against obvious improbabilities. And a little backslapping with Quicken Loans would help position Berkshire's HomeServices of America consumer unit to sell oodles of houses. What BNSF train derailments? When? Where?

Food for thought: Since Warren Buffett is such a huge advocate of "giving back" and doing his "fair share," does that mean he would willingly instruct his Berskshire Hathaway companies to give back their dominant market positions to their competitors so that it's a level playing field? Too parochial, you say. Buffett much prefers to keep strategic control of the return-on-investment game, as in bank bailouts by Congress to emancipate his Goldman Sachs investment from those toxic mortgage-related assets. With BH holding 13 million shares in GS and Buffett's personal undisclosed JPMorgan Chase stake, Warren was doubly guaranteed admission to Obama's presidential-appointment process.

Obama was in awe of Buffett's well-heeled contacts. During his presidential campaign, the self-effacing Barack portrayed himself as an unconnected outlier. Early in his life he shunned the opportunity to become a Gordon Gecko Wall Streeter and rose above the greedy multitudes to become a meek, hero-of-the-downtrodden, community organizer. One need only peruse the list of his 2008 contributors to comprehend Obama's personal fundamental transformation as he got closer to the White House—Goldman Sachs at #2, Citigroup at #6, and JPMorgan Chase at #8.

Even though Obama had an "unconscious bias" for working only with look-alike lawyers from his alma mater, he was dazzled by the sheer wealth the big bankers conjured up at will. With so many money-movers throwing bags of cash at him, Obama devised a system to select living-large, limousine liberals to work on his treasured project to remake America, nicknamed Obamanomics or twenty-first-century, American-made, collectivistic, central planning.

Eeny, meeny, miny, mo, which lackey stays and which foe goes? Immediately eliminated from his economic team was anyone who had military experience, had near or distant relatives, or any ancestors that might have even tried on a military uniform. Another resumé red-flag was genuine small, medium, and/or large business experience with actual profit & loss responsibility. These two exclusions, normally considered desirable traits, ensured that Obama's economic initiatives would never be realistic, pragmatic, budget-balanced, or accountable. Key CV phrases [PhD's only use curricula vitae] that Obama searched for were: registered Democrat, Obama bundler or contributor, Keynesian economist, U.S. Treasury Department, Goldman Sachs, Citigroup, the Clinton White House, Clinton's Treasury Secretary Robert Rubin, The Hamilton Project, London School of Economics, Oxford University, Yale, Princeton, any school at Harvard, University of California at Berkeley, Dartmouth College, preferably born between 1961 to 1970, lived in Africa, and whose father microfinanced Indonesian projects for Obama's mother. Oh, and they had to look dashing in Barack's Praetorian Guard uniforms.

The stars were aligned when Obama was elected in 2008. His top donors conveniently matched the attributes he was looking for in his fiscal-policy talent search. He walked into a one-year-old recession that arguably could be traced back to the subprime mortgage smorgasbord started under another Democrat, President Bill Clinton. Legacy flashback: Bubba and his progressive buddies social-engineered the housing bubble then hitchhiked on the dotcom rocket. Which boom went bust after Bubba left office? Both!

The day the risky-mortgage music died and the dotcom market crashed, President George W. Bush was left holding the government-sponsored obsession to offer loans to everybody even if they used their unemployment checks as a down payment. Tough noogies, 43! Rough-riding mountain bikes is child's play compared to surviving ultimate musical chairs, especially when the Democrats controlled both the Senate and the House. This gave Obama and his housing-for-all support team the blame-Bush excuse for everything that was wrong with America. They would right the cowboy's wrongs and restore the progressive dream. Abracadabra! Well, at least that was the grand illusion. Behind the curtains were the Republicans—President George W. Bush, Treasury Secretary Henry Paulson, and Federal Reserve Chairman Ben Bernanke—who worked the magic on the banking system. Paulson's "Blueprint for a Modernized Financial Regulatory Structure," dubbed the Hank Paulson Plan, staved off the second Great Depression, not Obama's infamous Stimulus package. The conservative trio saw the Dem's abracadabra and raised it with a David Copperfield.

If not for the turmoil and panic caused by the financial crisis, Senator John McCain and his running mate Governor Sarah Palin were cruising to a November 2008 presidential victory. But McCain had to pull one of his empty-suit, grandstanding tirades "to save America" without offering any solutions to correct the debacle. His Johnny-come-lately attacks infuriated his fellow senators; many Republicans withdrew their support to bring McCain-Palin across the finish line. Senator Obama stepped aside and demurely watched the "Country First" team implode.

The tables turned as Bush exited and Obama arrived. The bank bailout designed to restructure the financial system became a slush fund to payback Obama 2008 donors. Those responsible for creating and administering the Troubled Asset Relief Program, commonly referred to as TARP or the $700 billion bank bailout, didn't much stop the bleeding on Main Street but significantly enhanced their cronies at the fat-cat banks. The Old GM, the Old Chrysler, and their respective finance companies were thrown into the illiquid-mortgage hopper and walked away with $80 billion of the TARP funds. With an Obama wink and nod, a car loan was instantly converted to a home mortgage.

Another one of his "transform America" tricks was to finesse bankruptcy laws that forgave the automakers a ton of debt thus progressively assembling the New GM and the New Chrysler while rewarding his union brethren. Obama was against the TARP bailout prior to winning the election, not wanting to rescue those greedy bankers that caused the recession in the first place. At least that was his talking point for the voting masses that saw him as the savior of the 99%. But the 1% bankers got him elected and, before you knew it, he was handing out TARP money left and right.

After receiving $25 billion under TARP, Citigroup in a private deal behind closed doors was given an extra $25 billion cash infusion along with another $306 billion of U.S. government guarantees. Unbelievable but true. Apparently Citigroup was more screwed than the other banks due to troubled mortgages, toxic assets, derivatives, and God knows what else Citigroup's previous chairman, senior adviser, and director Robert Rubin had concocted. And by the way, Rubin was at one time a member of the board and co-chairman at Goldman Sachs. Birds of a financial feather? Having ascended to Economist in Chief without the regimentation of a PhD and proving himself in the world of charts and graphs, Obama took pity on them all and used taxpayer money as commiserating largesse.

During the 2012 president race, all—not just a few but all—the big Wall Street donors bet on Obama's opponent, Mitt Romney . . . and lost. Ouch! The reelected president felt betrayed. His Great Society dream was fading. When rocker Grace Slick saw The Great! Society!! dream disintegrating, she dropped acid and formed a new group. When he's disillusioned and down in the dumps, Obama drops out, too, but calls it "golfing." Turned on and tuned in, Obama wondered what would the resilient Jefferson Starship do? Enlightenment! The winds of hope & change started to blow; the Obama beasts went on the prowl.

Once dearly protected by Obama, the "too big to fail" financial institutions had their comeuppance when Obama's attorney general put them on notice that none of them were "too big to indict." They got the message and returned to their making-money knitting. By January 2014, five years after the big-bear-hug bailout, all of the major bailees beat the Street with their earnings except Citigroup, which obviously needed more of the Obama love-money to meet analysts' estimates. How low could Citigroup's tangible book value go before they had to beg Obama for more hugs and kisses? Love, money, parteeee! The TARP money was spent, however, in-kind access and hiring Citigroup employees and alumni reinforced the love triangle. So many Citigroup cupids, so little time.

The parade of Citigroup employees in and out of the White House never made the daily press releases. Michael Froman's name was on the roster of the 12-member advisory board for the 2009 Obama-Biden Transition Project. A classmate and *Harvard Law Review* partner of Obama's, Froman bundled and built connections during Obama's Senate run and later the 2008 campaign. As a managing director for Citigroup, he obligingly donated his time to serve on the transition team and recommended candidates. Not a particular suspect situation except while collecting a Citigroup salary, he was hiring Obama's economic team. Get the picture? While Froman was handpicking Obama's economic fortune-tellers, TARP funds were being dispensed and Citigroup got a pancreas-busting sweet deal. Sizeable 2008 bonuses were in the offing for Citi's management like Froman, but those last two months as Obama's white-shoe point man were priceless. Froman obligingly hired himself as Assistant to the President with National Economic Council duties where he made hay until June 2013. Then he was awarded a plum appointment—U.S. Trade Representative for the Executive Office of the

President acting as the "principal advisor, negotiator and spokesperson on international trade and investment issues." All aboard the Trans-Pacific Partnership Express for the pivot to Asia, excluding that juggernaut known as China. Sporting an attaboy halo with passport in hand, Froman traveled the globe working out deals while answering only to the president. But which one—the United States' or Citigroup's?

Froman worked mainly behind the scenes. The showstopping quartet was trotted out for the *Vanity Fair* March 2009 issue. Interviewed and photographed during inauguration week mid-January, Obama's economic team were days away from being confirmed in their new positions. Though lamenting how much work lay ahead of them, the fearless foursome had made it to the big time—an Annie Leibovitz photo spread!—and would show their undying appreciation.

The day after the Citigroup mega rescue hit the streets, Obama announced then-President of the New York Federal Reserve, Timothy Geithner, would be his nominee for Secretary of the Treasury taking over from the politically ambidextrous Hank Paulson. No private-sector experience nor law degree nor PhD, Geithner at least had an MA, was an understudy for former Treasury Secretaries Robert Rubin and Larry Summers, and was really tight with Wall Street. His finest quality though was his uncanny "see no evil, hear no evil, speak no evil" abilities having been privy to all the behind-the-scenes monkey business that was the TARP bank bailout.

Stroke of genius: When the Supreme Court decided *Citizens United* January 21, 2010 having argued it for the better part of Obama's first year in office, who was ultimately in charge of the IRS that conducted the witch-hunt on Tea Party groups? Good boy, Timmy! Here's your Cub Scout Leave No Trace patch. And don't forget your online certificate for having finally mastered the basics of credit default swaps backed by subprime loans so you can at least recognize a financial crisis when one stares you straight in the face. Does AIG ring a bell? After four years of guiding Obama through the world-of-finance maze and teaching him the fine art of weaponizing the IRS, Geithner joined a Wall Street private equity firm as president. Rubin even saved a spot for him on his Hamilton Project Advisory Council.

Two days after the munificent taxpayer infusion to Citigroup, Obama started getting his financial groove on. Peter Orszag, the 40-year-old Director of the Congressional Budget Office, had the perfect no-private-sector CV with *summa cum laude* from Robert Rubin. Orszag, too, was part of the bank-rescue cabal and equally practiced at keeping secrets. Obama believed that Peter would fit well into his White House Illuminati as his Director of the Office of Management and Budget. With a reputation for being a ladies' man, Orszag was also tasked with translating those hip-hop signs that Obama's daughters were using. When did the traitors Sasha and Malia join Jay-Z's Illuminati?

Orszag cinched the appointment when he branded himself with: "We've got to make government service cool again." By 2012, six of the top ten richest counties in the U.S. were feeding from the Washington trough. The richest county, Loudon County, Va., was just 46 miles from Orszag's office. Wahhh, wahhh, wahhh! Take your long congested commute and bank it! The median household income in Loudon County swimmingly boasted $119,525 while the overall U.S. median household income treaded water with a modest $43,000. The DC area as a whole clocked in at a strut-your-bureaucratic-stuff $74,710; Connecticut $58,908; California $46,000; Santa Clara & San Mateo Counties, Silicon Valley, $68,000. Continuous snow storms or endless sunshine—take your pick.

As the largest component of the Executive Office of the President, OMB was instituted to implement and enforce the president's vision. Obama and Orszag had a Vulcan mind meld: whip out the credit cards and ransack the place! Peter had five executive hammers to drive Obama's progressive vision—and he wielded all of them. He controlled the budget spreadsheets, oversaw Federal procurement including information/IT for programs like the big-data ObamaCare gateway, infused the utopian liberal worldview into all significant Federal regulations, delivered the spending ultimatums to Congress, and orchestrated Executive Orders and Presidential Memoranda. But something happened along the way to balancing the national budget.

Maybe the propeller-head babe magnet was having a hard time with that double-entry, debit-credit minutiae while juggling so many girlfriends. Or, maybe bow-before-me Valerie Jarret felt Peter's personal life was too much of a sideshow given the White House's squeaky-clean image—Orszagasm.com, really? Whatever it was, Orszag resigned from Obama's staff after eighteen months. Beating the big-spending drum for universal healthcare, climate-change teat-sucking, and pillaging the military, Peter's official OMB mission was accomplished. He was there just enough time to make a big name for himself, hookup with several new squeezes, father a love-child, and springboard to his next meat market. Citigroup welcomed him with an embarrassingly high salary that he tried not to reveal to the court and the press during his scrappy divorce. And, once again, Robert Rubin brought Peter R. Orszag back into the Hamilton Project sitting pretty on the Advisory Council.

One wonders, who really runs the White House's OMB, Obama or Rubin? After Orszag, the paradoxical economic-patriot Jack Lew, then Sylvia Mathews Burwell assumed the Director's position—both disciples of Robert Rubin. Jeffrey Zients filled in the gap before and after Lew's term. Though not a Rubin apprentice, functionally Zients shared the progressives' penchant for misleading the public on the effects of the White House budget and playing Congress small. Imagine Obama building a spreadsheet or working the keys on a calculator—never in a million years. Using the protective back-off! deference to the Office of the President to obscure facts, figures, and folly was the ultimate Obama play.

When not cycling in and out of positions at Harvard, Larry Summers tracked his mentor Robert Rubin in and out of government posts. Ever the inveterate academic, Summers was confirmed as Obama's Director of the National Economic Council the day of the inauguration. With his usual bull-in-a-china-shop bluster, he staked out his position emphatically: "It's very important to do as much as we can as fast as we can. There is only one post-inauguration period." Game on!

Bill Clinton appointed Summers his Treasury Secretary in 1999 with a net worth around $400k. Ten years later when he joined Obama's team he was worth between $17-39 million. He started racking up the big bucks when in 2006 he resigned his Harvard presidency in disgrace and joined hedge fund D.E. Shaw & Co. as a part-time managing director. A few mucky-muck connections between

Washington and New York; a speech or two at Citigroup, Goldman Sachs, JPMorgan Chase, Merrill Lynch, and Lehman Brothers; a casual call to senators to protect executive pay for stimulus-infused Wall Street banks; and before he knew it, he qualified as a multi-millionaire sophisticated investor. Summers's net worth was nothing compared to his part-time employer, Dr. "$3.5 billion King Quant" Shaw, but they both had friends in the highest political places—the Clinton and the Obama Oval Offices. Larry was in hedgie heaven.

Never shy about expressing his opinions, Summers coordinated and advised Obama on his version of economic policy with a vengeance, excluding the likes of former Federal Reserve Chairman Paul Volcker. But Summers wasn't there to make friends with those intellectually superior to him. He preferred the impressionable status-seekers, like Obama and Orszag, who were in awe of him. After two years at the NEC, he was bored. He resigned and left Obama to deal with the economic-policy time bombs that the two had set in motion. A social climber himself, he began having the time of his life as a newspaper columnist, board member, lowly Harvard professor, and any private sector position that paid him at least six figures. And at long last, so socially networked even his bossy protégée Facebook's Sheryl Sandberg would be proud, Larry Summers rejoined the Hamilton Project and his mensch—ta-da!—Robert Rubin.

Obama knew how Summers felt about women as aptitude-challenged beyond the multiplication tables, however, he chose to appoint a token female nonetheless. The president-elect was $1.6 million indebted to his biggest campaign donor, the University of California. Arriving Washington from UC

Berzerkeley without any private sector experience, Christina Romer was confirmed as Chairman of the Council of Economic Advisers. Her main responsibility was to provide Obama with objective economic advice on the formulation of both domestic and international economic policy based on economic research and empirical evidence. She came armed with her grandiose-government economic models, Etch A Sketches, Magic Drawing Slates, and her faithful crystal ball. Her ultimate mission hidden behind the lofty job description was to package her obtuse guesstimates as scientifically proven facts. The death of Keynesianism must be avenged! Predicting the economy is a stick-your-finger-in-the-air talent, though economists never want the paying public to know that, especially the elitist economists hand-picked by an even bigger elitist, Barack Obama.

When it came time to present President Obama with the economic team's recommendations, Romer wanted to go with $1.8 trillion to give themselves enough leeway to cover any specious assumptions common with soft-science pontificating. Obstreperous Summers urged staying in the billion-dollar range—just because. They used rock-paper-scissors to settle, either way, on a ginormous dollar amount. Summers won and they went with $788 billion that eventually grew to $840 billion.

Twenty months working in an administration dominated by MIT-disdaining Harvardians was about as much as Christina could handle. We'll have to wait for Romer's hell-on-earth book to find out if Larry Summers was as misogynistic as the female Cambridge professors said he was. Never daring to turn her back when Larry was around, Christina had a few misandristic moves of her own, yet practiced considerable restraint knowing Summers was way better connected and virtually untouchable. Romer returned to her economics professorship at UC Berkeley where campus politics was far simpler—tenured professors rule. Obama played defense for the rest of his term justifying Romer's erroneous employment projections. He got revenge on the University of California for sending him Romer when he arranged for his retired Secretary of Homeland Security Janet Napolitano to assume the position of president of the UC system. Short on leadership skills and devoid of inspiring the aspirational, Napolitano would have to prove herself with her administrative paper-pushing chops to UC professors that enjoy eating their own—unless you come packing a Nobel Prize.

The prix fixe menu had already been set: raise taxes, increase government spending, reduce the value of the dollar, print more money, borrow even more money with treasury bonds, and blame George W. Bush for every economic burp, belch, and release of intestinal gas. Obama's economic gang of four only needed to show up for the fiscal feeding frenzy. The calculation was simple: let Obama's favorite Wall Street bankers gorge themselves on TARP as a reward for funding his election; the second payback tier would dine off the Stimulus Package—unconditional grants to loyal voting believers, such as public and private unions, green-technology researchers, liberal academics, all shades of blue states, cities, and municipalities; then throw a few tax-consequential crumbs to the lowliest tier of uninformed-but-pulled-the-lever-for-Obama-anyway voters with ObamaCare. If the uninsured ingrates don't appreciate Obama's beneficence, the IRS will slap them with a maximum annual fine of $2,448 for individuals and $12,240 for families. Take that!

The role of the economic gurus was to prepare the noble Keynesian justification for the fearsome government spending spree never before seen in the history of the world, then . . . sell the hell out of it! Yowza! Yes, an experiment of gargantuan proportion funded with taxpayers' money. The Stimulus and ObamaCare were preordained—written, orchestrated, and set in motion—before Obama moved his toothbrush into the second-floor president's bathroom.

Rather than recount the entire nauseating roller-coaster ride that these two thank-you-for-voting-for-me porkfests inflicted on the country, grab your barf-bag as we summarize the shocking inflection points.

American Recovery and Reinvestment Act of 2009 (ARRA)
The Stimulus Package
The Recovery Act
Recovery.gov
$840 billion Stimulus

- October 1, 2008 – A press release in Washington from The Apollo Alliance introduced a clean-energy revolution plan assembled by business, labor, environmentalists, and social-justice advocates urging the new president and Congress to act boldly and implement their blueprint to save the planet from greenhouse gas emissions. The Apollo Alliance was tax-exempt sheltered under the 501(c)(3) nonprofit Tides Center, connected to the 501(c)(3) nonprofit Tides Foundation, connected to the profit-driven Drummond Pike, who was connected to the multi-billionaire profit-seeking missile George Soros—all pre-*Citizens United*. Another privileged child of the Sixties, Pike creatively moved unnamed donors' funds into environmental and social projects that magically appeared in The Stimulus Package. Some call it venture socialism. Others call it money-laundering with a tax-advantaged, charitable twist. Tweedledum and Tweedledee: Ever notice how a progressive philanthropic c3 organization usually has an aggressive political c4 partner just one web-click away?

- January 9, 2009 – CEA Chairman Christina Romer published "The Job Impact of the American Recovery and Reinvestment Plan" predicting unemployment **without** the Stimulus would peak around 9% in 2010; **with** the Stimulus unemployment would peak at just under 8% in 2009, or maybe even a heavily disclaimered 6%. Obama promised 4,000,000 jobs would be saved or generated.

- January 20, 2009 – President Barack Hussein Obama is sworn into office. Day One of the oceans receding and the planet healing, blah, blah, blah.

- February 17, 2009 – Only 29 days in office, President Obama signed the save-the-world Stimulus bill into law at the solar-paneled Denver Museum of Nature and Science. Messianically, he claimed he was keeping the American dream alive by feeding the multitudes shovel-ready projects thus delivering jobs, jobs, jobs. Eventually Colorado had to legalize marijuana to keep their own dreams alive having surrendered their personal identities and altered their normally well-grounded perceptions after being hypnotized by the Chosen One August 28, 2008 at Invesco Field during his I-will-forgive-your-white-guilt acceptance speech.

- February 17, 2009 – Senate Majority Leader Harry Reid publicly praised The Apollo Alliance for their help in developing and executing a strategy. Reid decoded: The Apollo Alliance wrote the Stimulus bill and hand carried it one mile to Speaker Nancy Pelosi's District 12 San Francisco office just in time to get invited to the inaugural festivities. Drummond Pike traveled but four miles to join Pelosi and pals for the *nom de plume* handoff. Democratic Senators Dianne Feinstein and Barbara Boxer joined in the celebration, clinking their Northern California sparkling wine glasses. Call the IRS inspectors: Did Pike's c3 tax-exempt charitable nonprofit organization influence legislation by developing, executing, and writing it, or were they just delivering pizza for the party?

Point of Information: Former Madame Speaker, can you explain the African American inequality between your 12th District power-base squarely in the middle of The City with only 6% black population, while just a short drive across the San Francisco-Oakland Bay Bridge the 13th District is 20% black? Maybe the 13th District's racism code-talker, Democrat Rep. Barbara "ashamed of

America" Lee, ought to have a sit down with the Speaker rather than spewing her bigoted invectives at Rep. Paul Ryan (R-WI) and Fox News' Bill O'Reilly. Sometimes California's Prop. 209, banning public institutions from discriminating based on race, works for you and other times it works against you—depending on which side of the bridge you live. Right, Nancy?

Point of Privilege – Emergency nose count, please: California's 33rd Congressional District including Beverly Hills and Hollywood is 3% black; California's 34th Congressional District including downtown Los Angeles is 4% black; Cali's 52nd including San Diego is 3% black; New York's 14th including NYC is 11% black; Illinois' 7th including Chicago is 55% black; District of Columbia's At-large Congressional District is 50% black. All of the aforementioned districts are represented by Democrats in the U.S. House of Representatives. Smells like White, Hispanic, and Asian guilt festering on those pristine California-dreamin' beaches. Obama handily won The Golden State voters in 2008 and 2012 by following his community-organizing instincts—follow the guilt, follow the gold.

- June 13, 2011 – Oops! President Obama admits to his audience at a meeting of the President's Council on Jobs and Competitiveness: "Shovel-ready was not as … uh … shovel-ready as we expected." Ba-da-bump! Obama casually laughed off the suffocating regulations that dragged on the very paycheck-providing, infrastructure-building jobs the Recovery Act was supposed to fund. The crowd roared with laughter. Keep in mind this was the summer of 2011 that followed Obama's 2010 "Summer of Recovery" marketing blitz. Median household incomes went down $2,400 instead of up in Obama's topsy-turvy universe. And on that note: Jeffrey Immelt, CEO of General Electric and Chairman of Obama's Jobs Council, calculated it was better to hold $108 billion in offshore tax-haven GE subsidiaries then letting President LMAO confiscate it. Economic patriotism?

- July 5, 2011 – Double oops! From the People's Republic of Berkeley faculty lounge, Professor Romer defended the central-planning boondoggle and—get ready to upchuck—said it should have been at least $2 trillion, maybe more depending on which rule-of-thumb model she used. And maybe they guessed wrong and added one or two too many zeros on Obama's four million jobs pledge. Fuhgeddaboudit!

- February 17, 2014 – Triple oops! At the 5th year anniversary of the Stimulus, Obama kept force-feeding Americans that his make-believe recovery did indeed happen. The papier-mâché recovery the Federal Reserve built with cellophane greenbacks was move-in ready and on the market for the last five years. Wellllllll, except when Obama erased the word "recovery" from the Dems' campaign scripts lest they suffer sure defeat in the upcoming midterm elections. Recovery? What recovery? Where? Use this "R" word instead; it's more destructive—Redistribution. Those living in the real world agreed with the Heritage Foundation's Chief Economist Steve Moore that "[The Stimulus] was maybe the most expensive policy mistake ever made in Washington."

- February 26, 2014 – Play it again, Uncle Sam. Since the first Stimulus never delivered on those jobs, jobs, jobs, Obama asked for another $302 billion stimulus package to repair and improve America's roads, bridges, and mass transit systems. The aftermath of the magical, mythical, Keynesian-multiplier math: The U.S. national debt was $17.4 trillion and rising; 10.5 million Americans were unemployed; real unemployment, including those underemployed and drop-outs, was stuck at 13%; the labor participation rate, those employed or actively seeking a job, was a ghastly 62.8%; GDP growth went south with a *negative* 3%. So, what's the problem? Give the guy a break. Prosperity is just around Obama's corner.

Wait. There's more. Life under Obama got even better with the lefties' cockup of the century—ObamaCare.

How many years had the progressives been pushing for national healthcare? Since 1912 when former President Theodore Roosevelt formed the Progressive Party trying to retake the White House, only to lose in an electoral-vote sweep to an even more committed progressive, Woodrow Wilson. On hiatus from his political career, Teddy didn't just shoot rare white Rhinos for the Smithsonian; he became one—**R**epublican **I**n **N**ame **O**nly.

In 1994, why did HillaryCare implode? It was the chart, stupid! "We never overcame the chart" lamented poor, abused, Dominatrix Hillary. The Clinton plan collapsed under its own convoluted, overreaching bureaucracy. The progressives believed they needed a better messenger—one less surly, one more savvy yet still a protected minority. Someday their multicultural prince would come.

How many end runs did the Obama Democrats attempt before passing ObamaCare? At least eight glory-seeking bills. The most frightening was the first. Perennially introduced by a group of Democrats since 2003 and re-introduced January 2009, the United States National Health Care Act proposed the single-payer system akin to the U.K. and Canada. It was always swiftly tabled and ignored, thus killed by the House members because of its blatant honesty. The liberals didn't want the insurance companies to know that the ultimate plan was to make private health insurance obsolete.

The tip-off to the insurance companies' demise was the planned cuts to Medicare Advantage. Meant to offset the cost of ObamaCare, the Medicare reductions would slash the profits of the largest health-insurance carriers by 30%. The Democrats were dismayed—their mission was to eradicate 100% of the capitalists' filthy, immoral profits. But alas, the planned cutbacks came to a screeeeeching halt April 2014. The Democrats running for reelection in November begged the president to do a U-turn on looting Medicare Advantage for two big reasons: 16,000,000 senior voters enrolled in Advantage were outraged at the ransacking and the insurance companies would impound all promised campaign donations. Obama caved—at least until 2015, a nonelection year.

Did the House Democrats ever pass any version of their momentous healthcare act? No, both versions of their focus-group tested Affordable [fill in the blank] Act failed either in the Senate or were abandoned for strategic, procedural, and/or budgetary reasons. And besides, lefty Senator Max Baucus was so hell-bent to have the Senate's version as the Ten Thousand Commandments that he monomaniacally forced the House to ditch their efforts temporarily—until they could jerry-rig the House Dems' wish list as the Reconciliation Act.

Did the House ever vote on the HR 3590 bill that the Senate approved as the Patient Protection & Affordable Care Act? No, the House voted unanimously for the Service Members Home Ownership Act (HR 3590) that the Senate received, completely gutted, then slapped on their my-way-or-the-highway version of a healthcare bill and renamed HR 3590 the "Patient Protection & Affordable Care Act." Under reconciliation, the Senate passed their cut-and-paste version of the law with just 51 progressive votes. The House never voted expressly for the actual wording of ObamaCare. Unbelievable but true story.

How many pages was the *mule* healthcare law HR 3590, formerly known as the Service Members Home Ownership Act, when it arrived the Senate for approval? Six irrelevant pages, double-spaced. How many pages was the "amended" HR 3590 when it left the Senate? The Patient Protection & Affordable Care Act was 2,409 pages, chock-full of progressive, mind-bending, booby traps. Only Democrats supported the law as it moved through the process leaving levelheaded Americans marginalized.

How many liberal lawyer legislators did it take to blow up one-sixth of the U.S. economy? Fifteen in gavel-wielding, “leadership” positions. Of these fifteen lawmakers, how many resigned, were defeated, retired, or died before the law could be fully implemented? Eleven; the twelfth remains as a useful idiot since his wife works at the EPA; the thirteenth is hanging around so he can be named the longest incumbent member of Congress as soon as his mentor is put out to pasture; former Speaker Pelosi and soon-to-be-former Senate Majority Leader Reid, both age 74 in 2014, will never leave Washington fearing irrelevance in their golden years. The executive branch “influencers,” President Obama and Vice President Biden, were destined for the history books in 2016.

Besides all having law degrees, what else did the liberal legislators that designed, wrote, and introduced the voluminous miscreations have in common? All were career politicians. Once they had their law degrees—bam!—it was off to DC where they could wallow around in endless legalese for 25, 30, 40, 50, 60 years. All of them parked their posteriors and lived off taxpayer money to the grave. Many of them came to Washington before or because of Watergate, the 1974 “Watergate Babies.” Not one, let me repeat, not one had any how-average-Americans-make-a-living experience beyond their law books and their political campaigns. Stunted mental, emotional, philosophical, and fiscal-responsibility growth? Their own bank accounts grew exponentially, however.

Polled outside the trial lawyer-industrial-congressional complex, what was the one correctable, definitive element of medicine that could have, should have, would have changed to lower the cost while maintaining the quality of healthcare for EVERYONE in America? Tort reform! No words, phrases, or references to tort reform exist in any of the healthcare bills put forward by the Democrats. The tort lawyers lobbied incessantly to keep the phrase "loser pays" out of ObamaCare and ban it completely from the American lexicon. What better way to improve the U.S. healthcare ecosystem then to put a loser-pays stake in the heart of the blood-sucking trial bar. Guess who has his good ol' boy thumb in the medical malpractice insurance pie? Little Warren Buffett and his Berkshire Hathaway conglomerate.

ObamaCare also nimbly dodged reversing the tax exclusion enjoyed only by businesses that compensate employees with in-kind health insurance benefits instead of paying them higher taxable wages. Don't dare poke a tea-party stick at that $250 billion subsidy else Corporate America's lobbying firm, the U.S. Chamber of Commerce in Washington, DC, will use its deep pockets to "make you feel the heat." Republican Senator Tom Coburn, MD revealed this to the *Wall Street Journal* after he had announced his early retirement from the Senate and was out of the line of fire. A medical doctor himself, he chose to use his energies to attend to his cancer diagnosis instead of fighting deficit spending and pork barrel projects with his famous *Wastebook*. If you really want to play with fire, try thwarting the Chamber's pet projects: extending the Export-Import Bank, comprehensive immigration reform with open-borders, and more tax revenues earmarked for the Highway Trust Fund. The Chamber protects the "establishment" at any cost. Money is no object.

Did you know that the PPACA (HR 3590) and HCERA (HR 4872) combined equal ObamaCare? The education component (HR 4872) of Obamacare was added to meet reconciliation rules, help pay for ObamaCare, and—an extra kicker for his Ivy Leaguers—block for-profit schools from access to federal loans and grants. HR 4872 was first introduced back on July 15, 2009 as HR 3221 Student Aid and Fiscal Responsibility Act of 2009. Presto chango! The Dems massaged the bill and stapled it to the HR 3590 nightmare. Just the law without the regulations instantly mushroomed to 961 single-spaced pages. Not one legislator read PPACA & HCERA before voting on ObamaCare. This monstrosity was fated to be a complete catastrophe: amateurish rollout, impossible to execute, difficult to manage, sheer hell for Americans that needed and wanted quality, affordable, and accessible healthcare.

Ode to HR 3590: O Patient Protection and Affordable Care Act! Why such a calamity? 3,590 "effective dates," count them, just try! No reason why, but to inflict confusion, distress, and veiled taxes on 317 million good-hearted souls, with no remorse. Must political battles be waged using human healthcare as a right, as your shield, as your sword? Be sure, it is but a personal responsibility.

The following competing bills were all proposed by Democrats either in the Senate or the House. The melee became a made-for-Hollywood clash of the peace-and-love titans. The diktats in each HR and S decree were arm-wrestled into what we now know as ObamaCare. The Dancing with the Statutes winner became an instant celebrity for delivering the unreachable star, with their names forever etched in the Progressive Walk of Favors—every liberal senator's pipe dream. Well, that was the high-and-mighty reason. The practical purpose was locking-up voter registration in the name of the big-government Democrats and securing votes with another mammoth entitlement that would keep progressives in control of our lives from now until eternity.

United States National Health Care Act (HR 676)
America's Affordable Health Choices Act of 2009 (HR 3200)
Affordable Health Care Choices Act (S 1679)
America's Healthy Future Act [BaucusCare] (S 1796)
Affordable Health Care for America Act (HR 3962)
Service Members Home Ownership Act of 2009 (HR 3590)
Patient Protection & Affordable Care Act (HR 3590)
The Health Care & Education Reconciliation Act of 2010 (HR 4872)
ObamaCare

- Late 1930s –"No enemies on the Left!" was adopted as a unity slogan amongst the Socialists and Communists of Europe. Progressives in the U.S. adopted it, *sotto voce*, as their fight-to-the-death pledge to pass ObamaCare.

- July 8, 2008 – Health Care for America Now announced its formation. Organized to campaign for socialized medicine, this c4 and its c3 partner, the Health Care for America Education Fund, were projects of The Tides Center. With $60 million, HCAN lead a progressive "grassroots" campaign working side by side with a coalition of nonprofits and political organizations to pass and implement ObamaCare. Legal liberal loophole: Billionaire George Soros contributed $5 million to HCAN having maxed out his $2,100 presidential campaign contribution to then-Senator Obama.

- November 12, 2008 – Eight days after Obama won the presidential election, then-Senate Finance Committee Chairman Max Baucus, D-Mont., published his healthcare manifesto "Call to Action," or the less Marxist-sounding Baucus Plan. The timing was critical to avoid sabotage by the right and the left—vying to sit on the progressive pedestal is backbiting business in Washington. Baucus's chief health counsel, Liz Fowler, quarterbacked the 87-page White Paper lifted from her recycled PhD thesis: "Tiptoeing through the DemocratCare tulips." Embellished with "risk adjustment" this and "adverse selection" that, Fowler's healthcare blueprint was a tome straight out of the second largest U.S. health insurer's public policy department. No wonder. She was WellPoint's VP and lobbyist before she rejoined Baucus to fulfill her lifelong goal of wreaking havoc on one-sixth of the U.S. economy and making a name for herself. Six years later, Wellpoint rebranded itself as the consumer-friendly Anthem—the celebratory song for ObamaCare.

- January 7, 2009 – Obama announced that Cass "opt out" Sunstein, a pal of his from the University of Chicago Law School, would be his nominee as Administrator for Office of Information and Regulatory Affairs (OIRA). Sunstein was confirmed eight months later, however, his "nudging" experiment began immediately with ObamaCare as the prototype. This brings us to the unbearable lightness of Sunstein's mental musings. With but an English minor and an I'm-incapable-of-comprehending-numbers law degree, Cass & Co. redefined his credentials as a behavioral economist which instantly made him an expert in psychology, economics, and mathematics, therefore, policy making. Tripping the light fantastic, Sunstein subjectively defined what healthcare Utopia should be for all Americans, proceeded to grant individuals the freedom to *opt out* of Sunstein's Utopia, and then declared that individuals had the freedom of choice to make their own healthcare decisions. You know you've been Sunsteinized when the food police sporting their "Nutrition Nudger" badges reprimand you for loading cookies, candy, and ice cream into your shopping cart; you buy them anyway sans food stamps; then your doctor chastisingly texts you about the cookies, candies, and ice cream you just charged to your credit card, having diagnosed you as pre-diabetic; and you never *opted out* of the bank's built-in right to share your personal purchases with data brokers who sell them to your doctor. Call it "proactive health management," "humanitarian interventionism," "forced choice," "choice framing," "welfare paternalism," . . . whatever! It was the exact opposite of fellow U. of Chicago Gary "the greatest social scientist" Becker's Nobel Prize work on valuing, protecting, and improving "human capital" rather than torturing humans to obey. The White House policy makers determined the choices based on the individual's "best interest" and then steered the individual to only *one option*. The goal was to control irrational Americans' behavior by formulating a selection based on the policy-makers' preferences that the guinea pigs were mandated to prefer, too—as an app on any product with the Apple logo. Now we know why the website's "front end" appeared a Likert psychometric scale that, by design, rendered the "backend" unnecessary. Just shove everyone into Obamacaid! One and done!

- February 28, 2009 – Obama offered the Secretary of Health and Human Services position to then-Kansas Governor Kathleen Sebelius. After all, the fly-over States have voters, too. Though not Obama's first choice, she was confirmed two months later. Her first assignment was to use her best late-term-abortion takedowns to pin the right-to-lifers to the mat during the ObamaCare brawl. Man, it was brutal—hand-to-hand combat with the "dirty" Little Sisters of the Poor and the Catholic hospitals! That proved to be her only talent. Beat down: In his concurring opinion in the June 2014 Supreme Court's decision to rule against HHS mandating death-to-fertilized-egg contraceptives in *Burwell v. Hobby Lobby*, Justice Anthony Kennedy questioned how Sebelius could decree sweeping requirements for all U.S. citizens when she was but an executive branch political appointee and not an elected official of the law-writing Congress.

- June 15, 2009 – During his song and dance at the 2009 annual meeting of the American Medical Association, Obama said: "If you like your doctor, you will be able to keep your doctor, period. If you like your healthcare plan, you'll be able to keep your healthcare plan, period No one will take it away, no matter what." After repeating it at least 36 times over the next four years, do you think it was Obama's intent to deceive?

- June 19, 2009 – Obama arranged a new position, Chief Performance Officer, and appointed another White House frat boy to the position. Working for OMB Director Peter Orszag, Deputy Director Jeffrey Zients's number one focus as CPO was to reform how the U.S. government buys and manages information technology. For projects like the 500-million-lines-of-code ObamaCare? For a website that cost taxpayers $840 million? Plus fourteen state-exchange websites at $1.2 billion? Another Obama fundamental transformation? After the botched rollout of the ObamaCare website that was ultimately blamed on Sebelius, Zients was summoned to fix the website by holding the various contractors accountable. Wasn't that Jeff-Z's main job when he was CPO, advising how to buy and manage government-scale IT projects? Zients was part of the White House brotherhood during the three years the ObamaCare infrastructure was supposedly under construction. Kneel before thee: Zeints was a member of the ruling class, the "management guru" preaching "best practice in management, strategy, and operations" and should never ever get his hands dirty. Did he not help design the logistics of Obama's legacy legislation? Where was he when it went live? We know he has powerful gods protecting him, but come on! Who really dropped the Healthcare.gov ball? Kathleen dear, do tell.

- September 9, 2009 – Addressing a Joint Session of Congress, Obama pledged: "First, I will not sign a plan that adds one dime to our deficits—either now or in the future. (Applause.) I will not sign it if it adds one dime to the deficit, now or in the future, period." U.S. National Debt Clock then: $11.8 trillion. U.S. National Debt Clock now: $17.7 trillion. The ballpark figure for 2016 when Obama leaves the White House: $20 trillion. Full stop.

- October 22, 2009 – When asked if the Constitution authorized Congress to mandate that every American must buy health insurance, then-Speaker Pelosi committed candor: "Are you serious? Are you serious?" Nancy, Nancy, Nancy, are you lost for words? Did your progressive Constitution-dissing handlers forget to prime you with the obligatory "faux-outrage" talking points?

- March 10, 2010 – Pelosi said: "But we have to pass the bill so that you can find out what is in it." She already had a stack of ObamaCare waivers, printed and ready to roll, for businesses in her district especially thirty-eight of her favorite high-end restaurants. And postmarked July 2014, an additional 4.5 million under-the-table exemptions gifted to the residents of the five U.S. territories: Puerto Rico, Guam, American Samoa, U.S. Virgin Islands, and the Northern Mariana Islands.

- March 23, 2010 – With twenty-two pens, Obama officially signed ObamaCare into law in the East Room of the White House on behalf of his deceased mother. At the White House press conference that afternoon, Vice President Joe Biden introduced the president at the podium then congratulated Obama on live television with: "This is a big f**king deal!" The crowd gave them both a standing ovation. His mother turned in her grave remembering how her son the lawyer watched her struggle during her illness and did nothing to help, never once interceded with the big bad insurance company on her behalf. Thanks for the nod, baby Barry, but don't you think it's too little, too late?

- May 25, 2010 – Obama signed the Reconciliation Act into law, the icing on the ObamaCare cake. Dizzy and giddy with emotion for the BaucusCare—whoops!—the ObamaCare victory, Baucus praised Fowler and only Fowler for writing, orchestrating, goading, intimidating, and general ballbusting to push ObamaCare over the finish line. So like-minded were the two that Baucus had tears in his eyes when he said that he was beholden to her "from the bottom of my heart."

- Tick tock, tick tock. Three years went by. During that time, many ambitious liberal mice ran into the White House. Fowler, Sunstein, and Zients were all there tossing the football around, comparing marathon stats, and besting each other's Fitbit activities. Hickory dickory dock! What was going on with ObamaCare? All the policy decisions were centrally controlled by an insular White House. Filled with Facebook-envy, the policy wonks lusted for control of a cross-channel portal that would put Zuckerberg to shame. Not the Amazon model that warehouses and ships physical inventories—that's hard work. Certainly not writing the Python or Ruby on Rails code—they were the movers and shakers! In their information-aggregating world, the federal government sits at the top of *all* American institutions, public and private. They would convert the hard-to-manage, unpredictable American people to scalable bits of information, content-richer than just their age, gender, interests, and location. The perfect algorithm! Capricious coefficients! The computer modelers' dream! First they would cross-link personal information from Healthcare.gov, insurance companies, mortgage records, the IRS, student loans, the NSA, the FBI—anywhere and everywhere because hyperscalers rule! The data-streaming would be endless! The physicians must use electronic health records or lose their EHR conversion subsidies and be penalized with lower reimbursements. The doctors play or no pay! Next, they would auction the data packs in the $17 billion global mobile advertising market. All funded with taxpayers' dollars—no risk for the government dweebs but what a tycoon-for-the-day rush. Up your Big Data, Google! Using their android-choice architecture reinforced with learned-helplessness cues, they could push and pull any product and service with but a swipe, tap, or click. Tick tock, tick tock. Well, it was fun to talk about over Starbuck lattes chased with Red Bulls. Towards the end of 2012, key White House staffers started quietly bailing—Fowler to a cushy senior-level position at Johnson & Johnson, Sunstein to a full professorship at the Harvard Law School, Zients became Director of OMB. Tick tock. The October 1st launch grew closer. All the mice had stuffed their rolodexes, expanded their resumés, lined up book deals, then scurried out the backdoor. None wanted their names associated with the Healthcare.gov big reveal. Mousetrapped: Sebelius never part of the inner circle, was left chomping the ObamaCare website cheese.

- April 17, 2013 – Dudley Do-Right choked: During a routine budget meeting, Senator Baucus biting his nails and trembling warned: "I just see a huge train wreck coming down."

- April 23, 2013 – Less than a week later, Baucus announced he would retire when his term ends in 2015.

- October 1, 2013 – ObamaCare was rolled out in the form of a website and guess what? Baucus's train did indeed wreck. Curses! Progressive healthcare foiled again!

- November 7, 2013 – The first wave of insurance policy cancellations started the initial kerfuffle. In an NBC interview, Obama gave a severely-selected, half-hearted apology: "I am sorry that they are finding themselves in this situation based on assurances they got from me. . . . Obviously we didn't do a good enough job in terms of how we crafted the law." As if healthcare was some crushed-candy game on his iPhone.

- November 14, 2013 – When unsuspecting responsible Americans, who bought and paid for their "subpar" policies, were deluged with cancellation notices, Obama admitted during a White House press briefing that "we fumbled the rollout on this healthcare law. . . . What we're also discovering is that insurance is complicated to buy." He admitted this on national TV. Whoopsie daisy!

- December 12, 2013 – Obama screwed the pooch: The *Washington Post* bestowed "If you like your healthcare plan, you can keep it," the Lie of the Year distinction.

- December 18, 2013 – Obama announced he would nominate Baucus as U.S. Ambassador to China.

- January 30, 2014 – On Jon Stewart's *The Daily Show*, Nancy Pelosi explained why the ObamaCare rollout was so botched: "I don't know. . . . It's not my responsibility." The liberals' finger-pointing scourge had spread beyond their fortified bunkers. Did Pelosi coach Sebelius on the fine points of flubbing her infamous, career-ending, October 7 Stewart interview?

- February 4, 2014 – Using fair-value accounting and not their legally-fraudulent federal bookkeeping, the CBO reported that ObamaCare will reduce the number of man-hours Americans work, equivalent to 2.5 million full-time jobs. Donning a powdered white wig for authenticity and to mask her lack of historical accuracy, Pelosi struggled to progressively recontextualize the Declaration of Independence as the "founders" way of endorsing the liberating effects of ObamaCare: "To give people life, a healthy life, liberty to pursue their happiness. And that liberty is to not be job-locked but to follow their passion." Sheesh!

- February 6, 2014 – Baucus, confirmed unanimously as U.S. Ambassador to China, admitted he was "no real expert on China." His spokesman brushed it off as Big Sky Country humility. Maxy Max now had 90 days to prepare for the Great Wall Marathon. He remembered to pack his "Made in China" Nikes, not the Vietnamese pair. Far more diplomatic, you know, the South China Sea oil & gas bonanza squabble. Baucus escaped the train wreck he Snidely Whiplashed on the American people by jumping on the royal gravy train—another taxpayer funded position, traveling the world as a U.S. dignitary, and an abundant pension when he retires.

- February 27, 2014 – Harry Reid on the Senate floor accused ObamaCare victims of lying: "There are plenty of horror stories being told. Stories made up from whole cloth. Lies distorted by Republicans to grab headlines or make political advertisements." Scary Harry, please go away—far, far away, deep in the Nevada desert.

- March 20, 2014 – At a news conference celebrating the fourth anniversary of the signing of ObamaCare, Nancy Pelosi stood by her lonesome and admonished the reporters for using the term "ObamaCare." Acting like Sister Mary Stigmata from *The Blues Brothers*, Pelosi repeated the word "affordable" fifteen times as if slapping the little boys and girls with her splintered ruler.

- March 31, 2014 – The deadline for ObamaCare open enrollment. Did the Dems achieve their goal? The administration's target was 7,000,000 fully-enrolled cash customers. On the verge of hurling Sebelius off the HHS Rock, the White House number-fudgers splashed 7,100,000 "sign-ups" to the media as mission accomplished. They rather precisely bumped the count just north of the target to make it appear an honest account. The rose-colored registrations included infants, toddlers, preschoolers, middle childhood, young teens, and teenagers. Net-net: Tallying those that were newly insured and actually paid the minimum first-month premium, the "new enrollee" sum of all the ObamaCare moving parts was more like 400,000. At least 85% were "bribed" with a subsidy. Golly! Seven of the fourteen state-exchange websites barely went live.

- April 10, 2014 – Sebelius resigned though she publicly stated a few weeks prior that she was planning on staying through the end of 2014. The Senate Dems had asked to "burn the witch" before the midterm-election circus began. Obama quietly compromised and allowed her to stay until her five-year anniversary to qualify for her lifetime, taxpayer-funded pension with health benefits of the non-ObamaCare variety. During her five years as an Obama Cabinet member—5 years!—Secretary Sebelius (big "S") never had a one-on-one with Obama. So much for her fair-weather, fellow Kansan. She had become the face of the ObamaCare flop even though she had "the best information from the best experts," from the esteemed policy team that set up the process. The hit-and-run super-nerds had already escaped. Cashin' in: Rumor has it that Sebelius and Christina Romer are co-authoring a provocative tell-all about Obama and his chauvinist buddies' secret war on women in the West Wing. The lead protagonist—chauvinista Valerie J. Should be yummy!

- April 15, 2014 – Tax Day. Twenty new ObamaCare taxes were unleashed on the taxpaying public. Yippee-ki-yay. IRS employees received $62.5 million in morale-boosting, performance bonuses for 2013—down from their down-in-the-dumps $89.1 million bonuses paid out in 2012. Taxpayer-funded ObamaCare state grants paid enterprising national tax-preparers sign-up bounties for every ObamaCare enrollee. Oregon, Maryland, and Massachusetts ditched their customer-repelling, ObamaCare-compliant, state-exchange websites for workable off-the-shelf software. The Democrat governors viewed the failures as accelerators on the autobahn to single-payer, healthcare serfdom—just like Liz Fowler predicted. The crippled ObamaCare websites cost more to fix than to build. Are we fundamentally transformed yet? Somebody break it to Obama: Fundamental transformation may be his sadistic erotica, but it will never happen. We are USA Strong . . . and taxed enough already!

The moral of the story is liberals make outrageously lucrative customers: they crave direction; they follow the crowd; need to belong; don't understand business; are swayed by emotional appeals; captivated by a good story; spellbound by enchanting leaders; easily distracted by the next new thing; don't care what things cost; naively believe people are looking out for their best interest; adore "brands," are easily branded, and don't care if they're psychographed, categorized, and monetized—it makes them feel part of the "like" crowd. Civil liberties—is that a new Netflix mini-series? Want to know what liberals look like? Apple's "1984" commercial—progressive zombies. The slavish mentality Steve Jobs mocked became the company's primary target market. Thirty years later post-Jobs, the same sleepwalkers are marching to the headphone beat of a new drummer—gansta rapper Dr. Dre.

What's the one word progressives mostly use to describe themselves? Don't laugh—intellectuals! And these "intellectuals" relish associating with other "intellectuals." It's a form of insider trading, status seeking, liberal apple-polishing, litterateurs' cheating—pitching each other's books, quoting one another's ruminations, collaboratively stuffing scholarly monographs, hiring only pedigreed progressives, exchanging blurbs. And, of course, they fancy themselves the arbiters of "the conversation" and the progenitor of all ideas. Discombobulated: As the taxed-enough-already-limited-government movement coalesced like wild fire across the country, the cognoscenti's sangfroid quickly melted. The "PhD" moniker places them in their own special 1% class, the best and the brightest. As a Columbia University professor and Keynesian economist, Joseph Stiglitz fortuitously pointed out with this unintended double-entendre: "Of the 1%, by the 1%, for the 1%"—the cast-off 99%ers are dreadful children of a lesser god.

Only enlightened liberals hold reasoned conversations, examine all sides, and reach rational decisions. It's the "take action" part that eludes them. Chin-wagging: Obama's "messy world" foreign policy proclamations speak for themselves.

Progressives even claim Aristotle as the first member of their movement. His ancient "truths" conveniently support their outmoded philosophies. Which gets to the heart of the matter: Is Obama really a paradigm shift, a revolution as seen in science or a retread of the progressives' tired old tirades? Our understanding of the world has crisscrossed through several scientific revolutions from Aristotle to Copernicus to Galileo to Newton to Darwin to Einstein. Adopting Obama's retrograde rants is equal to having lived in an open-ended Einsteinistic world, then being forced back by the power of the federal government to Aristotelian doctrines. What for all the experience, the building, the creating, the "blood, sweat, and tears" in between? Are we not wiser? Have we not learned that progressive programs are passé, on the verge of extinction?

Progressivism is on the decline for two specific reasons: 1) Chimeric liberals not only live in their lazy fool's paradise, but are also Democrat jackass-stubborn obstructionists when it comes to the #1 obligation to the American people—national security, and 2) Lefties are fixated on spending other people's money on their Utopian domestic programs, which eventually runs out as the "Iron Lady" Margaret Thatcher reminded us. But the progressive weenies talk a good game. The world has moved beyond sharing cultures. We get it. Technology took care of that, thank you very much. Now it's time to protect *all* civilizations. Can you say "global war on militant Islamic jihadist terrorism"?

The only contribution President Barack Hussein Obama made to advancing American Civilization was to inadvertently expose the multidimensional artifice used by liberals, progressives, and lefties to cast every conceivable "social" issue as guilt-ridden victimization solely to win *votes*.

Thank you, Barack, for lifting the veil. XOXO! Obama playing fast and loose with the truth while perverting American values will be the man's lasting legacy.

AMERICAN VALUES

By the age of sixteen, George Washington took to practicing "The Rules of Civility and Decent Behaviour in Company and Conversation" handed down to him by his father, who also practiced them as early as grammar school. There were 110 rules that offered direction on social behavior, character, and morality as well as philosophical and religious guidance. Washington built his character on duty, God, and country. The straight-talking Dave Hickey, UNLV professor and revered art critic, knew direct and down-to-earth cool when he saw it: "Washington's 'image' wasn't an image. He was that man—the incarnation of his own construction of virtue."

When Le Marquis de Lafayette, at the age of nineteen, secretly traveled to America to assist with the revolution against Britain, "the boy" saw General Washington for the first time and proclaimed: "That's the man I want to be like."

After Washington won the American War of Independence, he quietly retired to his Mount Vernon farm without seeking reward for risking his life to save the nascent

Republic. Noble to his core, the general took ownership of his life and his responsibilities. Principles were more important to him than personal gain. He demurred to be made king upon which King George III said: "If that is true, he must be the greatest man in the world."

Washington, without giving a single speech to the Continental Congresses or the Constitutional Convention, directed these important debates by his very presence and demeanor. With a quiet nod here and an encouraging whisper there, he steered the crafting of the U.S. Constitution on its intended course—to regulate the government, not the people. He became the indispensable cornerstone, the de facto president, the center for democracy because of his integrity, accomplishments, and respect of his peers. He lived his life based on his reserved moral authority and set an example for the world and for many generations. Who better than George Washington to become the first President of the United States of America?

October 11, 1976, Lieutenant George Washington of Virginia was promoted posthumously to the full grade of General of the Armies of the United States by President Gerald R. Ford and Congress. This made Washington the most senior U.S. military officer, forever outranking any and all other military officers. Washington's appointment was effective July 4, 1976 in celebration of the nation's bicentennial. His uplifting spirit lives on and is an indelible part of our nation's DNA, never to be eradicated even during the chaotic Obama years.

In contrast, by the age of sixteen, Barack Obama was already preparing his own otiose rules. He knew there were at least 110 ways to get high, inhale reefer, drink booze, snort cocaine, smoke cigarettes, cut class, quit studying, hang out at the beach, befriend junkies, shoot hoops, glorify disaffection, become cynical, whine, play his mother small, and his grandfather even smaller. And the "civility and decent behavior" part of his education, Obama played hooky from kindergarten the day they taught how to make nice with others. Yes, these were the early ideals of the 44th president of the United States.

George Washington personifies American values, the First Principles that defined our nation. George Washington is cool. Barack Obama doesn't even come close.

On the next several pages are some of the treasured American values that built the strongest and most free nation in the world. Perhaps they will inspire you to write your own Cool Rules. Another option might be to follow the Golden Rule or the Ten Commandments enhanced with Adam Smith's *mutual sympathy* and *invisible hand* supported by Milton Friedman's *free markets*. By serving your own interests, you serve the interests of society. Give it some thought, after all it is your life. YOLO! And in America, you are free to choose—as is everyone else—to be yourself, to be the best that you can be without government dictates. The American dream is alive—liberty and justice for all.

American Values

Accountability

Achievement

Advancement

Aesthetics

Affectionate

Beauty

Boldness

Bravery

Character

Charity

Civility

Clarity

Community

Compassion

Competition

Confidence

Congruent

Constancy

Courage

Creativity

Curiosity

Daring

Decency

Democracy

Dignity

Diligence

Discipline

Discovery

Education

Empathy

Entrepreneurship

Equality

Ethical

Excellence

Excitement

Exploration

Fair

Faith

Fearlessness

Fellowship

Flexible

Forgiveness

Fortitude

Free enterprise

Freedom

Friendship

Fun

Future-oriented

Generous

Gravitas

Happiness

Hardworking

Health

Honesty

Honor

Hope

Humanitarianism

Humility

Idealism

Inclusive

Independence

Individualism

Ingenuity

Initiative

Innovation

Integrity

Intelligence

Intensity

Intrepidity

Justice

Knowledge

Leadership

Legacy

Liberty

Love

Loyalty

Maximize potential

Meritocracy

Modesty

Open-minded

Openness

Opportunity

Optimism

Patient

Patriotism

Peace loving

Perseverance

Persistence

Possibility

Pragmatic

Pride

Privacy

Productive

Promise

Realism

Resiliency

Respect

Responsibility

Security

Self-control

Self-effacement

Self-fulfillment

Self-knowledge

Self-reliance

Self-sacrifice

Simplicity

Sincerity

Sobriety

Strength

Success

Teamwork

Tenacity

Tolerance

Tradition

Unity

Verve

Victory

Wealth

Winning

Wisdom

Work ethic

THE CIGARETTE AFTER

Tomorrow is the most important thing in life. Comes into us at midnight very clean. It's perfect when it arrives and it puts itself in our hands. It hopes we've learned something from yesterday.

John "Duke" Wayne

Thank you for reading

COOL WET KISS

www.ingramcontent.com/pod-product-compliance
Lightning Source LLC
Chambersburg PA
CBHW072113270326
41931CB00010B/1541